BEST of the BEST
from
NEW ENGLAND

Selected Recipes from
the FAVORITE COOKBOOKS of
Rhode Island, Connecticut, Massachusetts,
Vermont, New Hampshire, and Maine

Best of the Best
from
NEW ENGLAND

*Selected Recipes from
the FAVORITE COOKBOOKS of
Rhode Island, Connecticut, Massachusetts,
Vermont, New Hampshire, and Maine*

EDITED BY
Gwen McKee
AND
Barbara Moseley

Illustrated by Tupper England

QUAIL RIDGE PRESS

Drake; *A Taste of Hallowell* © 1992 Alice Arlen; *A Taste of New England* © 1990 Junior League of Worcester, Inc.; *A Taste of Providence* © 1989 Terrence Gavan and Gillian Drake; *A Taste of Provincetown* © 1991 Gillian Drake; *Tony Clark's New Blueberry Hill Cookbook* © 1990 Arlyn Patricia Hertz and Anthony Clark; *Traditional Portuguese Recipes from Provincetown* © Mary Alice Cook and Gillian H. Drake; *Uncle Billy's Downeast Barbeque Book* © 1991 Jonathan St. Laurent; *Vermont Kitchens Revisited* © 1990 Vermont Kitchen Publications; *Washington Street Eatery Cookbook* © 1993 Washington Street Eatery; *What's Cooking at Moody's Diner* © 1989 Nancy Moody Genthner; *Windjammer Cooking* © 1989 Pen & Ink Press

Library of Congress Cataloging-in-Publication Data

McKee, Gwen.
  Best of the best from New England: selected recipes from New England's favorite cookbooks/by Gwen McKee and Barbara Moseley.
      p.   cm.
  Includes index.
  ISBN 0-937552-50-X : $16.95
  1. Cookery, American—New England style. I. Moseley, Barbara.
II. Title.
TX 715.2.N48M37   1994
641.5974--dc20   94-5578
                                                                        CIP

Copyright 1994 by
Quail Ridge Press

ISBN 0-937552-50-X

First printing, October 1994
Second printing, February 1997
Third printing, September 1999

Manufactured in Canada
Designed by Barney and Gwen McKee

Chapter opening photos courtesy of:
Connecticut Department of Economic Development; Fayfoto/Greater Boston
Convention and Visitors Bureau; Boston, Massachusetts Office of Travel and Tourism;
Vermont Department of Travel and Tourism; Kim Fuller/Newport Yachting Center;
Maine Department of Economic and Community Development;
Arthur Bouffard/New Hampshire Office of Travel and Tourism Development;
Michael Baz/Rhode Island Tourism Division;
Gwen McKee and Barbara Moseley/Quail Ridge Press

Cover photo courtesy of
Paul Spezzeferri/State of New Hampshire Tourism

QUAIL RIDGE PRESS

P. O. Box 123 • Brandon, MS 39043 • 1-800-343-1583
Email: info@quailridge.com • Website: www.quailridge.com

*A grand view of boats at their moorings from the only pedestrian drawbridge
in America, at picturesque Perkins Cove, Ogunquit, Maine.*

CONTENTS

Editors Gwen McKee and Barbara Moseley enjoy an early morning stroll behind the Breakers, summer cottage of the Vanderbilts, on the Cliff Walk in Newport, Rhode Island.

The mere mention of New England brings delightful images to mind...of lighthouses on rocky coastlines, of white-steepled churches in Currier-and-Ives villages, of winding country lanes exploding with spectacular fall foliage. And names come to mind...Martha's Vineyard, Mystic Seaport, Bar Harbor, Plymouth Rock, Montpelier, Franconia Notch, Newport Beach, the Berkshires, the Ivy League schools...and songs..."You're sure to fall in love with Old Cape Cod"...well, we did. In fact, we fell in love with *all* of New England.

We cannot begin to tell you the whole story of the compilation of this cookbook, nor to be able to thank all the delightful New England people who helped us with it, but we want to share with you some of the experiences of our quest so that you may be able to enjoy it vicariously with us. The research primarily consisted of always looking for bookstores, gift and kitchen shops, local restaurants, libraries, churches and civic organizations, and talking to people about the foods they eat and the cookbooks they enjoy using to prepare them; and all the while absorbing the culture, the food, the places, the people...the *feeling* of beautiful, breathtaking New England.

We began our search for cookbooks in Boston (after an irresistible lobster salad at Faneuil Hall). Arnold at Boston Cooks was an immediate help, with so many fascinating cookbooks to devour that we lingered much of the drizzly afternoon. We encountered local people at every turn, like very Italian Voto, who suggested, "Add a little lobster water to your spaghetti sauce, then put a can of minced clams over the sauce"—this said, of course, with vigorous Italian gusto.

Cape Cod was bigger than we had thought: full of rotaries (traffic circles) with drivers who drove fast and made quick turns, where there were few street signs, fewer highway signs, and "up" is not necessarily north. The beaches were delightful—sea breezy and sunshiny and sand-duney. We were enthralled with the market's assortment of fruits, clams, mushrooms—so many varieties we had not seen before. We purchased car goodies and were tickled to be enjoying a sandwich when we got to the town of Sandwich.

Newport, Rhode Island, was decadent fun, driving down avenues of stately mansions, many overlooking the ocean, each one so impeccably landscaped and manicured. Helpful Evan and pretty Gail told us not to miss Muriel's award-winning chowder. We didn't, and it most definitely got our blue ribbon award.

Mystic, Connecticut, is a storybook setting, as interesting as it is charming. Boating and whaling and marine life are so interestingly explored and explained and displayed. Nearby Stonington is a Brigadoon-like fishing village wedged into a narrow peninsula of quaint shops and cozy tearooms. Bill in Rocky Hill was quite proud of his state and eager to help us with pictures and information.

Innkeeper Shirley in Williamstown, Massachusetts, told us about local cookbooks and the nearby theatre. We just missed the opening night performance, but talked to several patrons outside at the gala celebration who cordially offered insights to our research.

Beautiful Vermont is interlaced with scenic highways through the Green Mountains with so many couldn't-resist-pulling-off-to places. We encountered savvy Sue in the biggest country store you could ever imagine in Westin, who told us—with the delightful music of Roy Rogers and the Sons of the Pioneers in the background—that she couldn't wait to see the outcome of our project.

We next drove into the picturesque White Mountains of New Hampshire through Shaker Villages and sleepy fishing-lake settings. The curvy backroads there and into western Maine are thickly wooded with beautiful spruce and birch trees—so pretty and green—and signs that say "Watch for Moose"—which, of course, we diligently did.

Duncan and his fluffy cat, Albert, welcomed us to their bed and breakfast in Camden, Maine, graciously showing his cookbooks and giving us needed information. We met another handsome cat, Sir Thomaston, named for the town, who eyed us curiously in "his" bookshop where owner, Marti, helped us and was fascinated by our quest. Coastal Maine is so gorgeous that we couldn't resist making frequent side trips to lighthouses on foggy fingers of land that stretched hauntingly out into the ocean.

The New Englanders we met were salt-of-the-earth people who graciously gave us information, directions, and their opinions for the asking, especially about their cooking. Most prefer good old basic cooking without too many frills. Soups, chowders, and pot roasts help take the chill off a blustery day; and the abundant cranberries, blueberries, apples, and potatoes are prepared in every imaginable way. They like things fresh—fresh basil, fresh spinach, fresh pumpkin, and freshly grated ginger replace packaged varieties—and sauces or flavored vinegars provide flavor enhancements. Recipes (sometimes called *rules* or *receipts*) frequently use salt pork and molasses for seasoning. Baked beans cooked in a stoneware pot with steamed brown bread are still traditional fare on Saturday night. "Blow on a few in a spoon...their skins should break" is instructed for just how long to bake them. Molasses replaces sugar for the sweetener, and sometimes maple syrup replaces molasses. Indian pudding is still a New England favorite.

But foods that are healthier and quicker-cooking are high on the priority list of today's cooks. We learned from Diane and Colleen at the Marshmallow Kitchen in Falmouth that with the availability of foods, condiments, and more fresh produce to choose from, New England cooks are also willing to try less familiar cuisine.

All of the above resulted in the discovery of hundreds of cookbooks, 107 of which we invited to be contributors to this fifteenth volume in our "Best of the Best" series. We want to especially thank all the cooks who created these recipes—please know that you are very much appreciated. We are grateful to these authors, editors, chairpersons, and publishers for their cooperation in making this book possible. Each and every one of them was cooperative and enjoyable to work with. The complete catalog showing and describing each book, along with ordering information, begins on page 329—you may order their individual books directly from them. Please forgive us if we have inadvertently overlooked any books that might have been included in this collection.

Special thanks to our "Best" artist, Tupper England, who captured the flavor and charm of New England in her lovely drawings. We are grateful to the food editors from newspapers across the New England states who helped us with our research, and to some enthusiastic radio announcers who spread the word that we were looking for cookbooks. All the book and gift store managers who answered our questions and allowed us to delve into their knowledge of area cookbooks are appreciated and will be remembered for their kindnesses. We thank the very courteous people at the various tourism departments (listed on copyright page) for graciously providing us with pictures and information. And thanks to all the New Englanders we met along the way, who smiled and responded and eagerly offered to help...they are forever in our memories.

New England is made up of six separate states, each with its own uniqueness. But together they are a region of similarities in lifestyles and cuisine. We truly loved the experience of getting to know its people, its culture, its food and fancies. Perhaps our enjoyment will transcend through the pages of this book. We hereby invite you to partake of the glorious cuisine of incomparable New England.

Gwen McKee and Barbara Moseley

CONTRIBUTING COOKBOOKS

All-Maine Cooking
All-Maine Seafood Cookbook
All Seasons Cookbook
Another Blue Strawbery
Apple Orchard Cookbook
The Art of Asian Cooking
As You Like It
Baba À Louis Bakery Bread Book
The Bed & Breakfast Cookbook
Berkshire Seasonings
The Best from Libby Hillman's Kitchen
Best Recipes of Berkshire Chefs
The Blue Strawbery Cookbook
The Book of Chowder
Boston Tea Parties
A Cape Cod Seafood Cookbook
Cape Cod's Night at the Chef's Table Cookbook
Cape Collection - Simply Soup
Celebrities Serve
The Chef's Palate Cookbook
Chicken Expressions
Chris Sprague's Newcastle Inn Cookbook
Christmas Memories Cookbook
Clams, Mussels, Oysters, Scallops & Snails
Classic New England Dishes from Your Microwave
Come Savor Swansea
Connecticut Cooks
Connecticut Cooks II
Connecticut Cooks III
The Cookbook II
Cooking with H.E.L.P.
Country Inns and Back Roads Cookbook
The Country Innkeepers' Cookbook
Cuisine à la Mode
A Culinary Tour of the Gingerbread Cottages
Dining on Deck
Favorite New England Recipes

CONTRIBUTING COOKBOOKS

The Fine Art of Holiday Cooking
The Fine Arts Cookbook I
The Fine Arts Cookbook II
Fresh from Vermont
From Ellie's Kitchen to Yours
From the Inn's Kitchen
The Gardner Museum Café Cookbook
Good Maine Food
Great Island Cook Book
The Hammersmith Farm Cookbook
A Hancock Community Collection
The Harlow's Bread & Cracker Cookbook
Hasbro Children's Hospital Cookbook
Heritage Cooking from the Kitchen of Mary Pauplis
Heritage Fan-Fare
Home Cookin' is a Family Affair
Homespun Cookery
Hospitality
The Island Cookbook
J. Bildner & Sons Cookbook
The King Arthur Flour 200th Anniversary Cookbook
The Legal Sea Foods Cookbook
The Loaf and Ladle Cook Book
The Lymes' Heritage Cookbook
The Maine Collection
Maine's Jubilee Cookbook
The Marlborough Meetinghouse Cookbook
The MBL Centennial Cookbook
Memories from Brownie's Kitchen
Merrymeeting Merry Eating
More Than Sandwiches
Moveable Feasts Cookbook
Mrs. Appleyard's Family Kitchen
My Own Cook Book
Off the Hook
The Parkview Way to Vegetarian Cooking
Perennials

CONTRIBUTING COOKBOOKS

Peter Christian's Favorites
Peter Christian's Recipes
Plum Crazy
Provincetown Seafood Cookbook
Recipes from a Cape Cod Kitchen
Recipes from a New England Inn
Recipes from Smith-Appleby House
, The Red Lion Inn Cookbook
Rhode Island Cooks
RSVP
Sandy Hook Volunteer Fire Company Ladies Auxiliary Cookbook
Savory Cape Cod Recipes & Sketches
Seafood Expressions
Seafood Secrets Cookbook
Seasoned with Grace
Stillmeadow Cook Book
A Taste of Boston
A Taste of Cape Cod
A Taste of Hallowell
A Taste of New England
A Taste of Newport
A Taste of Providence
A Taste of Provincetown
A Taste of Salt Air & Island Kitchens
Tasty Temptations from the Village by the Sea
Tony Clark's New Blueberry Hill Cookbook
Traditional Portuguese Recipes from Provincetown
Uncle Billy's Downeast Barbeque Book
Vermont Kitchens Revisited
Visions of Home Cook Book
Washington Street Eatery Cook Book
What's Cooking at Moody's Diner
Windjammer Cooking

Appetizers

"Where everybody knows your name," the television show, "Cheers" got its inspiration from the The Bull & Finch Pub in Boston, Massachusetts.

Chocolate Almond Coffee

When I was a little boy, my mother showed me how to float heavy cream on top of black coffee—sliding it off a spoon that was ever-so-lightly sitting on the surface, just barely resting against the side of the cup. She called it "French coffee," and assured me that it was a certain test as to whether or not the cream you had been served was really cream— something that was before light cream, half-and-half, heavy cream, whipping cream, ultra-pasteurized, and whatever else they've come up with since. There was milk, and there was cream—that was it.

Coffee isn't even coffee anymore. Trendy shops are promoting flavored coffees which are great to have, but you needn't spend six dollars a pound for them. Perk up your own coffee—and your life—for half the price.

Splash 3 pounds of coffee beans with an ounce and a half of chocolate extract. Let it dry, add a handful of chopped almonds, and grind it just as you'd grind normal coffee. I do about a fourth of the mixture at a time in a blender on the "grind" setting. Store it in a cold place.

If Chocolate Almond Coffee seems too pedestrian, do the same 3 pounds of beans, add an ounce and a half (a shot or two) of Vandermint, Amaretto, or Frangelico and throw in black walnuts, pecans, or filberts. If you topped them all with flavored whipped cream, the coffee could become the dessert itself.

Another Blue Strawbery

Brick Alley Pub & Restaurant Irish Coffee

Winner of the 1983 Jameson's Irish Whiskey Cup.

Dip the rim of an Irish coffee cup ¼-inch deep in a shallow saucer of Grand Marnier liqueur. Dip the rim into a saucer of granulated sugar. Caramelize the sugar on the rim of the glass over an open flame. Add ½ teaspoon of superfine sugar. Add 1½ ounces Jameson's Irish Whiskey. Fill to ½ inch of top with freshly brewed coffee. Top with whipped cream. Drizzle Bailey's Irish Cream liqueur over the whipped cream. Sprinkle shaved Ghiardelli chocolate over the whipped cream. Serve with a rolled wafer cookie and a sip stick.

A Taste of Newport

Hot Mocoa

¼ cup baking cocoa	3 cups milk
1 tablespoon sugar	2 teaspoons Kahlua
Pinch of salt	¼ cup whipped cream
⅓ cup water	1 teaspoon Kahlua

Combine cocoa, sugar, salt, and water in saucepan. Simmer for 2 minutes, stirring constantly. Add milk. Heat to serving temperature, stirring frequently. Do not boil. Stir in 2 teaspoons Kahlua. Pour into 4 preheated mugs. Combine whipped cream and 1 teaspoon Kahlua in bowl. Top each serving with whipped cream. Yield: 4 servings.

Approximately Per Serving: Cal 179; Prot 7 g; Carbo 17 g; Fiber 2 g; T Fat 10 g; 49%; Calories from Fat; Chol 35 mg; Sod 81 mg.

Rhode Island Cooks

Once Washington's headquarters (1775-76), the home and grounds of Henry Wadsworth Longfellow in Cambridge, Massachusetts, is open to the public.

Harvard-Yale
Hot Buttered Rum Mix

Some hearty tailgaters we know served this with smashing results one freezing afternoon prior to the annual Ivy League football game. The game turned out to be rather humdrum, but everyone was clamoring for the hot rum recipe. A hint: save any leftovers for the holidays and skating parties. Here's to the lads in crimson and blue...

½ cup (1 stick) butter, slightly softened
1 cup brown sugar
1 heaping teaspoon ground cinnamon
1 heaping teaspoon ground nutmeg

⅛ teaspoon ground allspice
¼ teaspoon powdered ginger
½ teaspoon angostura bitters (in the condiments section)

To make the mix, place the softened (but not melted) butter in a medium bowl. Add the brown sugar gradually, and cream the butter and the sugar together, mixing well. Mix in the spices and bitters. Store tightly covered in the refrigerator for up to several months, or use immediately.

To use the mix, stir 1-2 teaspoons of the butter/spice mix into 2 ounces of dark rum and 4 ounces boiling water for each serving. Yield: Enough for 20 servings.

J. Bildner & Sons Cookbook

Hot Buttered Rum

This is supposed to have been the Pilgrims' brew and, when made in quantity, it was kept hot by dipping a hot iron in the bowl—the iron was called a loggerhead. Hot buttered rum was a remedy for everything from chills to snakebite and is still a help when the thermometer drops below zero.

1 teaspoon confectioners' sugar
¼ cup rum

1 tablespoon butter
¼ cup boiling water

Heat the glass you will serve in or use a hot mug. Put the sugar in, and add the remaining ingredients. Fill the glass or mug with boiling water and serve at once. You may sprinkle the top with nutmeg—I use cinnamon. Serves 1.

My Own Cook Book

Boiled Cider

"A native Vermonter, I (a cookbook committee member) managed to get through over half a century without tasting boiled cider. I didn't know what I was missing! It was mentioned as a logical inclusion in this book, so the search was on for a recipe. To no avail. I figured that boiled cider must be just that, so I poured 1 gallon fresh apple cider into a large stainless steel stockpot and boiled it.

"Here's my method: Bring cider to a rolling boil and then turn down to a good simmer so that it continues to evaporate. You can then go about your business and forget about it for a few hours. I simmered mine for about 5 hours, or until it was syrupy. No trick to it—just simmer it until it achieves a consistency that pleases you. It has a wonderful, tart, apple taste, and is a surprising treat on a number of things."

Try this on puffy pancake, cottage cheese pancakes, apple pie, or custard pie, for starters. And the pièce de résistance is a dollop on top of the hard sauce on top of figgy pudding!

HOT MULLED CIDER:
To make hot mulled cider, drop into a quart of cider a cheesecloth bag or tea ball filled with ½ teaspoon whole allspice, ½ teaspoon whole cloves, and 2 broken sticks of cinnamon. Simmer 15 minutes, remove spices, and enjoy in front of the crackling fire.

Vermont Kitchens Revisited

Hot Mulled Cider

You can use a crock-pot, but it will take longer to heat. This is the recipe we use at the annual Harvest Craft Fair.

1 quart hot tea	3 sticks cinnamon
1 gallon cider	1 teaspoon allspice
Juice of 5 lemons	1 teaspoon whole cloves
Juice of 5 oranges	½ teaspoon salt (optional)
1¼ cups brown sugar	Pinch of mace

Simmer, uncovered, for 15 minutes in a large 10-12-quart pan, stirring from time to time. Serve hot with thin slices of oranges in each cup. Makes 20-30 servings.

This cannot be frozen, but it can be refrigerated and reheated.

Tasty Temptations from the Village by the Sea

Brew

2 cups cranberry juice	2 cups apple juice
4 cups decaffeinated or	1 cup orange juice
regular tea	Honey to taste
½ teaspoon cloves	1 teaspoon cinnamon
½ cup lemon juice	

Combine all ingredients in saucepan. Heat until warm.

Hasbro Children's Hospital Cookbook

Scooter's Punch

Scooter was the name of the pet owl who lived behind the bar at The Moors for many years.

2 ounces light rum	½ ounce grenadine
1½ ounces dark rum	1 ounce Myers Dark Rum
3 ounces pineapple juice	½ ounce Cointreau
2 ounces orange juice	

Fill a 24-ounce hurricane glass with ice. Pour in the first 5 ingredients in order and shake. Then float the Myers and Cointreau on top. Garnish with a red long-stemmed carnation.

A recipe from The Moors, Provincetown, MA.

A Taste of Provincetown

Irish Cream

A delicious after-dinner drink, it makes a great gift.

1 teaspoon coffee powder
2 tablespoons boiling water
1 (14-ounce) can sweetened
  condensed milk

2 cups coffee creamer
1 teaspoon vanilla flavoring
6 shots whiskey or to taste

Combine ingredients in blender container; blend well. Chill. May be stored in refrigerator several weeks. Yields 1¼ quarts.

Connecticut Cooks II

Cranberry-Orange Eggnog

6 eggs, separated
¾ cup sugar
2 cups heavy cream, chilled
1 quart cranberry juice,
  chilled

½ cup orange juice,
  chilled
Nutmeg

Beat egg whites and ¼ cup sugar until stiff. Beat egg yolks and ½ cup sugar. Fold whites and yolks together and add cream and juices. Garnish with nutmeg.

Visions of Home Cook Book

Hammersmith Bull

½ cup vodka
½ cup bouillon
1 tablespoon fresh lemon
  juice
1 teaspoon horseradish

Sprinkle of fresh ground
  pepper
A few drops of Worcestershire
  sauce
1 celery stalk

Shake everything except celery. Serve hot or cold. For cold, shake with ice. Stir with celery stalk.

The Hammersmith Farm Cookbook

 Summer home of the Auchincloss family for four generations, Hammersmith Farm, established in 1640, is the last working farm in Newport. It was the setting for daughter Jacqueline Bouvier and John F. Kennedy's wedding reception. They were married in St. Mary's Church in Newport, Rhode Island, in 1952.

Best Crab Dip Ever

1 (8-ounce) package cream
  cheese
1 tablespoon milk
1 can crabmeat, drained
2 tablespoons chopped onion

½-1 teaspoon horseradish
¼ teaspoon salt
2 tablespoons sherry
Slivered almonds (optional)

Mix the cream cheese and milk. Add other ingredients and mix well. Put in a small baking dish with a cover. Bake at 350° for 20-30 minutes. Garnish with almonds, if desired. Serve in a chafing dish (or one that can be kept warm) with crackers.

A Taste of New England

Slates Warmed Artichoke Heart Dip

2 small-medium cloves garlic
¼ teaspoon white pepper
Pinch of cayenne pepper
4 sprigs parsley, chopped
  (optional)
1 teaspoon mustard, Dijon
  style
1 (8-ounce) package cream
  cheese, softened

2 ounces white wine or
  orange juice
Juice of ½ lemon
½ cup Parmesan cheese,
  grated
1 can artichoke hearts,
  drained and quartered
Bread crumbs and scallions
  for garnish (optional)

"Cuisinart" or combine garlic, pepper, cayenne, parsley, mustard, softened cream cheese, wine, lemon juice, and ¼ cup Parmesan cheese. Stir in artichoke hearts. Pour into an ovenproof casserole and top with the rest of the Parmesan cheese. Bread crumbs and scallions are additional optional toppings. Bake at 375° for 15 minutes or until lightly browned and bubbly. Serves 6-8.

A recipe from Slates Restaurant, Hallowell, ME.

Note: Serve with French bread and assorted raw vegetables. For a change, add ½ pound crabmeat (well drained) for Warmed Artichoke Heart Crabmeat Dip.

A Taste of Hallowell

Delish Dip

1 (8-ounce) package cream
  cheese (lite)
2 tablespoons milk

½ cup sour cream
1 (2½-ounce) jar dried
  beef, chopped

Soften and mix cream cheese, milk, and sour cream. Mix in dried beef.

2 tablespoons minced onion
2 tablespoons chopped green
  pepper
Dash of pepper

½ teaspoon horseradish
  (optional)
Crushed walnuts

Add onion, green pepper, pepper, and horseradish. Place in pan. Sprinkle with crushed walnuts. Bake at 350° for 15 minutes, covered. Serve with crackers or vegetables.

Cooking with H.E.L.P.

Spinach Dip

Assorted vegetables for
  dipping
1 package frozen spinach,
  thawed, drained, and chopped
1 package dried vegetable
  soup mix

1 cup mayonnaise
1 cup sour cream
1 cup water chestnuts,
  drained and chopped

Cut up vegetables, e.g. yellow squash, zucchini squash, sweet potatoes, celery, cauliflower, carrots, broccoli, red or green peppers, cucumber, cherry tomatoes, etc.

Combine in a bowl, spinach, soup mix, mayonnaise, sour cream and water chestnuts. Mix well. On a large platter, arrange fresh cut-up vegetables. Place spinach dip in small glass bowl in center of platter. Makes 1 quart. Serve cold.

Moveable Feasts Cookbook

Shrimp Pâté

Smooth and scrumptious.

1 (4-ounce) can small shrimp
1 (3-ounce) and 1 (8-ounce)
   package cream cheese
2 teaspoons curry
2 tablespoons Worcestershire
   sauce

¼ teaspoon Tabasco
Dash cayenne pepper
1 (10½-ounce) can
   consommé

Drain, wash, and dry shrimp. Put in blender with cream cheese, curry, Worcestershire sauce, Tabasco, cayenne, and half of consommé. Reserve remaining consommé. Blend until smooth. Pour into 6 small ramekins and refrigerate overnight. Next morning, drizzle remaining consommé over ramekins. Refrigerate until set. Serve with crackers. Serves 6.

The Cookbook II

Smoked Bluefish Pâté

1 pound smoked bluefish
   fillets
¼ pound cream cheese
3 tablespoons butter
2 tablespoons Cognac
1 tablespoon minced onions

¼-½ teaspoon Worcestershire
   sauce
1 tablespoon lemon juice
Salt
Freshly ground black pepper

Purée the bluefish, cream cheese, butter, and Cognac in a food processor. Add the onions, Worcestershire sauce, and lemon juice and pulse the machine on and off until the ingredients are combined. Taste and correct the seasonings with salt and pepper.

Pack into a crock and serve with crackers or thinly sliced pieces of toast. The pâté will keep in the refrigerator for 4-5 days, or may be frozen for up to 3 months. (Makes about 3¼ cups.)

The Legal Sea Foods Cookbook

Kate's Last-Minute Artichoke Spread

A house classic, this recipe is in constant demand by our guests who try to guess the secret flavorings. There aren't any. It's fast, simple, and just plain wonderful.

1 (14-ounce) can artichoke
  hearts, water packed
1 clove garlic, peeled and
  mashed

3 tablespoons good mayonnaise
Hungarian paprika

Drain the artichokes and squeeze out the water from each one. Chop finely and transfer them to a small saucepan. Add the garlic and mayonnaise. Blend well.

To blend and enhance the flavors, warm over low heat, stirring constantly. Do not let it boil. Turn spread into a serving bowl, sprinkle with paprika, and offer with your favorite crackers. Serves 10-12.

Recipes from a New England Inn

Asparagus Canapés

½ loaf white bread slices
½ cup butter, melted
1 (8-ounce) package cream
  cheese

1 can asparagus spears,
  drained and cut in halves
8 slices cooked, crisp
  bacon, crumbled (optional)

Halve bread slices and place on a cookie sheet. Brush with melted butter. Next, spread small amount of cream cheese on bread. Place half of an asparagus spear on top of the cream cheese. Roll bread around asparagus spear and brush top with melted butter.

Set oven to broil position. Broil asparagus rolls until golden, 2-3 minutes. Optional: Sprinkle top of canapé with crumbled bacon. Serve immediately.

Heritage Cooking

Old Saybrook, Connecticut, was the original home of Yale University in 1701. Yale moved to its present New Haven location fifteen years later.

Suzan's Eggplant Antipasto

3 cups peeled, cubed
  eggplant
1/3 cup chopped green pepper
1 medium onion, chopped
3/4 cup sliced mushrooms
2 cloves garlic, crushed
1/3 cup salad oil
1 (6-ounce) can tomato paste
1/4 cup water

2 tablespoons wine vinegar
1/2 cup sliced stuffed
  olives
1 1/2 teaspoons sugar
1/2 teaspoon oregano
1 teaspoon salt
1/8 teaspoon freshly ground
  pepper

Put eggplant, green pepper, onion, mushrooms, garlic, and oil in skillet. Cover and cook slowly for 10 minutes, stirring occasionally. Add remaining ingredients and cook an additional 30 minutes. Refrigerate overnight or longer in a covered dish. Serve on wheat crackers or warm Syrian bread.

A Taste of New England

Eggplant Caviar
(Potlijel)

I use eggplant year round, whether it is grown locally or not. Eggplant Caviar and roasted peppers are staples in my refrigerator. Soon you will be wondering about the size of my refrigerator. It is just average, but I have kept a 40–year-old one in our garage for overflow.

1 eggplant	Salt and pepper, to taste
1 green pepper	2 tablespoons wine vinegar or
2 or 3 sweet red peppers	lemon juice
1 small onion	1 tablespoon olive oil (optional)
⅛ teaspoon red pepper flakes	

Puncture the skin of the eggplant in 4 or 5 places. Place a rack 4 or 5 inches below the broiler, and heat the broiling unit in the oven. Put the eggplant and peppers on a baking tin. Broil them for 15 or 20 minutes, turning them occasionally. The eggplant should be soft when pierced with a fork. If the peppers are charred before the eggplant is finished, transfer the peppers to a brown paper bag. Fold the top of the bag to enclose the peppers and allow to cool slowly. Do the same with the eggplant when it is soft. Remove the skin and seeds from the peppers. Cut the eggplant in half, vertically, and scrape the flesh from the skin (it will practically slide off).

Chop the onion in the food processor for 10 seconds until minced. Add the green pepper, half the amount of red pepper (reserve the remainder), the eggplant, and the red pepper flakes. Turn the machine on and off to chop ingredients roughly; do not purée them.

Transfer the mixture to a bowl. Season with salt and pepper. Vinegar or lemon juice and oil may be added at this time. Sometimes I omit them. Serve in a bowl as a spread. Cover and store in the refrigerator for up to 1 week. Makes about 2½ cups.

Slice the reserved red pepper into strips. Place in a jar and cover with olive oil. Refrigerate for garnishes.

Suggestions: For a spicy touch, char a tiny hot green pepper with the sweet ones. Add with the rest.

Add a few tablespoons tomato salsa to the Eggplant Caviar. Toss ½ cup Eggplant Caviar with a green salad. An oil dressing will be unnecessary for people counting calories.

The Best from Libby Hillman's Kitchen

Spinach and Cheese Angelicas

1 large egg, plus 2 egg
  whites, beaten well
6 tablespoons whole wheat
  flour
2 cups low-fat cottage
  cheese
1 (10-ounce) package frozen
  chopped spinach, thawed
  and well drained

2 cups Soya Kaas Cheddar
  cheese or Soyco Parmesan
  cheese
Freshly ground pepper, to
  taste
1 small onion, chopped
3-4 tablespoons Italian
  seasoned bread crumbs

Beat eggs with flour. Process remaining ingredients. Bake in oiled 13x9x2-inch baking dish at 350° for 45 minutes. Let stand before cutting. Yield: about 54 squares.

The Chef's Palate Cookbook

Spinach Squares

Expect requests for this recipe!

2 (10-ounce) packages frozen
  chopped spinach
3 tablespoons butter or
  margarine
1 small onion, chopped
¼ pound mushrooms, sliced
4 eggs
¼ cup fine dry bread
  crumbs

1 (10¾-ounce) can cream
  of mushroom soup, undiluted
¼ cup grated Parmesan
  cheese
⅛ teaspoon pepper
⅛ teaspoon dried basil
⅛ teaspoon dried oregano

Place spinach in wire strainer; rinse under hot water to thaw. Press to remove water. Melt butter in skillet; add onion and mushrooms; cook until onion is soft. Beat eggs with a fork. Add bread crumbs, soup, 2 tablespoons cheese, pepper, basil, oregano, spinach and onion mixture; mix well. Pour into well-greased 9-inch-square baking pan. Sprinkle with remaining cheese. Bake, uncovered, at 325° for 35 minutes or until firm when touched lightly. Cool slightly; cover and chill. Cut into 1-inch squares for appetizers and serve cold, or reheat at 325° for 10-12 minutes. Yields 7 dozen.

Connecticut Cooks II

Sausage Quiches

1 (8-ounce) package
  refrigerated crescent rolls
½ pound hot sausage,
  crumbled
2 tablespoons dried onion
  flakes
2 tablespoons minced chives
4 eggs, lightly beaten

1 pint cottage cheese, small curd
2 cups grated Swiss or
  Cheddar cheese
⅓ cup grated Parmesan
  cheese
Paprika

Generously grease 4 miniature muffin tins. Separate dough pieces and cut up to fit into tins about ⅔ way up the sides. Brown sausage lightly with onion. Drain well. Add chives. Spoon equally over dough. Mix eggs and cheeses. Fill tins with mixture. Sprinkle top with paprika. May be frozen at this point, tightly covered. Bring to room temperature. Bake at 375° for 20 minutes. Makes 48 small quiches.

Connecticut Cooks

Fancy Mini Quiches

1 package refrigerated
  butterflake dinner
  rolls (12)
1 (4½-ounce) can shrimp,
  drained
1 beaten egg

½ cup light cream
1 teaspoon brandy
½ teaspoon salt
Dash pepper
1⅓ ounces Gruyère cheese

Grease 2 dozen 1¾-inch muffin tins. Separate each dinner roll in half; press into muffin pan to form shell. Place 1 shrimp in each shell.

Combine egg, cream, brandy, salt and pepper; divide evenly among shells, using about 2 teaspoons for each.

Slice cheese into 24 small triangles. Place 1 on top of each appetizer. Bake in 375° oven for 20 minutes or until golden brown. Serve immediately or cool. Makes 24.

Cuisine à la Mode

Bow House Brochettes

Flavor lives up to its wonderful aroma!

½ pound sliced bacon
1 pound sea scallops, rinsed
  and drained
2 tablespoons unsalted
  butter, melted

1½ tablespoons firmly
  packed brown sugar
1 teaspoon ground cinnamon

Cut bacon slices in half. Wrap bacon around scallop and secure with wooden toothpick. Combine butter, brown sugar, and cinnamon. Brush on bacon-wrapped scallops. Broil, turning as necessary, until bacon is crisp on all sides.

Scallops and bacon may be assembled early in day and chilled. Recipe may be doubled. Yields 1½ dozen.

Connecticut Cooks II

Terrine of Scallops and Salmon

1½ pounds scallops
1 cup cleaned and sliced
  leeks
3 egg whites, chilled
3 tablespoons bread crumbs
1½ tablespoons grated
  lemon rind
½ teaspoon ground nutmeg
1 tablespoon tomato paste

3 tablespoons minced parsley
Dash of Tabasco sauce
6 ounces skim evaporated
  milk
1 teaspoon salt
Dash of pepper
1 pound salmon fillets,
  diced
1 cup frozen peas

Place all the ingredients in the bowl of a food processor, except for 6 of the scallops, the salmon, and the peas, and process until smooth. Transfer the mixture to a large bowl and stir in the diced salmon, peas, and the whole scallops. Check for seasoning. Fill a 9-inch loaf pan with the mixture, cover with aluminum foil, and set the pan into a larger pan. Fill the larger pan with water until it reaches halfway up the sides of the loaf pan. Bake at 350° for 45 minutes. The terrine is done when it reaches an internal temperature of 130°.

Cool to room temperature and refrigerate overnight. To serve, briefly warm the bottom of the pan (in warm water or with a hot wet towel) and run a knife around the edge. Turn out onto a platter. Slice the terrine and serve with a Dijon mayonnaise sauce. Serves 12.

As You Like It

Cold Salmon Mousse

1 (16-ounce) can red salmon; drain, remove bones, and flake

1 (8-ounce) package cream cheese (room temperature)

1 tablespoon lemon juice

¼ teaspoon salt

1 tablespoon horseradish, grated

2 tablespoons onion, grated

½ tablespoon liquid smoke (optional)

6 tablespoons chopped pecans

½ cup chopped fresh parsley

Blend all ingredients except pecans and parsley. Chill for at least 4 hours. Make 2 balls by dividing mixture in half. Roll each ball in 3 tablespoons of chopped pecans mixed with 3 tablespoons of chopped parsley just before serving. Serve with French bread. Garnish with small pickles, tomatoes, cucumbers, and whatever you have. Flavors improve if made the day before.

Note: This dish is also great molded in individual molds (line molds with plastic wrap) and used as a first course. Press pecans and parsley on molded salmon.

Seafood Expressions

Smoked Mackerel and Horseradish Cream

This is a terrific spread on crackers or crisp toasts.

1 pound smoked mackerel

½ pound butter

½ pound cream cheese

2 tablespoons grated horseradish

½ pint heavy cream

Peel the skin off the smoked fish and pick out the bones. In a food processor, soften the butter and cream cheese together with the horseradish. When these ingredients begin to meld, add the fish and purée everything. Whip the cream and fold it into the puréed fish mixture. No additional seasonings should be required, as the smoked flavor of the fish will be strong enough.

The Harlow's Bread & Cracker Cookbook

 Before the advent of refrigeration, salt mackerel was the most eaten fish in the world.

Clam Tart Appetizer

On the Eastern seacoast, we eat clams in a variety of ways. This recipe makes a highly popular appetizer.

2 (6½-ounce) cans minced
  clams
½ cup (1 stick) margarine,
  melted
½ teaspoon dried oregano

¾ cup fine bread crumbs
½ cup grated Parmesan
  cheese
8 ounces shredded mozzarella
  cheese

Combine undrained clams, margarine, and oregano with bread crumbs. Spread in an 8-inch pie pan. Sprinkle with Parmesan and mozzarella cheeses. Bake in a preheated 350° oven for 20 minutes or until hot and bubbly. Serve with melba toast rounds. Makes about 2 cups.

The Lymes' Heritage Cookbook

Lobster Tarts

1 pie crust
2 tablespoons butter
1 (6-ounce) can frozen
  lobster, or 8 ounces fresh
  lobster
2 tablespoons finely chopped
  onion
1 tablespoon finely chopped
  parsley

2 tablespoons lemon juice
1 tablespoon flour
½ cup warm light cream
1 egg yolk
2 tablespoons brandy
Cheddar cheese

Make 36 mini-tarts using either tart pan or small muffin pan. Lightly bake. Melt butter; add lobster, onion, and parsley. Sprinkle with lemon juice and flour. Add cream, which has been blended into yolk and brandy. Fill tarts with mixture and sprinkle with cheese. Bake at 375° for about 20 minutes.

A Taste of New England

Crab Rangoons

1 (8-ounce) package cream
cheese softened
8 ounces crabmeat or surimi
(imitation crab)
¼-½ teaspoon cayenne
pepper, or crushed dried red
pepper flakes, to taste

2-3 tablespoons water
Oil for frying
1 pound wonton wrappers or
1 pound egg roll wrappers,
cut in quarters

Combine all ingredients except wonton wrappers. Place ½-1 teaspoon crab mixture in a corner of the wonton and roll up on the diagonal. Moisten tips of wonton wrappers with water to seal. Place seam-side-down in 1½-2 inches hot oil and fry until golden on one side. Turn over and fry until second side is golden. Remove from oil and drain on paper towels. Yield: approximately 64 rangoons.

Hint: Serve with duck sauce or hot mustard. These may be frozen. To reheat, place frozen rangoons in a 350° oven and bake until hot, about 10 minutes. You can substitute a 6½-ounce can of tuna for the crab.

From Ellie's Kitchen to Yours

Pepperoni Puffs

Very easy and freeze beautifully!

1 cup all-purpose flour
1 teaspoon baking powder
1 cup milk
1 egg

¼ cup grated Cheddar
cheese
1 cup diced pepperoni

Combine first 5 ingredients and mix thoroughly. Add pepperoni and mix until evenly distributed throughout the mixture. Allow batter to stand for 15 minutes. Grease mini-muffin pans or spray with nonstick vegetable spray. Fill each cup ¾ full. Bake at 350° for 25-35 minutes or until browned. Yields 60 puffs.

Connecticut Cooks III

 Mystic Seaport is Connecticut's most popular tourist attraction. It is a nationally acclaimed "living museum" featuring a restored 19th-century village, authentic whaling ships, and working craftspeople.

Shrimp Puffs

They have an intriguing "melt-in-the-mouth" quality that you'll find quite delicious.

1 egg white	½ cup mayonnaise
¼ cup sharp Cheddar cheese, grated	24 slices round party rye bread
⅛ teaspoon salt	24 small shrimp, cooked, shelled, and deveined
⅛ teaspoon paprika	

Beat the egg white until stiff. Fold in the cheese, salt, paprika, and mayonnaise.

Heap this mixture on the party rye rounds. Top each round with 1 shrimp. Broil the puffs until light brown. Serve hot. Makes 24 canapés.

The Country Innkeepers' Cookbook

Scallop Puffs

One of the great pleasures of living at the eastern end of Long Island Sound is the scallops, both the bay scallops from the waters at Niantic, and the large sea scallops. This recipe is a splendid way to use them.

½ pound sea scallops	1 heaping cup mayonnaise
2 tablespoons butter	⅛ teaspoon black pepper
1 teaspoon grated lemon rind	6 dozen 1½-inch bread rounds, lightly toasted
1½ garlic cloves, minced	
½ teaspoon dried dill weed	Paprika
1 cup shredded Swiss cheese	

Cut scallops in quarters. Melt butter. Add scallops, grated lemon rind, and garlic. Cook for 2-3 minutes. Add dill and cook 30 seconds more. Cool to room temperature. Add cheese, mayonnaise, and pepper and mix well. (Can be prepared up to a week in advance; cover and refrigerate.)

Place mixture on toast rounds, sprinkle with paprika, and run under broiler for 2-3 minutes. Serve hot. Puffs can be frozen after broiling. Makes 72 puffs.

The Lymes' Heritage Cookbook

Angels on Horseback

STUFFING:

½ cup fresh parsley,
  chopped
1½ tablespoons onion,
  finely minced

1 teaspoon fresh garlic,
  minced

SAUCE:

3 tablespoons fresh-squeezed
  lemon juice
½ cup heavy cream

½ pound unsalted chilled
  butter, cut into half-
  tablespoon-sized pieces

Prepare the stuffing by mixing stuffing ingredients until well mixed. Set aside. Prepare the sauce by placing the lemon juice in a heavy-gauge saucepan and cooking while stirring, until juice reduces to slightly less than half. Add the heavy cream and, over medium heat, reduce mixture to half, whisking frequently. Slowly add the chilled butter, whisking, 1 piece at a time. Add the next piece when the previous piece of butter is half-melted, to maintain a consistent temperature. When the last piece of butter has been added, remove sauce immediately from heat and whisk until it has melted completely. It is very important to make sure the sauce gets neither very hot nor very cold.

15 strips bacon
30 oysters, shucked

6 slices country-style white
  bread

Cut the raw bacon strips in half to make 30 short pieces. Place 1 oyster in the middle of each piece of bacon. Spoon about ½ teaspoon of stuffing over each oyster. Roll up so that the stuffing is covered by bacon. Secure with a toothpick. Place the oysters under a broiler for 3-4 minutes on each side, until bacon is cooked.

Toast bread and remove crusts. Cut toast in half, diagonally, and place 2 toast points on each plate in a "stretched-out" rectangle. Place 5 bacon-wrapped oysters, toothpicks removed, on each plate, spoon sauce over oysters, and serve. Serves 6.

A recipe from The Impudent Oyster, Chatham, MA.

Cape Cod's Night at the Chef's Table

Mustard Seed Shrimp

A different twist to marinated shrimp.

1½ cups mayonnaise
⅓ cup lemon juice, freshly
  squeezed
¼ cup sugar
½ cup sour cream
1 large red onion, finely
  chopped
4 tablespoons chopped fresh
  dill, or 2 teaspoons dry dill

1 tablespoon mustard seed
1 tablespoon Worcestershire
  sauce
2 pounds medium shrimp,
  cooked and peeled

In a large bowl, mix mayonnaise, lemon juice, sugar, sour cream, onion, and seasonings. Stir in the shrimp; cover and refrigerate overnight. Spoon into a crystal bowl or family heirloom and serve with wooden picks. Serves 6-8. Must be made ahead.

Seafood Secrets Cookbook

Brie in Crust

When salad is the main course for luncheon or supper, this is a delicious accompaniment hot from the oven. Or, with plenty of paper napkins, it can be used for a cocktail or buffet party. This recipe is for two loaves—if you don't need both, wrap one in plastic and freeze it.

2 round bread loaves, 3
  inches larger than cheese

1 brie (about 2 pounds), cut
  in half to make 2 disks

Preheat oven to 350°. Cut bread loaves in half horizontally and place cheese disks between them. Fasten with toothpicks or tie securely with kitchen string. Bake 10 minutes, until cheese has melted. Remove toothpicks or string. Cut in wedges at the table. Yield: 2 loaves.

Favorite New England Recipes

 A 4-foot, 39-pound copper gilded grasshopper weathervane has been spinning atop Faneuil Hall in Boston since 1742. Nobody seems to know why a grasshopper was chosen. Legend has it that the grasshopper is a symbol of good luck and prosperity.

Linda's Savory and Sweet Surprises

1 cup butter, softened
1 pound grated sharp
  Cheddar cheese

2 cups flour
1 pound pitted dates, halved
  lengthwise

Blend the butter and cheese together. Gradually add the flour to the butter and cheese mixture. Chill the dough overnight. Bring to room temperature and roll out the dough thinly. Cut into small rounds. Place a date half on one side of each dough round, and fold over the remaining dough. Pinch the edges together. You will have a bite-size turnover. Bake on a nonstick baking sheet at 250-300° for 30 minutes. Serve warm. Serves 30-45.

As You Like It

Chinese Barbecued Spareribs

2 pounds lean spareribs, cut
  into 2-inch lengths
Salt
½ cup water
⅓ cup soy sauce
⅓ cup light brown sugar
2 tablespoons cider vinegar

¼ teaspoon freshly grated
  ginger root
1-2 cloves garlic, very
  finely minced
1 tablespoon cornstarch
2 tablespoons water

Place the lightly salted ribs in a roasting pan with the ½ cup of water. Cover and bake at 350° for 1¼ hours. Drain off all water and grease, cool slightly, and cut into individual ribs. Can do this several days ahead.

Combine the soy sauce, sugar, vinegar, ginger, and garlic in a saucepan and bring to a boil stirring constantly. Boil 1 minute. Combine cornstarch and water well and add to the sauce. Cook over medium heat stirring constantly until sauce is thick and clear. Cool slightly and then pour over ribs to coat completely. Place coated ribs in a flat baking dish and bake for 20 minutes at 350°. Yield: about 20 ribs.

RSVP

Spinach-Wrapped Chicken with Oriental Dip

2 whole chicken breasts	1 pound fresh spinach
1¾ cups chicken broth	Lettuce leaves
¼ cup soy sauce	
1 tablespoon Worcestershire sauce	

In a 3-quart saucepan, simmer the chicken breasts in the chicken broth, ¼ cup soy sauce, and 1 tablespoon Worcestershire until tender, about 15-20 minutes. Remove the chicken breasts from the broth and cool.

Thoroughly wash and remove the stems from spinach leaves. Reserve smaller spinach leaves for another use, and pour 2-3 quarts of boiling water over the larger ones. Completely drain and set the spinach aside to cool.

When the chicken breasts are cool, discard the bones and skin. Cut the meat into 1-inch cubes.

To assemble, place a chicken cube at the stem end of a spinach leaf. Roll over once, fold leaf in on both sides, and continue rolling around the chicken piece. Secure the end of the leaf with a toothpick and chill in the refrigerator.

Cover a serving plate with lettuce leaves. Place Oriental Dip in a small bowl in the center and surround it with the spinach-wrapped chicken pieces.

ORIENTAL DIP:

1 cup sour cream	4 teaspoons soy sauce
2 teaspoons toasted sesame seeds	2 teaspoons Worcestershire sauce
½ teaspoon ground ginger	

In a small serving bowl, combine the sour cream, sesame seeds, ground ginger, soy sauce, and Worcestershire. Stir gently to combine the ingredients. Chill 4 hours in the refrigerator. Yield: 3-4 dozen.

Hospitality

Daniel Webster was one of this country's most famous statesmen. Educated at Exeter, New Hampshire, and Dartmouth, New Hampshire, Webster served in the U.S. Senate and was Secretary of State under Presidents Harrison and Fillmore.

Chinese Chicken Wings

3 cloves of garlic, minced
1 small onion, minced
3 tablespoons fresh parsley,
  chopped
1 cup soy sauce
½ cup vegetable oil

1 tablespoon Dijon mustard
1 tablespoon honey (or ½
  tablespoon sugar)
3-5 pounds chicken wings,
  disjointed

Combine garlic, onion, parsley, soy sauce, oil, mustard, and honey. Mix thoroughly in food processor or with wire whisk. Marinate wings for several hours at room temperature or overnight (covered in refrigerator).

Bake wings on a cookie sheet or jelly roll pan at 300° for 45 minutes, turning once, and broil for approximately 5 minutes or until wings are brown and bubbly.

A Taste of Salt Air & Island Kitchens

Tasty Toasts

"I always keep these wonderful herb toasts in my freezer. They are a good accompaniment for soups, salads, or any beverage. Quite my favorite canapé and possibly my most popular."

1 cup (2 sticks) margarine,
  softened
½ teaspoon dried oregano
½ teaspoon dried basil
½ teaspoon dried rosemary

½ teaspoon dried thyme
4 tablespoons minced fresh
  parsley
24 slices melba-thin white
  bread, crusts removed

Cream margarine with all seasonings; blend well. Spread bread slices generously with mixture. Cut each slice into 4 even pieces and place on 2 cookie sheets. Bake in a preheated 250° oven for 1 hour. Cool, pack in closed container, and store in freezer. Use them as needed, served at room temperature. Makes 96 toasts.

The Lymes' Heritage Cookbook

Corn Chips

These make great dipping crackers.

6 cups bread flour
3 cups corn flour
2 teaspoons salt
2 teaspoons garlic powder

1 teaspoon cumin
1 teaspoon chili powder
1 teaspoon baking powder
3 cups water

Mix the dry ingredients together, then add the water. Wrap and refrigerate the dough. When ready to roll, preheat the oven to 350°. This dough will oblige by rolling out easily and very thin. Place the sheets on parchment-lined cookie sheets, cut to size, and bake 7–10 minutes.

The Harlow's Bread & Cracker Cookbook

Cracked Pepper Crackers

The first one is good, the second better, and by the third you are positively addicted. These crackers are great served with Bloody Marys, as they are closely related.

1 tablespoon crushed
  peppercorns
1 tablespoon salt
¼ cup vegetable oil
2 tablespoons horseradish

2 teaspoons Tabasco sauce
1 teaspoon Worcestershire
  sauce
2 cups tomato juice
7 cups bread flour

Mix the peppercorns and salt in a large bowl, then add the rest of the ingredients except for the flour. Mix until they are thoroughly distributed. Work in the flour a cup at a time. (If you are mixing by hand, you may not be able to work in all the flour.) Wrap the dough in plastic and chill for at least 60 minutes.

Preheat oven to 350°, roll the dough as thin as it will go, place on parchment-lined baking sheets, and cut into squares. Bake approximately 8–10 minutes. The tomato color will yellow a bit and the crackers will be quite crisp when they are done.

The Harlow's Bread & Cracker Cookbook

Dense and bland but crunchy, common crackers were first made in Montpelier, Vermont, in 1828.

Bread and Breakfast

Boston's Beacon Hill, with its gaslamps, brick sidewalks, and narrow cobblestone streets, still looks like a 19th-century neighborhood.

Boston Brown Bread
(Microwave)

If you have a lot of spare time, you might want to make this bread conventionally. One traditional recipe calls for steaming the batter in coffee cans for three hours!

⅓ cup light molasses	½ cup whole wheat flour
1 cup sour milk or	½ teaspoon salt
buttermilk	1 teaspoon baking soda
½ cup rye or white flour	1 cup seedless raisins or
½ cup yellow cornmeal	cut-up dates

Grease a 2-cup ovenproof glass measuring cup with shortening.*

Mix the molasses and milk together; set aside. Mix the rye or white flour, cornmeal, whole wheat flour, salt, and baking soda in a large bowl. Add the milk mixture, stirring until well blended. Add raisins or dates; mix well.

Pour half of the batter (about 1 cup) into the greased cup. Cover with vented plastic wrap. Heat at MEDIUM (50%) power for 3 minutes; rotate cup a half turn. Heat at MEDIUM for another 2–4 minutes, or until the bread is not doughy looking. When done, the bread will start to pull away from the cup edge.

Let stand on a flat surface for 5 minutes before uncovering. Carefully run a knife around the edge of the cup; unmold onto a plate. Microwave the remaining batter as above. Serve the bread warm with butter or softened cream cheese. Wrap any unused bread in plastic wrap before storing. Makes 2 small loaves.

*This bread may be baked in a greased 5- or 6-cup microwaveable ring mold if you wish. Pour all the batter into the mold; cover with vented plastic wrap. Heat at MEDIUM (50%) power for 5 minutes; rotate the mold a half turn.

Heat at MEDIUM for another 5–7 minutes, or until the bread is not doughy looking. Let the mold stand on a flat surface for 10 minutes before removing the plastic wrap. Carefully run a knife around inner and outer edges of mold. Gently unmold onto a serving plate.

Classic New England Dishes from Your Microwave

Boston Brown Bread

1 cup yellow cornmeal
1 cup graham flour
1 cup rye flour (2 cups
  cornmeal, if no rye)
¾ cup molasses

1½ cups sour milk with
  1 teaspoon soda and
  1 teaspoon salt
1 cup raisins

Mix and sift dry ingredients and stir in the rest. Add raisins. Pour into tin cans, fill only ⅔ full, cover, and steam on a rack in a kettle of boiling water 2½ hours.

Stillmeadow Cook Book

Quick Brown Bread

A traditional New England bread that is especially good with chicken, ham, and baked beans. Hard to go wrong making this.

2 cups whole wheat flour
1 teaspoon salt
½ teaspoon soda
1½ teaspoons baking
  powder

1 egg
1 cup buttermilk
½ cup molasses
¼ cup shortening

Mix the flour, salt, soda, and baking powder thoroughly. Beat the egg and add to it the buttermilk, molasses, and shortening. Add the liquid to the dry ingredients and stir only enough to barely mix. Bake in a well-greased loaf pan at 350° for 30 minutes. Cut in slices and serve hot. Makes 1 loaf.

The Country Innkeepers' Cookbook

Rhode Island Johnnycakes

Made with white cornmeal and cooked on a hot griddle. Some Rhode Island cooks would omit the sugar, others the eggs.

3 eggs
2 cups stone-ground white
   cornmeal
2 teaspoons baking powder
2 tablespoons flour
1 teaspoon salt

2 tablespoons sugar
   (optional)
1 tablespoon melted butter
   or shortening
Milk (1-2 cups)

In medium bowl, beat eggs well. Add remaining ingredients, stirring in enough milk to make thin batter. Pour batter onto hot griddle (use ¼-cup measure to dip batter). Cook until brown on one side; flip and brown on other side. Serve with butter and maple syrup.

Variation: Break completely with tradition! Try serving johnnycakes topped with smoked salmon and Crème Fraîche or sour cream; sprinkle with plenty of fresh snipped dill. Yield: about 12 (4-inch) cakes.

All Seasons Cookbook

Indian Bread

1 cup Indian meal (coarsely
   milled cornmeal)
½ yeast cake
2 cups boiling water

¼ cup shortening
¼ cup molasses
1 pinch salt
¼ cup sugar

Scald meal in boiling water and mix in other ingredients. Add in enough white flour to allow the mixture to be kneaded. Allow to rise as with white bread. Bake in medium 350° oven for about 45 minutes.

Recipes from a Cape Cod Kitchen

Sour Cream Corn Muffins

1 cup yellow cornmeal
1 cup flour
¼ cup sugar
2 teaspoons baking powder
1 teaspoon salt

½ teaspoon soda
1 cup sour cream
2 eggs, slightly beaten
¼ cup butter, melted

Butter 12 muffin tins. In a medium bowl, combine cornmeal, flour, sugar, baking powder, salt, and soda. In a small bowl, combine sour cream, beaten eggs, and melted butter; blend well. Add to dry ingredients and stir until evenly blended; do not overmix. Drop batter into prepared muffin tins and bake at 425°, 25-30 minutes. Cool in pans for 5 minutes before removing. Serve hot.

Memories from Brownie's Kitchen

Best Ever Oatmeal Bread

2 packages dry yeast or
    2 yeast cakes
½ cup warm water
1½ cups boiling water
1 cup quick-cooking rolled
    oats
¼ cup honey

¼ cup molasses
⅓ cup shortening
2 teaspoons salt
5½–6 cups flour
2 eggs, beaten, or ½ cup
    frozen egg product (thawed)

Dissolve yeast in warm water. Combine boiling water, rolled oats, honey, molasses, shortening, and salt. Cool to lukewarm. Stir in 2 cups of flour and beat well. Add yeast and eggs or egg substitute. Mix thoroughly. Stir in enough flour to make a soft dough.* Turn out on floured surface and knead 6-7 minutes, until smooth and elastic. Place in a greased bowl, turning once to grease top. Cover and let rise until double in bulk. Punch down; divide dough in half. Cover and let rest 10 minutes.

Grease two 9x5-inch bread pans and coat inside with rolled oats. Shape dough into loaves and place in pans. Cover and let rise until double. Mix 1 egg white with 1 tablespoon water and brush tops of loaves. Sprinkle with rolled oats. Bake at 425° for 15 minutes. Reduce heat to 325° for 30 minutes more.

*Be sure to use enough flour, because otherwise oatmeal bread has a tendency to "fall" on the sides after it is baked.

Homespun Cookery

No-Knead Shredded Wheat Bread

2 large shredded wheat
  biscuits
2 cups boiling water
1 teaspoon salt
1/3 cup sugar

1/3 cup molasses
3 tablespoons margarine
1 yeast cake
1/2 cup warm water
5-6 cups flour

Crumble shredded wheat in 2 cups boiling water. Add salt, sugar, molasses, and margarine; let stand until cool. Add yeast cake dissolved in warm water. Stir in the flour. Mix thoroughly. Cover with a damp cloth; let rise until doubled in bulk.

If necessary at this time, add more flour to make stiffer dough. Divide dough and put into 2 greased 9x5-inch pans. Let rise until above rim of pan. Bake at 400° for 15 minutes; reduce heat to 350° and bake 30 minutes longer. Remove from pans and brush tops of bread with margarine.

The Parkview Way to Vegetarian Cooking

Squash Yeast Bread

This bread is a delicious loaf made in the shape of a French bread. It also may be made with mashed potatoes in place of the squash. If potatoes are used, substitute 1/2 cup minced chives for the cinnamon and cloves in the squash bread.

2 tablespoons dry yeast
2 tablespoons honey
1 1/2 cups warm water
2 1/2 cups mashed squash
1/4 cup oil
3 tablespoons maple syrup

2 teaspoons salt
1 teaspoon cinnamon
1/2 teaspoon cloves
8-10 cups flour, half white, half
  whole wheat

Dissolve yeast and honey in water. Add mashed squash, oil, maple syrup, salt, spices, and 2 cups of the flour. Stir in remaining flour. (Add last of flour slowly so as not to get too much.) Knead for 10 minutes. Let rise for 1 hour, punch down and shape into 2 large loaves or into French-bread-shaped loaves. Place in 2 greased loaf pans or in 2 long loaves on a cookie sheet. Let rise until double in size. Bake at 375° for 45-50 minutes. Cool on wire rack.

Memories from Brownie's Kitchen

Popovers

These crisp and airy creations, hot from the oven, accompanied by a bowl of chilled summer soup or a steaming winter stew, are guaranteed to lift your spirits.

2 large eggs	**1 cup King Arthur Unbleached**
1 cup milk	**All-Purpose Flour**
½ teaspoon salt	

Beat the eggs into the milk until frothy. Add the salt and flour. Beat the mixture about 1 minute or until you begin to see large bubbles develop. If you have time, let it sit for 30-45 minutes at room temperature and then beat again.

Fifteen minutes or so before the second beating, preheat your oven to 400° and liberally grease an 8-cup muffin tin with butter. To bake, fill the cups ⅔ full of batter and place in the hot oven. Bake for 35-40 minutes until the popovers are blown up and lightly browned. Make sure not to open the oven to look while they're baking. Until they're completely done, the airy structure of the popovers will collapse without much provocation.

After they're done, remove them from the oven and prick them with a knife to let the steam escape. Make sure you time your baking so you can eat them while they're still warm. A cold popover loses much of its charm.

Variations: For Cheese Popovers, add a few shakes of paprika, cayenne pepper, or dry mustard and ½ cup of grated cheese to your batter. Fresh Parmesan would be wonderful, or equally good would be Asiago, Romano, plain or smoked Cheddar. For Bacon Popovers for Sunday breakfast, put a bit of crisp, crumbled bacon in the bottom of each cup before you pour in the batter. Or combine the two for Cheese & Bacon Popovers.

The King Arthur Flour 200th Anniversary Cookbook

Onion, Cheese, and Walnut Muffins

1¾ cups flour
¼ cup sugar
2 teaspoons baking powder
1 beaten egg
¾ cup milk

⅓ cup cooking oil
1 onion, coarsely chopped
½ cup shredded Cheddar
   cheese
½ cup chopped walnuts

Preheat oven to 400°. In a large mixing bowl stir together the flour, sugar, and baking powder. Make a well in the center. Combine egg, milk, and oil. Add egg mixture all at once to flour mixture; stir just until moistened. Stir in onion, cheese, and walnuts. Grease or line muffin cups and fill approximately ⅔ full. Bake at 400° for 20-25 minutes or until golden. Makes 12 muffins.

The Maine Collection

Herb Rolls

1 package active dry yeast
¼ cup warm water
¾ cup milk, scalded
3 tablespoons butter
3 tablespoons granulated
   sugar
1½ teaspoons salt

3-3½ cups all-purpose
   flour
1 egg, beaten
¼ teaspoon mace
1 tablespoon sage
1 egg white, slightly beaten

Soften yeast in warm water. Blend milk, butter, sugar, and salt thoroughly in a large bowl; cool to warm. Add 1 cup flour and beat thoroughly. Beat in egg, mace, and sage; then yeast. Mix in enough remaining flour to make a soft (but not sticky) dough.

Turn onto a lightly floured surface and knead until smooth and elastic. Put into a greased deep bowl; turn dough to bring greased surface to top. Cover; let rise in a warm place until doubled, 1 hour. Punch down dough and let rest about 10 minutes.

Shape dough into 12 round rolls. Place in greased muffin tin cups and let rise again 45 minutes or until doubled. Brush with egg white. Bake in 375° preheated oven 15 minutes or until browned.

Dining on Deck

Open Sesame (à la Baba)

The one thing crucial to this recipe is to make sure the sesame seeds are roasted. Sesame seeds are not often sold roasted, so it will require roasting some ahead. The sesame seeds should be taken out of the oven when lightly browned. (Darker roasted seeds are also good if that is your preference.) The sesame taste is present throughout, and the crust has a crackly surface for the first day.

½ **pound roasted sesame seeds, hulled or unhulled (¾ cup)**
1 **pound whole wheat flour (3 cups)**
1 **pound unbleached white flour (3¼ cups)**

1½ **teaspoons dry yeast**
2 **cups + 2 tablespoons water, anywhere from body temperature to 120°**
1½ **tablespoons sea salt**

Set the sesame seeds aside. Mix the flour, yeast, water, and salt until a nice firm ball of dough is formed. Place in a covered container to rise for 12 hours. When the 12 hours are up, knead in the roasted sesame seeds. Cut the dough in 2 and roll each piece of dough into a ball by stretching the top outside surface and tucking the side edges underneath while pinching the bottoms of the loaves together with the 2 outer edges of your palms. Set on a tray sprinkled with cornmeal and allow 2-4 hours for the loaves to double in bulk. They will look like water balloons on a flat surface.

Egg-glaze the top of the crust, if you wish, and sprinkle the top with roasted sesame seeds. Slice the top with a knife or razor blade in the form of a flapping wing or any other design.

Cook for about 40 minutes at 375°; the bread will acquire a dark crisp crust in an oven at 450°. Regardless of how the outside looks, the inside of the bread must be allowed to cook. The bottom of the bread knows best how to tell you if the bread is cooked through. Tapping on the bottom and hearing a hollow sound is the true indicator of the bread's being done. Makes 2 loaves.

Baba À Louis Bakery Bread Book

Cinnamon Raisin Bread

1½ cups raisins
1½ cups water (or cider)
2 packages dry yeast,
   proofed
¼ cup oil

1 tablespoon sugar
1 tablepoon salt
6–8 cups bread flour
Whole-egg wash
Cinnamon sugar for top

PROOFING THE YEAST:
Put a small portion—1 tablespoon to ¼-cup—of the total water required by the recipe into a small bowl with a pinch of sugar, which acts as a catalyst to wake up the yeast. The water should be luke-warm; yeast will be killed at 138°. Open the package(s) and float the yeast on the sugar-water. Go on assembling the dry ingredients of the recipe in a large bowl, and then look at your yeast. If it has gone cloudy and started to bubble, you know that it is very much alive and you can get on with your bread-making. If there is no such response, then borrow from your neighbor or go to the store, and start again.

Soak the raisins in water or cider for at least 60 minutes. Drain the raisins and reserve the liquid. To the proofed yeast add the raisin water, oil, sugar, and salt, and work in 6-8 cups bread flour. Knead in enough flour to make an elastic, tender dough.

Raise the bread, covered, in a lightly oiled bowl until doubled. Punch it down, divide the dough, and form into 2 flat rectangles. Brush with some of the whole-egg wash and spread the raisins over the dough, pushing them down slightly. Sprinkle cinnamon sugar over the raisins and roll up jelly-roll fashion. Pinch the seams to-gether—any raisins that stick out will burn in the baking process.

Place the loaves into 2 greased loaf pans, or lay them out on lightly oiled cookie sheets, brush the tops with remaining egg, and sprinkle once more with cinnamon sugar.

Preheat oven to 325° while loaves are rising again. Then bake for 15 minutes, then at which point increase the heat to 350° and bake for 30 minutes more.

The Harlow's Bread & Cracker Cookbook

The first street in America to be illuminated by gaslight was Pelham Street in Newport, Rhode Island, in 1806.

Lemon Puffs

½ cup hot water
1 package active dry yeast
5 eggs, beaten
2 tablespoons powdered milk
¼ cup melted butter
⅓ cup sugar, plus sugar
  for topping

Finely grated rind of 1
  lemon
½ teaspoon salt
4½ cups flour
1 egg yolk, beaten
Finely chopped walnuts

Combine water and yeast and set aside to dissolve. In a large mixing bowl, combine eggs, powdered milk, melted butter, ⅓ cup of the sugar, lemon rind, and salt. Add dissolved yeast and mix well. Stir in flour. Allow dough to rise in a bowl, until it is doubled in volume. Punch down, remove from bowl and knead lightly on floured board. Dough will be smooth and soft. Place in a clean bowl and set aside to rise again until doubled in volume. Punch down again and knead out the bubbles. Preheat oven to 350°. Grease 2 baking sheets. Shape dough into 1-inch balls and place them 1 inch apart on prepared baking sheets. Brush the tops with egg yolk and sprinkle with sugar and finely chopped walnuts. Bake 15 minutes and serve at once. Yield: 30 rolls.

A recipe from Stafford's in the Field, Chocorua, NH.

Country Inns and Back Roads Cookbook

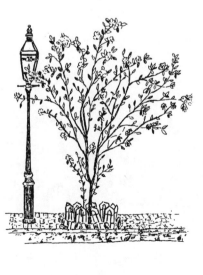

Lemon Layer Loaf

One of my favorites, this spectacular bread combines lemon and raspberry in a unique flavoring. It is perfect for afternoon tea.

½ cup soft butter
⅔ cup sugar
2 eggs
1½ cups flour
1 teaspoon baking powder
1 teaspoon salt
½ cup milk

3 tablespoons fresh lemon juice
1½ tablespoons grated lemon rind
½ cup seedless raspberry jam

Preheat oven to 325°. In a large bowl cream together butter and sugar. Beat in eggs. In a separate bowl sift together the flour, baking powder, and salt; mix into the creamed mixture, along with the milk. Beat well, adding lemon juice and rind.

Pour half the batter into a greased and floured 9x5x3-inch loaf pan. Carefully spread jam over the top. Pour remainder of batter over the layer of jam, being careful not to disturb it.

Bake at 325° for 50 minutes, or until a toothpick inserted in center comes out clean. Cool in pan for 10 minutes and then turn out onto rack to cool thoroughly. Cool completely before slicing.

A recipe from Eastover Farm, Bethlehem, CT.

The Bed & Breakfast Cookbook

Morning Cake Delight with Topping

CAKE:

1 pound butter	1½ teaspoons almond
2 cups sugar	extract
6 eggs	4 cups flour
½ cup sour cream	1 tablespoon baking powder
½ cup milk	1 cup berries (raspberries,
1 banana, mashed	blueberries, or blackberries)

Preheat oven to 350°. In a large bowl cream together the butter and sugar. Beat in eggs. Then add sour cream, milk, banana, and almond extract. Mix well. In a separate bowl combine flour and baking powder. Add to creamed mixture and blend well but do not overbeat.

Pour half the batter into a greased and floured 12-inch Bundt pan, sprinkle with berries, and cover with remaining batter. Bake at 350° for 50-60 minutes. This is a big cake, so be sure to test with a toothpick to be certain it's done.

Cool in pan for a few minutes, and then turn out of pan to cool completely on a rack.

TOPPING:

½ cup whipping cream	½ cup sour cream
½ cup yogurt with fruit	

Whip the cream. Fold in the yogurt and sour cream. Serve each portion of cake with a generous dollop of the topping.

A recipe from Hawthorne Inn, Concord, MA.

The Bed & Breakfast Cookbook

 During the late nineteenth century, the Astors, Vanderbilts, Belmonts and many more of America's wealthiest families built mansions they called "cottages" overlooking the ocean along Bellevue Avenue and Ocean Drive in Newport, Rhode Island.

Butterscotch Pecan Rolls
Sticky Buns

DOUGH:

1 package active dry yeast
¼ cup warm water
¼ cup sugar, white or
 brown
¾ cup lukewarm milk
1 egg
¼ cup soft shortening,
 butter, or margarine

1 teaspoon lemon rind,
 grated
1 teaspoon salt
3½-3¾ cups unbleached
 or bread flour

FILLING:

½ cup plus 2 tablespoons
 butter or margarine, divided
½ cup sugar mixed with 1
 tablespoon cinnamon

½ cup brown sugar
1 cup pecan halves

In a medium-sized mixing bowl, dissolve yeast, warm water, and 1 teaspoon of the sugar. Let stand about 5 minutes or until proofed. Add milk, remaining sugar, egg, shortening, rind, salt, and half the flour. Mix until smooth. Add enough remaining flour to handle dough easily. Turn onto a floured board. Knead until smooth and elastic, about 5 minutes. Add small amounts of flour if necessary. Cover and let rise until double, about 1 hour. Rising temperature of 85° is best.

Punch dough down and proceed as follows: Roll dough into a rectangle 15x9 inches. Spread with the 2 tablespoons softened butter and sprinkle with the cinnamon-sugar mixture. Roll up tightly beginning at wide end. Seal well by pinching the long end. Cut into 18 buns.

Melt ½ cup butter and put into 9x13-inch pan. Stir in brown sugar and pecans. Place buns on top, cut-side-down. Cover and let rise until double, 45 minutes. Bake at 375° until rolls are golden brown. Turn out onto a large serving dish. Or turn out onto a large cooling rack, cool completely, wrap, and freeze. Makes 18 rolls.

The Fine Art of Holiday Cooking

Berry Patch Coffee Cake

1 (8-ounce) package cream
  cheese
1 cup sugar
½ cup vegetable shortening
  or margarine
2 eggs
1 teaspoon vanilla
1¾ cups all-purpose flour
  (not self-rising)

1 teaspoon baking powder
½ teaspoon soda
¼ teaspoon salt
¾-1 teaspoon cinnamon
¼ cup milk
½ cup chopped pecans
½ cup raspberry or
  blackberry preserves

Soften cream cheese at room temperature. Combine with sugar and shortening, mixing until well blended. Add eggs one at a time, mixing well after each addition. Blend in vanilla. Sift dry ingredients together and add alternately with the milk. Blend thoroughly. Stir in pecans.

Pour into a greased and floured 9x13-inch pan. Dot with preserves and cut through batter several times for a marbled effect. Bake at 350° for 35 minutes until done.

Heritage Fan-Fare

Filling Station
Sour Cream Coffee Cake

Sara Dix's original bakery was located in the building at the base of Winthrop Hill. One day a tractor-trailer lost its brakes coming down the hill and crashed into the bakery, fell through the floor, and landed in the basement. Needless to say, this was a real crimp on "business as usual." However, Sara adapted, sold baked goods and sandwiches/ soups out of her house, and then relocated to her current location—a converted gas station with an art deco look.

1½ cups sugar
¾ cup butter
1½ teaspoons vanilla
3 eggs
3 cups all-purpose flour
1½ teaspoons baking
   powder

1½ teaspoons baking soda
¾ teaspoon salt
1½ cups dairy sour cream
1 cup blueberries

Heat oven to 325°. Grease a tube pan. Beat sugar, butter, vanilla, and eggs in a bowl at medium speed. Add flour, baking powder, baking soda, salt, and sour cream. Fold in blueberries. Bake 45-50 minutes. Test with a toothpick; if it comes out clean, the coffee cake is done. Cool 20 minutes and remove from the pan.

A Taste of Hallowell

Apple Honey-Buns

½ cup butter
1 cup brown sugar
1 teaspoon cinnamon
1 tablespoon honey
⅓ cup milk
1 (16-ounce) package Hot
   Roll Mix

¾ cup very warm water
⅓ cup sugar
1 egg
½ cup chopped nuts
1½ cups chopped apples

Combine butter, brown sugar, cinnamon, honey, and milk in a small saucepan. Stir over low heat until butter melts and mixture is smooth. Pour half of the mixture into an ungreased 13x9x2-inch baking pan; reserve the remaining mixture.

Dissolve the yeast from the Hot Roll Mix in warm water in a large bowl; stir in sugar, egg, and nuts. Add flour mixture from Hot Roll Mix and apples; blend well.

Drop dough by heaping tablespoonfuls on top of the brown sugar mixture in the pan, forming 15 rolls. Drizzle with remaining brown sugar mixture.

Cover; let rise in a warm place for 45-60 minutes or until light and doubled in bulk. Bake for 30-35 minutes or until golden. Let stand a few minutes; remove from pan. Yield: 15 honey-buns.

Apple Orchard Cookbook

Old-Fashioned Doughnut Balls

2 eggs
1 cup sugar
1 teaspoon salt
1 teaspoon nutmeg
½ teaspoon cinnamon
¼ cup butter, softened
1 cup buttermilk

3¾ cups flour
1 teaspoon baking powder
1 teaspoon baking soda
1 cup grated apple
Fat or oil for deep frying
Cinnamon and sugar

Beat eggs, sugar, salt, spices, and butter together well. Add buttermilk. Combine flour, baking powder, and baking soda and stir into batter; add grated apple. Let set in refrigerator while fat heats.

Heat fat to about 370°. Drop batter by teaspoonfuls into the hot fat, turning once. Roll doughnut balls in a mixture of cinnamon and sugar while still slightly warm. Yield: 5 dozen doughnut balls.

Apple Orchard Cookbook

Golden Raisin Buns

1 cup water
½ cup butter or margarine
1 teaspoon sugar
¼ teaspoon salt
1 cup flour

4 eggs
½ cup golden raisins,
   plumped*
Lemon Frosting

Preheat oven to 375°. Grease cookie sheet. Combine water, butter, sugar, and salt in saucepan; bring to boil. Add flour all at once. Over low heat, beat with wooden spoon about 1 minute, or until mixture leaves sides of pan and forms a smooth, thick dough. Remove from heat. Continue beating about 2 minutes to cool slightly. Add eggs 1 at a time, beating after each until mixture has a satiny sheen. Stir in raisins. Drop by heaping measuring tablespoons about 2 inches apart on greased cookie sheet. Bake 30-35 minutes, or until doubled, golden, and firm. Remove to wire rack to cool slightly. While still warm, gently spread frosting over tops and sides. Makes 20. Best served warm.

*To plump raisins, cover with hot water. Let stand 5 minutes; drain well.

LEMON FROSTING:

1 tablespoon butter or
   margarine
1½ tablespoons heavy
   cream

1 cup confectioners' sugar
½ teaspoon lemon juice
½ teaspoon vanilla

Melt butter and stir in heavy cream. Remove from heat. Stir in confectioners' sugar until smooth. Stir in lemon juice and vanilla; add more cream, if necessary, to make of spreading consistency.

Tasty Temptations from the Village by the Sea

Leslie's Blueberry Cinnamon Muffins

Preheat the oven to 375°. Grease the muffin pan with butter or cooking spray. In one bowl, blend the liquids:

1 egg, lightly beaten	¾ cup milk
2 tablespoons soft butter or vegetable oil	

In another bowl, blend the solids:

½ cup sugar	¼ teaspoon ground cloves
1 cup flour	½ teaspoon salt
1 teaspoon baking powder	1½ cups fresh or frozen
½ teaspoon ground cinnamon	wild blueberries (if frozen, drain well)

In a small cup, mix the topping:

2 tablespoons sugar	1 teaspoon ground cinnamon

Add the liquids to the solids and quickly blend the ingredients with a rubber spatula. Do not overmix. Fill the muffin cups, sprinkle with the topping, and bake for 20-25 minutes. Have some sweet butter and a mug of coffee ready—you're in for a glorious morning! Makes 8 muffins.

Recipes from a New England Inn

Morning Glory Muffins

2 cups flour	1 apple, peeled and grated
1 cup sugar	½ cup raisins
2 teaspoons baking soda	½ cup shredded coconut*
2 teaspoons ground cinnamon	½ cup chopped pecans
½ teaspoon salt	3 eggs, lightly beaten
2 cups grated carrots (3 medium)	1 cup vegetable oil
	2 teaspoons vanilla

Grease 18 muffin cups. Set oven at 350°. In a large bowl, sift flour, sugar, baking soda, cinnamon, and salt. Stir in carrots, apple, raisins, coconut, and pecans. In another bowl, stir together the eggs, oil, and vanilla; add these to the flour mixture just until the batter is moist and smooth. Divide the batter among the muffin cups and place in the center of the heated oven. Bake for 30-35 minutes or until firm and puffed. Loosen from muffin cups and serve with apple butter or sweet butter.

*Can use 1 tablespoon of Miller's Bran instead of coconut.

Heritage Fan-Fare

Blueberry Muffins

¼ cup oleo	3 teaspoons baking powder
½ cup sugar	½ teaspoon salt
1 egg	1 cup milk
2 cups flour	1½ cups blueberries

Cream together oleo and sugar; add egg and beat well. Mix in dry ingredients, then stir in milk. Dust blueberries with flour and fold into batter. Spoon into 12 greased muffin tins, ⅔ full, and bake 25 minutes at 350°.

What's Cooking at Moody's Diner

Blueberry Hill
Wild Blueberry Pancakes

This was and continues to be the most-requested breakfast entrée, as attested to by the many "blue" smiles of guests leaving the dining room. Serve them up with Country Apple Sausage for a truly Vermont-style breakfast.

1¼ cups unbleached white flour	2 cups milk
1 tablespoon sugar	¼ cup sweet butter, melted
1 tablespoon baking powder	1 cup wild blueberries, rinsed and picked over
½ teaspoon salt	Butter
4 eggs, separated	Maple syrup

In a large mixing bowl, mix together all the dry ingredients. Set aside. Lightly beat the egg yolks, then add the milk and melted butter and mix well. Set aside.

Beat the egg whites until they form stiff—but not dry—peaks. Set aside. Make a hollow in the center of the dry ingredients. Pour in the milk mixture and blend batter well. Don't worry about a few lumps—they will work themselves out. Carefully fold in the egg whites until well incorporated. Gently stir in the blueberries.

Ladle the batter onto a lightly greased hot skillet or griddle to form 3-inch circles. Cook till bubbles form, flip, and cook until golden brown, about 1 minute. Serve with butter and heated Vermont syrup. Serves 4.

Tony Clark's New Blueberry Hill Cookbook

King Arthur Flour Pancake "Mix"

To be prepared for those rushed mornings, or the lazy ones, you can either measure out just the right ingredients ahead of time or go one step further and make this all-natural King Arthur Pancake "Mix." (You could even take this on your next camping trip.)

6 cups King Arthur
  Unbleached All-Purpose
  Flour
3 cups King Arthur Stone
  Ground Whole Wheat Flour
½ cup wheat germ or bran
  (optional)
1½ cups nonfat dry milk
  or 1½ cups dry buttermilk
  powder

1 tablespoon salt
¼–½ cup sugar, white or
  brown
¼ cup baking powder
1 cup vegetable shortening

In a large bowl, combine flours, wheat germ or bran, dry milk, salt, sugar, and baking powder, and mix well. Cut in the shortening until it is evenly distributed. (It is important to use shortening rather than butter because it remains stable at room temperature.) To store this "Mix," place it in a large, airtight container, or put it up in premeasured (don't pack it) 2-cup portions. It will make approximately 7.

PANCAKES:
1 egg, slightly beaten
1–1¼ cups water
  (depending on how thick or
  thin you like pancakes)

2 cups King Arthur Flour
  Pancake "Mix" from above,
  not packed

Combine the egg and water in a bowl. Stir in the "Mix" until it's just moistened. Cook the pancakes on preheated, greased griddle. Makes about a dozen 5-inch pancakes.

The King Arthur Flour 200th Anniversary Cookbook

 The Mark Twain Memorial in Hartford, Connecticut, a 19th-century brick-and-stick Victorian mansion where Twain penned some of his greatest works, is as delightfully eccentric as the author who once lived there.

Individual Baked Pancakes

These pancakes, served directly from the oven, are impressive in shape and size. The oohs and aahs from the dining room always make me smile. I can't tell you how many times guests have run to their rooms to get their cameras.

3 eggs	**Pinch salt**
½ cup milk	**2 tablespoons unsalted**
½ cup all-purpose flour	**butter, melted**

Whisk the eggs with the milk until well blended. Add the flour and the salt and whisk well. Add the melted butter and whisk well again so that the batter is smooth.

Grease two 6-inch round cake pans, unless they are the nonstick kind. Pour the batter into the pans. Bake in a preheated 450° oven for 15 minutes. Quickly turn the pancakes out of their pans, put them right-side-up, and garnish them. Serve them immediately while they are still tall.

GARNISHES:

We usually serve these pancakes with lemon zest and lemon juice sprinkled over the middle, and confectioners' sugar dusted over the tops. Guests top them off with our Maine maple syrup.

You might instead sprinkle sliced strawberries over the middle, then dust confectioners' sugar over the tops. Sautéed apples also go nicely with these pancakes. Try other fruits, too, depending upon the season. I usually serve these pancakes with sausage links. Serves 2.

Chris Sprague's Newcastle Inn Cookbook

Apple Pan Dowdy

White bread	**½ cup dark brown sugar**
Melted butter	**½ teaspoon cinnamon**
4 large green apples	**½ cup water**

Remove crust from bread and slice into fingers. Dip each finger into melted butter and line bottom and sides of a baking dish with fingers. Peel and core apples. Slice. Place in center of bread fingers. Sprinkle apples with mixture of the sugar and cinnamon. Add ½ cup water and cover the top with a layer of well-buttered fingers of bread. Sprinkle top with additional sugar. Cover and bake 1 hour in a 350° oven. Serve hot with whipped cream. Serves 6.

Recipes from Smith-Appleby House

Berkshire Apple Pancake

This popular Red Lion Inn recipe uses two products from the bounty of the Berkshires—apples and maple syrup.

3 apples
3 eggs, beaten
3 cups flour
1½ tablespoons baking
  powder
¾ teaspoon salt
5 tablespoons sugar
2 cups milk

¾ teaspoon vanilla
¾ teaspoon ground cinnamon
5 tablespoons butter, melted
¼ cup light brown sugar,
  firmly packed
Warm maple syrup, for
  serving

Preheat the oven to 450°. Peel and core the apples. Coarsely chop 2½ of the apples. Slice the remaining half apple into thin spirals for garnish on top. Brush the spirals with lemon juice to prevent them from darkening, and set them aside.

Mix the eggs, flour, baking powder, salt, sugar, milk, vanilla, cinnamon, and the chopped apples together in a bowl. Beat until they are combined, although the batter will remain lumpy. Melt the butter in a 10-inch cast iron frying pan. Pour the batter into the pan, and arrange the reserved apple spirals on top.

Bake the pancake in the oven at 450° for 15 minutes. Then turn the oven down to 350° and continue to bake the pancake an additional 40 minutes, or until a toothpick inserted in the center comes out clean. Remove the pan from the oven and allow it to rest for 5 minutes. Sprinkle the brown sugar over the top of the pancake, cut into wedges, and serve with the warm maple syrup. Serves 6.

The Red Lion Inn Cookbook

Steamed Apple Dumpling

BAKING POWDER BISCUITS:

2 cups flour, unbleached	2 tablespoons butter
4 teaspoons baking powder	¾-1 cup milk
½ teaspoon salt	

Sift dry ingredients and rub in the shortening. Add the milk slowly and mix thoroughly but quickly. Turn onto floured board, knead slightly, and pat into a round large enough to cover layer of apples in saucepan, making a small, round air vent in the center.

6-8 peeled, cored, sliced apples (preferably tart, firm, baking apples, e.g. R.I. Greenings) or enough to make a generous layer in the bottom of a heavy-bottomed saucepan with a tight cover	½ cup water
	Approximately ²/₃ cup sugar, depending on tartness of apples
	Grated nutmeg and a few slices of butter
	Baking powder biscuit dough

Slice apples into saucepan; add water, sugar, and grated nutmeg and butter. Cover and bring to gentle boil, being careful not to scorch. Place soft biscuit dough over apple layer, leaving an air vent in middle of dough, and continue cooking, covered, for approximately 25 minutes or until the biscuits are done. Remove cover and turn contents onto large plate, with biscuit on bottom and apples on top. Serve warm with sweetened whipped cream lightly flavored with vanilla.

Variation: The steamed apple dumpling may be made as an Apple Slump by replacing all or a part of the sugar with heavy, dark molasses and adding 1 teaspoon cinnamon and ½ teaspoon ginger to the apple layer and continuing as above.

The Hammersmith Farm Cookbook

Old White Church Apple Crisp

¾ cup Quaker Oats	1 teaspoon cinnamon
¾ cup brown sugar	4-6 large Cortland or
½ cup butter or margarine	Macintosh apples (or one
½ cup flour	half of each kind)

Prepare apples as for pie; slice thin.

Combine other ingredients. Sprinkle over apples. Bake 35-40 minutes at 350°. Serve with cream. Serves 6-8.

Come Savor Swansea

Apple Crisp

6 Baldwin apples, peeled,
    sliced
1 cup each sugar and flour
1 teaspoon baking powder

½ teaspoon salt
1 egg
½ cup butter or margarine
Cinnamon and nutmeg

Arrange apples in an ungreased 9-inch pan. Preheat oven to 350°. In a medium bowl, mix together sugar, flour, baking powder, and salt with a fork. Add egg and continue mixing with fork. Put this mixture on top of apples. Melt butter, pour over apple mixture. Sprinkle with cinnamon and nutmeg. Bake 25-30 minutes. Serve warm or cold.

The Island Cookbook

Raspberry Crumble

3 cups crushed raspberries
1¼ cups granulated sugar
Juice of ½ a lemon
¼ cup butter or margarine,
    softened

¾ cup flour
Pinch of salt

Preheat oven to 350°. Coat 1-quart quiche dish with vegetable spray. Sprinkle raspberries with half of sugar, add lemon juice, and stir well. Place in prepared soufflé dish.

Blend butter with remaining sugar, flour, and salt and spread over raspberries. Bake 40 minutes. Yield: 4 servings.

Favorite New England Recipes

Down East Blueberry Crisp

4 cups fresh blueberries
2-4 tablespoons sugar
2 teaspoons lemon juice
¼ cup margarine
¼ cup packed brown sugar

⅓ cup all-purpose flour
¼ teaspoon cinnamon
Dash of salt (optional)
¾ cup old-fashioned rolled
    oats

Preheat oven to 375°. Place blueberries in a greased (margarine) baking dish. Sprinkle with sugar and lemon juice. In a medium bowl, combine margarine, brown sugar, flour, cinnamon, and salt; mix until crumbly. Stir in rolled oats and sprinkle evenly over blueberries. Bake in 375° oven for 35-40 minutes. Serve warm. Yield: 6-8 servings.

A Taste of New England

Blueberry Buckle

½ cup shortening
½ cup sugar
1 egg, beaten
2 cups flour

½ teaspoon salt
½ cup milk
2½ cups blueberries

Cream shortening with sugar; add egg and beat. Sift flour with salt and add to the creamed mixture alternately with the milk. Spread in an 8x8-inch pan and spread blueberries over top. Cover with the following topping.

TOPPING:
½ cup sugar
½ cup flour

½ cup margarine
¾ teaspoon cinnamon

Bake at 375° 45 minutes.

Maine's Jubilee Cookbook

Ellen's Blueberry Delight

This recipe should be made a day ahead. The caramelized topping of this cool, creamy fruit dish is unusual and delicious. The variations listed at the end of the recipe make this a good dish all summer long.

3 cups fresh blueberries
1 cup sour cream
1 teaspoon vanilla extract

1 cup brown sugar, firmly
packed

Preheat oven to broil. Divide the blueberries evenly among 6 serving-size ramekins or custard dishes. Set aside.

In a small bowl combine the sour cream and vanilla. Pour over the fruit. Sprinkle evenly with the brown sugar. Broil until the sugar caramelizes. Watch carefully! The sugar needs to melt but not burn. Cover and refrigerate several hours or overnight before serving.

Variations: This recipe may be made with seedless green grapes, peaches or strawberries.

A recipe from Kenniston Hill Inn, Boothbay, ME.

The Bed & Breakfast Cookbook

Buttery Waffles

4 eggs
2 cups all-purpose flour
1 teaspoon salt
1 teaspoon baking soda

1 teaspoon baking powder
1 cup milk
1 cup sour cream
1 cup butter, melted

Preheat waffle iron. Beat eggs until light. Sift together flour, salt, soda, and baking powder. Mix milk and sour cream. Add flour mixture and milk mixture alternately to beaten eggs, beginning and ending with flour mixture. Add melted butter and blend thoroughly.

For each waffle, pour batter into center of lower half of waffle iron until it spreads to 1 inch from edge—about ½ cup. Lower iron cover on batter; cook as manufacturer directs, or until waffle iron stops steaming. Carefully loosen edge of waffle with fork; remove.

Cool. Place waxed paper between waffles. Freeze in airtight container. To serve, remove from freezer and toast until heated through.

Dining on Deck

Stuffed French Toast

A delicious variation from a Cape Cod inn.

1 (8-ounce) package cream
  cheese
½ cup chopped walnuts
1 teaspoon vanilla extract
12 thin slices bread
4 eggs, beaten

¾ cup heavy cream
1 teaspoon vanilla
Grated nutmeg
Butter for grilling
3 large bananas, sliced

Combine cream cheese, walnuts, and vanilla. Spread mixture on 6 slices of bread, covering with remaining slices to make a sandwich. Combine eggs, cream, vanilla, and nutmeg to taste. Dip each sandwich into egg mixture and grill in butter, as for French toast.

APRICOT SAUCE:

12 ounces apricot jam   ½ cup orange juice

Combine jam and juice and heat. To serve, cut toast in points and arrange with bananas. Top with sauce. Serves 6.

Merrymeeting Merry Eating

Rum Raisin French Toast

¾ cup rum raisin ice
  cream, melted
3 large eggs, beaten
1 tablespoon dark rum
¼ teaspoon cinnamon
5 tablespoons finely ground
  walnuts

5 tablespoons sweet butter
6 (or more) slices raisin
  bread
Vermont maple syrup
Scoops of rum raisin ice
  cream

Combine melted ice cream, eggs, rum, cinnamon, and nuts in a bowl. Beat with a wire whisk until well mixed. Dip raisin bread into egg mixture, coating well on both sides. Sauté in butter over medium-low heat until "toasted." Serve with a scoop of rum raisin ice cream napped with Vermont maple syrup. Serves 3-4.

From the Inn's Kitchen

Baked French Toast with Blueberry Sauce

This is a delicious and easy-to-prepare breakfast or brunch dish, especially during blueberry season. If, however, you use frozen berries, do not defrost them. You can start making this the night before by soaking the bread and finish assembling it in the morning. By the time the table is set and the coffee is made, the blueberry French toast will be ready to come out of the oven! You can use your imagination by trying strawberries, raspberries, or sliced peaches or apples to vary the flavor of your Baked French Toast. Also, cholesterol-free egg substitutes work very well in this recipe!

1 (8-ounce) loaf French or
   Italian bread
4 eggs
½ cup milk
¼ teaspoon baking powder
5 cups (approximately 1½
   pounds) fresh or frozen
   blueberries

1 teaspoon vanilla
½ cup sugar
1 teaspoon cinnamon
1 teaspoon cornstarch
2 tablespoons melted butter
   or margarine
Confectioners' sugar

Slice the bread into 12-14 slices about ¾-inch thick. Place on a 10½x15½x1-inch cookie sheet. Whisk eggs, milk, baking powder, and vanilla together and slowly pour it over the bread, turning to coat the bread completely. Cover with plastic wrap and refrigerate for 1-2 hours, or overnight.

Combine blueberries, cinnamon, sugar, and cornstarch and place in a greased 9x13-inch baking pan. Place bread, wettest side up, on the berry mixture. Wedge slices in tightly, cutting some pieces to fit, if necessary.

Brush tops of bread with melted butter or margarine. Bake at 450° for 20-25 minutes or until the toast is golden and the berries are bubbling around the sides. Remove from the oven and sprinkle with confectioners' sugar. Let rest for 5 minutes before serving. To serve, lift toast onto plates and spoon blueberry sauce over it.

From Ellie's Kitchen to Yours

 Maine grows 98 percent of the nation's wild, low-bush blueberries. It is ranked third in the nation for production of potatoes, worth $150 million.

Irish Scones

2 cups flour	4 tablespoons butter
4 tablespoons sugar	1 egg
½ teaspoon salt	¾ cup milk
1 tablespoon baking powder	½ cup currants (if desired)

Mix dry ingredients. Add butter and cut through with a knife until butter becomes small particles. Add egg, milk, and currants and mix lightly with wooden spoon. Turn out onto a floured table and just handle lightly until together. Flatten out to about an 8-inch round. Cut in half, then cut in triangles, 4 to each half. Place on an ungreased cookie sheet. Bake for 20 minutes at 350°. Makes 8 scones.

"Delicious served the Irish way with butter, jam, and whipped cream at tea time or for breakfast, just plain, or with butter and jam!"

Tasty Temptations from the Village by the Sea

Sausage Whirls

1 pound hot bulk sausage	½ teaspoon salt
½ cup onion, chopped	3 teaspoons baking powder
1 tablespoon oil	5 tablespoons butter
2 cups flour	⅔ cup milk

In a large fry pan, sauté sausage and onion in 1 tablespoon oil until browned. Set aside. In a large bowl, combine flour, salt, and baking powder. Cut in butter with pastry blender until mixture resembles coarse crumbs. Stir in milk to make soft dough. Divide dough in half. Roll out each half on a floured surface making 2 (10x15-inch) rectangles ½-inch thick. Spread evenly with sausage and onion. Roll up as for jelly roll. Seal edges.

Wrap in plastic wrap and freeze until ready to use. Thaw bread and preheat oven to 400°. Bake "loaves" on greased baking sheet 10 minutes until golden. Cool 10 minutes before slicing. Serve warm. Makes 40 pieces.

Moveable Feasts Cookbook

Country Apple Sausage

Make a special breakfast even more special by presenting these sausages baked with apples. They're easy to serve to a crowd, as you can prepare them ahead of time just to the point when you'd put them in the oven. Another bonus is the drippings—they're delicious, and can be used to baste other meats.

**4 large sweet Italian pork sausages
3 Cortland apples, cored and cut into wedges**

⅓ cup Vermont made syrup

Preheat the oven to 400°. In a heavy skillet, with no fat added, sauté the sausages over medium to high heat until brown. Transfer the sausages to a small baking dish, cover them with the apple wedges, and drizzle with the maple syrup. Cover and bake for 10 minutes. Decrease the temperature to 350° and continue baking until done, about 15–20 minutes. (The apples should not fall apart.) Serves 4.

Tony Clark's New Blueberry Hill Cookbook

Mushroom Supreme

**1 pound mushrooms, chopped
Butter for sautéing
½ cup chopped onions
½ cup chopped celery
½ cup chopped green pepper
½ cup mayonnaise
¾ teaspoon salt
¼ teaspoon pepper**

**2 eggs, beaten
1½ cups milk
8 slices buttered bread, crust removed and cubed
1 (10¾-ounce) can condensed mushroom soup, undiluted
¾ cup grated cheese**

Cook the mushrooms in a small amount of butter for 3 minutes. Add the vegetables and sauté for 4 minutes, covered. Drain well. Combine all ingredients up to and including half of the bread cubes (reserve half the bread cubes for the top). Place in a greased 13x9-inch baking dish and refrigerate overnight.

Just before cooking, spread the mushroom soup on top and top with the remaining bread cubes. Bake in a 325° oven, covered, for about 50 minutes. Sprinkle with the grated cheese and brown for another 10 minutes, uncovered. Serves 8.

As You Like It

Sausage and Wild Rice

This savory dish has been a hit as breakfast, but I've also enjoyed it for a light dinner with salad. Louise Sims says this is one of her most frequently requested recipes. She likes to serve it with scrambled eggs, baked apples, and scones.

1 (6-ounce) package Uncle Ben's Long Grain & Wild Rice
1 pound bulk breakfast sausage
1 medium-sized onion, chopped
½ cup sliced mushrooms
¼ cup butter
¼ cup flour
1½ cups chicken stock
1 teaspoon ground black pepper
¼ cup heavy cream

Preheat oven to 350°. Cook the rice according to the directions on the package. Set aside. Cook the sausage, breaking into small pieces as it cooks. Drain off all fat and add the onion, mushrooms, and butter to the sausage. Sauté just until the onion is tender.

Sprinkle with the flour and mix well. Add the chicken stock and pepper. Stir and cook until thickened. Mix in the cream and remove from heat. At this point you may refrigerate the cooked rice and the sausage mixture (separately) until the next day. If you do this, bring the ingredients to room temperature before baking.

When you are ready to complete the casserole, combine the rice with the sausage mixture and pour into a 2-quart casserole. Bake at 350° for 30-45 minutes, until the casserole is hot and bubbly. Serves 10.

A recipe from The Bells Bed & Breakfast, Bethlehem, NH.

The Bed & Breakfast Cookbook

Breakfast Meatloaf

½ pound ground chuck
2 apples, peeled, cored, and cut into ¼-inch cubes
2 pieces white bread, toasted and diced into small pieces
1 large egg
¼ cup raisins
1½ tablespoons tomato sauce or catsup

½ teaspoon cinnamon
¼ teaspoon ginger
⅛ teaspoon nutmeg
⅛ teaspoon cloves
1 teaspoon sugar
Salt and pepper
1½ teaspoons lemon juice
2 teaspoons rum
5 strips of bacon

In large bowl, blend by hand, ground beef, apples, bread, egg, raisins, and tomato sauce. Add spices, sugar, salt and pepper, lemon juice, and rum. Blend again by hand. Set loaf in 1-quart casserole and drape bacon over the mound. Flatten mound so that it pushes against sides of casserole and so bacon covers the sides and top of the loaf. Bake at 350° for 45 minutes. Serves 4.

Perennials

Katie's Cheese Dish

Perfect for lunch or brunch.

6-8 slices white bread (trim crust) cut in cubes
⅓ cup melted butter or margarine
6 ounces (about) sharp cheese grated (Kraft's Vermont is excellent)

2 slightly rounded teaspoons mustard
Salt and pepper to taste
3 eggs
1¼ cups milk

In buttered pie pan or square pan, evenly scatter ⅓ (2 slices) bread cubes, ⅓ melted butter, half of the grated cheese and half of the mustard, salt and pepper. Repeat layer. Top with remaining bread and melted butter.

Beat eggs and milk and pour over mixture. Wait about 2 minutes, then tilt the pan. If milk is not easily visible, pour in a bit more milk and tilt again. Bake at 350° about 1 hour. Dish should be good and moist but not runny.

A Taste of Hallowell

Charlie's Cuckoo's Nest

Named by one of our guests...is one of Charlie's big breakfast favorites!

French bread (thinly sliced) Vermont Cheddar cheese,
2 eggs   shredded
1/3 cup milk   Butter

Butter an 8-ounce round ramekin. Fan thin slices of yesterday's French bread (overlapping slightly) on bottom of ramekin. Pour over the bread a mixture of eggs and milk. Sprinkle generously with cheese and dot with butter. Cover tightly with clear wrap and refrigerate overnight.

Bake at 375° for 20-25 minutes. Serve with cooked bacon criscrossed on top of "nest." Serves 1. Adjust the recipe to serve as many as you wish.

From the Inn's Kitchen

Oyster Omelet

1 slice bacon   1 teaspoon cream or milk
4 oysters   Salt and freshly ground
2 eggs   black pepper to taste

Fry the bacon brown, drain and crumble it. Pour off most of the bacon fat in the skillet, add the oysters, chopped in quarters, and cook for 1 or 2 minutes. Add the crumbled bacon and mix it in. Set aside. Mix the eggs with the cream and beat lightly; pour into a small buttered skillet or omelet pan. Make the omelet in the usual manner using the bacon-oyster mix for the filling. Serves 1.

Clams, Mussels, Oysters, Scallops & Snails

Maple Syrup Substitute

1 cup water   1 teaspoon maple flavor
2 cups sugar   1/4 teaspoon butter flavor
2 teaspoons molasses

Heat sugar-water mixture to dissolve sugar. DO NOT overcook or mixture will turn to candy. Add remaining ingredients and refrigerate.

Great Island Cook Book

Vermont Blueberry Sauce

A simple but delicious sauce with many uses: on vanilla ice cream, orange sherbet, pound cake or angel food, pancakes or johnnycakes, sliced fresh peaches or nectarines, or frozen lemon mousse.

1½ cups blueberries,
   fresh or frozen
¼ cup sugar

¾ teaspoon cinnamon
¼ teaspoon nutmeg

Combine all ingredients in saucepan over low heat; cook, stirring frequently, for about 10 minutes. Serve warm or cold. Yield: about 2 cups.

All Seasons Cookbook

Beach Plum Jam

6 cups beach plums
7 cups sugar

1 box Sure-Jell pectin

Have jelly glasses or Mason jars scalded and ready.

Wash beach plums and put them in large pot with enough water to barely cover. Cook until berries are soft. Drain, and mash them through a strainer to remove pits and skin. This is time consuming, but worth it!

Return the pulp to the pan and add sugar. Boil together 5 minutes. Pour into the boiling mixture 1 box pectin. Skim foam off the top and ladle jam into jars. Seal jelly glasses with paraffin (melted over boiling water) or seal Mason jars according to directions.

Savory Cape Cod Recipes & Sketches

Your Own Butter

Making butter is quite simple. Using the large chopper blade in your food processor, pour in a quart of cream and just let it go. It will become whipped and then just keep getting thicker and thicker until it finally separates. Put it all into a mixing bowl, squeeze the liquid [skim milk] from the fat with your (clean) hands, and there you are—a lump of butter. I have found that the best results occur if you let the cream sit in the refrigerator for a week before you churn it and then let it warm almost to room temperature.

The skim milk that's left is sweeter, more wholesome, and far more delicious than any I could buy in a supermarket. It could only be fresher if the cow were making it herself. That skim milk goes into soups, sauces, and custards, and no one knows that what they are eating is good for them.

WHAT TO DO WITH YOUR LUMP OF BUTTER:

Break it into 1-inch pieces and throw it back into the processor. This is the point where you make the butter into any fantasy that pleases you. I generally add about two tablespoons of fresh herbs and a little nutmeg, black pepper, and salt. Spin it just long enough to smooth the herbs and soften the butter into a "whip." You now have what is probably the most wonderful herb butter you've ever eaten.

After you learn the herbs, the rest comes easily. Ripe pears whipped into fresh butter, or blackberries, or maple syrup, or lobster meat. The possibilities are endless. Imagine whipping a handful of wild strawberries into your butter and squeezing it through a pastry bag onto French toast points that have been sautéed in Grand Marnier and dusted with vanilla sugar. That, and a cup of coffee, would be a wonderful way to celebrate the first morning of a romance—or the last.

Excerpt from James Haller's entire chapter on butter.

Another Blue Strawbery

Portsmouth, or Strawbery Banke at the time, was the first Colonial capital of New Hampshire. The name Strawbery Banke came from when early settlers climbed the banks of the Piscataqua River looking for fresh water and found their hands stained red from strawberries.

Soups

*Enjoying a sunny day on the slopes of Ski Sundown
in New Hartford, Connecticut.*

Chilled Peach Soup with Watermelon Purée

6 large ripe peaches,
  peeled, pitted, and sliced
1 (1-inch) piece of
  gingerroot, peeled
1 teaspoon ground nutmeg
½ teaspoon ground mace
1 teaspoon grated lemon rind
3 cups dry white wine

1 cup water
4 cups puréed or minced
  watermelon flesh
1 cup peach brandy
3 tablespoons chopped fresh
  mint
1 cup heavy cream (optional)

In a large, uncovered Teflon-coated or non-corrodible saucepan, simmer the peaches, ginger, nutmeg, mace, lemon rind, wine, and water over moderate heat. Let cook until the liquid is syrupy and the peaches and ginger are soft, about 45 minutes. Remove from the heat; let cool 1 hour.

Remove the ginger, and purée the mixture in a food processor or in small batches in a blender. Strain through a fine sieve.

Add the watermelon purée and the peach brandy. Ladle into bowls and garnish with chopped mint. Serves 6-8.

Variation: Heavy cream may be added to produce a smoother, richer soup.

The Gardner Museum Café Cookbook

Superb Scandinavian Apple Soup

2 cups chicken broth
1 tablespoon cornstarch
3 cups diced apples
½ teaspoon cinnamon
Dash of salt
½ cup sugar

½ cup sweet red wine
3-4 drops red food coloring
  (optional)
Whipped cream (garnish)
Cinnamon (garnish)

Stir together the chicken broth and cornstarch. Combine with the diced apples, cinnamon, and salt in a saucepan and simmer for about 25 minutes or until apples are soft. Pass through a strainer. Add sugar, red wine, and food coloring.

Taste for sweetness (this will depend on the kind of apples used) and add more wine or sugar if needed. Chill well.

Top each serving with a dab of whipped cream and sprinkle with cinnamon. Yield: 4-6 servings.

Apple Orchard Cookbook

Chilled Cherry Soup

4 (16-ounce) cans pitted
   tart cherries
1 cup sugar
3 pieces cinnamon stick
20 pieces of clove
20 pieces of allspice

1 slice lemon
2 pinches salt
1 pint medium or heavy cream
1 tablespoon flour
½ bottle red Burgundy wine

Combine 2 whole cans of tart cherries and only the juice from the other 2 cans in a large pot. Add the sugar, spices*, lemon slice, and a pinch or two of salt to taste. Bring to boiling point.

Add the flour to the cream and blend in well, using a wire whisk. Add the cream and flour mixture to the cherries, and then the wine, and bring to boiling point again.

Remove from flame, let cool, and then refrigerate. Serve chilled with a tablespoon of whipped cream on top of each serving. This soup will keep in the refrigerator for at least 2 weeks. Serves 12.

*Tie spices in cheesecloth for easy removal.

A recipe from Café Budapest, Boston, MA.

A Taste of Boston

Cold Beet Soup

Quick and easy!

WHAT YOU NEED:
2 cups sliced beets, fresh
   or canned
1 quart buttermilk

1 teaspoon salt
½ cup chives, chopped
White pepper

WHAT YOU DO:
If you use fresh beets, boil them until tender, then peel and slice them. In a food processor or blender, purée the beets with the buttermilk. Stir in chives, salt, and white pepper. Chill, serve, and enjoy!

Cape Collection–Simply Soup

Dairying is the primary farm industry in Vermont, producing more than two billion pounds of milk annually.

Chilled Blueberry Soup

1 cup fresh or frozen unthawed blueberries	1 teaspoon ground coriander
½ cup water	¼ teaspoon cinnamon
¼ cup sugar	½ cup plain yogurt
½ cup lemon juice	½ cup sour cream
	½ cup dry red wine

Purée blueberries in blender until smooth. In medium saucepan, combine puréed blueberries, water, sugar, lemon juice, and spices. Cover and simmer over low heat for 10 minutes. Whisk in remaining ingredients, blending until smooth. Chill for several hours before serving. Makes about 6 servings, ½ cup each.

Hasbro Children's Hospital Cookbook

Iced Lemon Soup

5 cups chicken stock	2 tablespoons flour
Grated rind of 4 lemons, plus juice of 4 lemons	½ cup sugar
	4 tablespoons lemon extract
2 tablespoons butter	1 pint heavy cream

In a large saucepan, bring chicken stock to a boil; add half the lemon rind and the lemon juice and boil 5 minutes longer. Meanwhile, in a small saucepan, in a small amount of water, boil the remaining rind until soft; strain and reserve the rind. In another large saucepan, melt the butter, then whisk in the flour and cook 2-3 minutes, whisking constantly. Pour in the hot chicken stock, and stirring, add sugar and lemon extract. Continue to cook 5-8 minutes until sugar is dissolved. Chill. Add heavy cream and strain the soup through cheesecloth or a very fine strainer. Serve in chilled bowls garnished with the reserved rind, powdered sugar, or sour cream. Serves 6.

A recipe from Spalding Inn Club, Whitefield, NH.

Country Inns and Back Roads Cookbook

Vermont has 114 covered bridges. The roofs and walls were built to protect the wooden trusses from rot.

Cream of Cucumber Soup

I served this soup cold at one of our first dinner parties. Guests always ask for it!

WHAT YOU NEED:

1 medium onion, chopped
5 cucumbers, peeled, seeded, and chopped
½ cup butter
½ cup flour
1½ quarts hot beef or chicken stock

2 cups hot milk
1 cup light cream
Chives, chopped
Salt and pepper

WHAT YOU DO:

Sauté the onions and cucumber in butter. When soft, add the flour and blend thoroughly to form a roux. Add the hot stock and simmer for 15 minutes. Add the hot milk and simmer for an additional 10 minutes. Remove from heat, place in a blender, and blend on high speed for 30 seconds (or rub through finest possible sieve). Add cream; season with salt and pepper. Serve immediately or chill and serve cold. Garnish with chopped chives.

Cape Collection–Simply Soup

Cream of Green Soup

1 cup chopped celery
½ cup chopped onion
¼ cup butter
4 cups chicken stock
2 cups chopped broccoli
1 diced potato
¼ teaspoon salt

¼ teaspoon white pepper
1/16 teaspoon nutmeg
½ cup peas
1½ cups spinach
1 cup milk
1 cup cream
Chopped raw carrot

Sauté celery and onion in butter. Add chicken stock, broccoli, potato, and spices and simmer for 30 minutes. Add peas and spinach. Simmer for 10 minutes more. Purée in blender, then add milk and cream. Top each bowl of soup with 1 teaspoon chopped raw carrot.

A Taste of Salt Air & Island Kitchens

Carrot Soup

2 tablespoons butter
1 bunch scallions, chopped
3 cloves garlic, minced
½ teaspoon thyme
4 cups chicken broth

1 pound carrots, peeled and
 sliced
3 medium potatoes, peeled
 and sliced
Salt and pepper to taste

Sauté scallions, garlic, and thyme in butter until tender. Add chicken broth, carrots, potatoes, and salt and pepper. Simmer until vegetables are fork-tender. Separate into thirds and purée in blender one-third at a time. Return to pan and reheat.

Recipes from Smith-Appleby House

Potato Soup

6 potatoes
2 slices bacon
1 chopped onion
2 tablespoons chopped
 parsley
1 tablespoon flour

1 quart scalded milk
1 cup grated American cheese
1 teaspoon Worcestershire
 sauce
1 tablespoon celery salt
¼ teaspoon pepper

Boil potatoes and put through ricer. Cut bacon fine, cook in frying pan until crisp, then drain on brown paper. Sauté onion and parsley in bacon fat; add flour, scalded milk, bacon, potatoes, cheese, Worcestershire sauce, and seasonings. Serves 6.

Good Maine Food

Potage de Vermont

This smooth and creamy soup does justice to our wonderful Vermont Cheddar cheese. Although I always served it as a first course, it would make a delicious dinner of its own, accompanied by a loaf of crusty bread and a simple salad.

2 tablespoons sweet butter
½ cup chopped carrots
½ cup chopped onion
½ cup chopped fresh dill
   weed
½ cup chopped celery
5 tablespoons unbleached
   white flour

5 cups chicken stock
3 cups grated Vermont
   Cheddar cheese
2 cups half-and-half
Salt and freshly ground
   white pepper to taste
Toasted sesame seeds for
   garnish

Sauté the carrots, onion, dill, and celery in the butter in a large saucepan. Sprinkle in the flour 1 tablespoon at a time, stirring after each addition.

Add the stock. Bring to a boil over medium heat, and cook for about 5 minutes. Strain out the vegetables, purée them in a food processor fitted with a steel blade, then return the puréed vegetables to the stock. Continue to cook over medium heat until the soup boils, then reduce the heat and let it simmer slowly for 15 minutes. Add the grated cheese, stirring constantly with a large wire whisk until it is melted. Slowly add the half-and-half and stir until well blended. Add the salt and pepper to taste. Serve at once garnished with the toasted sesame seeds. Serves 8.

Tony Clark's New Blueberry Hill Cookbook

Tomato Cognac Soup

No doubt, this is one of our most popular soups and an honored classic.

1 large Spanish onion
3 ounces butter
3 pounds canned, peeled
   plum tomatoes
1 tablespoon dried basil
1 pint heavy or all-purpose
   cream

1-2 tablespoons dark brown
   sugar
5 tablespoons cognac
Salt and pepper to taste
Minced parsley for garnish

Chop the onion and sauté in butter for 20 minutes until soft and translucent but not brown. With your fingers, squash the tomatoes; add them and all the liquid in the can to the onion. Add the basil and stir. Bring the soup to a boil, then simmer, covered, for 30 minutes. Set aside and cool slightly, then purée the soup in a food processor.

In a small saucepan heat the cream with the sugar, whisking often. Pour this mixture into the soup. Reheat, but do not boil.

Just before serving, add the cognac and season with salt and pepper. Garnish with parsley and serve. Just great! Serves 6.

Recipes from a New England Inn

Pumpkin Soup

We wish we had a dollar for every time we've handed out this recipe!

2 pounds fresh pumpkin
3 cups scalded coffee cream
   or milk
1 tablespoon butter

2 teaspoons maple syrup
1 teaspoon salt
1/8 teaspoon nutmeg

Steam the fresh pumpkin, then mash. (Three cups canned pumpkin may be substituted.) Stir into the milk, then add the remaining ingredients. Heat, but do not boil, and serve immediately. Makes 6-8 servings.

The Country Innkeepers' Cookbook

The first American in space, Alan Shepard, was born in Derry, New Hampshire. His historic flight was made in 1961. The first private citizen passenger in the history of space flight was Christa McAuliffe, a New Hampshire school teacher. A planetarium in her honor can be visited in Concord.

Pumpkin-Lentil Soup

In the early 1960s, I introduced Pumpkin Soup to our family at the Thanksgiving table. I brought it to the table in a scooped-out pumpkin used as a tureen. The children loved the idea and everyone enjoyed the soup. The lentils in combination with the pumpkin add another dimension for taste and nutrition.

2-4 tablespoons unsalted
   butter or olive oil
2 large onions, diced
1 rib celery, sliced
1 carrot, sliced
½ cup lentils, rinsed in
   water
5 cups chicken stock
1½ cups cooked or canned
   pumpkin

¼ teaspoon marjoram
⅛ teaspoon thyme
¼ teaspoon freshly ground
   pepper
Dash Tabasco sauce
1 cup half-and-half
   (optional)
Salt to taste

Melt butter or heat oil in a soup kettle. Add onions and cook until lightly colored but not browned. Add celery and carrot; cook for another minute. Stir in lentils and chicken stock. Add pumpkin, herbs, pepper, and Tabasco. Simmer about 1 hour.

Allow to cool, then purée in a food processor. At this time, the soup can be refrigerated for up to 3 days or frozen for up to 2 months.

Add half-and-half when you reheat the soup before serving. Adjust seasoning.

Variations: The pumpkin may be used as a tureen. Cut across the pumpkin 2 inches below the top. Scoop out the seeds and pulp. Warm the pumpkin in a 300° oven for 5 minutes before filling with soup. Use the pumpkin top as a cover. Serve at the table, ladling out portions.

Of course, Pumpkin-Lentil Soup is delicious year round. Add tiny meatballs for a one-bowl dinner.

Since lentils contain a fair amount of protein, this soup is a favorite with vegetarians. Substitute vegetable stock or water for cold chicken stock.

Additions of rice or canned corn niblets are interesting variations. Serves 8-10.

The Best from Libby Hillman's Kitchen

Escarole Soup

1 pound lentils, washed
8 cups water
3 tablespoons olive oil
1 onion, chopped
1 clove garlic, minced
1 tablespoon fresh parsley,
  minced

1 pound escarole, trimmed,
  cleaned, and cut into 1-inch
  pieces
¼ cup grated cheese

Place lentils and water in large pot. Cover and bring to a boil. Lower heat and simmer for 1 hour, until almost all of the liquid is absorbed.

Sauté onion, garlic, and parsley in olive oil. Add drained escarole leaves. Cover and simmer for 15 minutes, stirring occasionally. Add escarole and pan juices to lentils. Season with salt and serve hot with grated cheese sprinkled over top.

Tasty Temptations from the Village by the Sea

Portuguese Kale Soup

This is a genuine Portuguese recipe from the Arruda family.

1 quart chicken broth
1 quart beef broth
2 chicken breasts
1 pound chourico or linguica
  or half and half, cut in
  ½-inch-thick pieces
1 small onion, chopped
3 small potatoes, cubed

2 bunches fresh kale or 2
  boxes frozen
1 can stewed tomatoes
2 cans red kidney beans
2 teaspoons fresh or dry
  mint
Salt and pepper, to taste

Heat 2 quarts of broth; add meat and cook 1 hour. Remove chicken and take meat off bones; replace in pot. Add onion, potatoes, kale, and tomatoes. Cook 20 minutes. Add red kidney beans and mint at the end. Salt and pepper to taste. Serve hot with crusty Portuguese or Italian bread. Serves 8-10.

A Culinary Tour of the Gingerbread Cottages

Yankee Bean Soup

This is a soup that could be made from scratch, but I doubt that you would bother. Rather, it is a perfect way to stretch leftover baked beans to make a full meal instead of a snack.

Purée leftover baked beans with beef stock to thin the purée slightly. Heat the soup and add sliced, cooked hot dogs. Molasses, ketchup, and mustard may be added if you want to accentuate the Yankee bean flavor.

The Loaf and Ladle Cook Book

White Bean with Roasted Garlic Soup

2 cups navy or white beans
  (cleaned well)
4-5 cups water or stock
1 bulb fresh garlic
2 tablespoons oil
2 carrots (peeled and diced)

1 large onion (diced)
1 bay leaf
1 tablespoon dried thyme
  leaves
Salt and pepper to taste

Soak beans overnight in water. Drain and rinse well in colander. Place in a soup pot with water or stock. Bring to a boil, then simmer for 1-1½ hours, skimming the surface from time to time. Separate the bulb of garlic into individual cloves, keeping skin on. Toss garlic in oil and wrap loosely in aluminum foil. Roast in a 450° oven for 10-15 minutes or until cloves become soft. Cool. Add prepared vegetables, bay leaf, thyme, and salt and pepper, to the beans. Squeeze the cloves out of their skins and mash with a fork. Stir into the soup. Simmer until vegetables are tender. Add more liquid if too thick. Serve with unseasoned croutons. Yields: 6-8 servings.

Washington Street Eatery Cook Book

Shaker Vegetable Soup

1 quart boiling water	1 stalk celery, sliced
2 potatoes, medium, diced	2 tablespoons barley
1 carrot, sliced	¾ cup light cream
1 turnip, small, diced	1 teaspoon butter

To boiling water, add vegetables and barley. Cook until done. Season and add cream and butter. Ten minutes before serving, make batter. While soup is still boiling, pour batter into it slowly. It will float around on top and will have the taste of vermicelli.

BATTER:

1 egg	Flour
1 cup milk	

Mix egg and milk together and add flour until the mixture drops off a spoon easily. Serves 6.

Seasoned with Grace

Curry Soup

A beautiful soup for a company luncheon or dinner. There couldn't be any soup much easier to make. There couldn't be any much tastier.

1 (10¾-ounce) can beef consommé	1 soup can half-and-half
	½-1 teaspoon curry powder
1 cooking apple, peeled, cored, and sliced	Salt and pepper
	Minced fresh parsley

Pour consommé into top of a double boiler set over boiling water. Add apple and cook until it is quite soft. Pour mixture into a blender or food processor and process until smooth. Return to double boiler and add half-and-half. Stir in curry powder and a very small amount of salt and pepper to taste.

All this can be done ahead of time. When ready to serve, heat in double boiler, stirring occasionally. Garnish each serving with minced parsley. Serves 4.

Note: The soup tastes much more peppery when you eat 6-8 ounces of it in a soup bowl than when you test it by the spoonful during cooking, so don't use too much curry.

The Lymes' Heritage Cookbook

Church Fair Minestrone Soup

This soup is served at our Church Fair each fall.

1 pound hamburg	1 package frozen peas
1 large onion, chopped	1 package frozen corn
2-3 quarts water	Pepper to taste
4-5 beef bouillon cubes	1 tablespoon Italian herbs
2 stalks celery, sliced	½ teaspoon garlic powder
1 large can chopped tomatoes	1 cup orzo, #47
3 carrots, sliced	1 teaspoon vinegar
1 package frozen mixed vegetables	Shredded Parmesan cheese for topping

Brown hamburg and onions in 6-quart pan. Add water and bouillon cubes. Bring to a boil and add fresh vegetables and tomatoes. Simmer until carrots and celery are half-cooked, then add frozen vegetables and seasonings. Bring to a boil, add orzo, and simmer for 15-20 minutes. Add vinegar.

When serving, top with Parmesan cheese. Serves 8-10.

Come Savor Swansea

Hungarian Pork Stew

2–3 pounds cubed pork
2–3 large potatoes
1 large onion
2–3 carrots
4 cups chicken stock
1 large green pepper
1 (1-pound) can tomatoes

1 pound mushrooms
½ teaspoon thyme
Salt and pepper
1 tablespoon sweet Hungarian
  paprika
1 pint sour cream

Simmer the cubed pork starting with cold water to cover. As the meat cooks, skim occasionally. Peel and dice the potatoes, onion, and carrots and cook in a large pot with the chicken stock. When the meat is tender and the carrots almost soft, combine the two. Halve the peppers, remove the seeds, and dice. Add to the stew with tomatoes, whole mushrooms, thyme, salt, pepper, and paprika and simmer for another half hour, stirring from time to time.

Just before serving, stir in the sour cream. Serves 6–8.

The Loaf and Ladle Cook Book

Lobster Stew

The lobster feed is enjoyed by inlanders as well as those on the coast. One of the delicious aftermaths of a lobster feed is a lobster stew. The coral (eggs in some lobsters) and tomalley (lobster liver) add good flavor, plus the meat from claws and body of the crustacean, picked by patient lobster "pickers." We find that it takes about 5 (1¼-pound) lobsters to make 1 pound or 3 cups of clear meat.

¼–½ cup butter or
  margarine
2–3 cups lobster meat

2 quarts milk
Salt and pepper to season
Coral and tomalley

In a kettle, melt butter over low heat and sauté the lobster meat, stirring until meat is pink in color. Add milk and continue cooking, stirring frequently. Reduce heat; do not boil. A double boiler at this stage is recommended. The stew will have blossomed to a rosy color. Add tomalley and coral. Heat to serve hot. Many cooks prepare the stew early in the day, refrigerate and reheat when needed.

Memories from Brownie's Kitchen

Cape Cod Oyster Stew

1 quart oysters with their liquor	1 cup hot cream
½ cup butter	Seasoned salt and pepper to taste
3 cups hot milk	Paprika

Heat the oysters in a heavy kettle just until the edges begin to curl, adding the butter as they begin to heat. Add milk and cream and seasonings. Turn the heat off as the milk and cream are added. When the oysters begin to rise in the stew, serve at once in heated bowls with paprika on top. Serves 4.

My Own Cook Book

Portuguese Fish Soup

Gather the vegetables from your summer garden.

2 onions, chopped	2 cups water
3 cloves garlic, mashed	4 tomatoes, peeled and chopped
3 tablespoons olive oil	2 green peppers, chopped
1½ pounds haddock or scrod, cut into 1-inch pieces	½ teaspoon salt
2 (10¾-ounce) cans chicken broth	1 teaspoon oregano
	½ teaspoon ground red pepper

Sauté onions and garlic in oil until onions are translucent. Add remaining ingredients. Bring to a boil. Reduce heat to simmer. Cover and cook for 5 minutes, or until fish flakes easily. Serves 8.

The Cookbook II

Broccoli and Crab Bisque

Good for weight-watchers and cholesterol-counters. Tastes creamy and elegant—but good for you!

1 head broccoli	¾ cup chopped celery
4 potatoes	½ teaspoon black pepper
1½ cups diced carrots	1 teaspoon lemon juice
1 pound crab meat (imitation) or sea legs	¼ teaspoon thyme
	1 bay leaf
1½ cups chopped onion	¾ teaspoon or less salt
2 teaspoons margarine or oil	2 cups skim milk
5 cups broth (fish, chicken, or vegetable)	

Slice broccoli stems crosswise and reserve flowerets. Peel and dice potatoes and carrots. Slice crab meat into ½-inch pieces.

Sauté onion in margarine until soft. Add broth (fish bouillon cubes best), broccoli stems, half of potatoes and carrots, celery, pepper, lemon juice, thyme, bay leaf, and salt. Bring to boil, reduce heat, simmer for 15 minutes or until vegetables are tender.

Remove bay leaf. Purée vegetables and broth in blender. Return purée to pot. Add remaining half of diced potatoes and carrots; cook soup over low heat about 10 minutes or until vegetables are tender.

Add broccoli flowerets and cook for 5-10 minutes until broccoli is tender-crisp. Add milk and crab meat; heat but do not boil. Serve with favorite croutons, if desired.

The Marlborough Meetinghouse Cookbook

Easy Clam Chowder

This tastes pretty authentic!

3 slices bacon, minced
1 small onion, minced
1 can Campbell's Cream of
  Potato Soup
1½ soup cans milk

1 can minced clams,
  undrained
1 tablespoon butter or
  margarine
Salt and pepper

Fry bacon in a large saucepan until crisp. Remove bacon and set aside. Discard all but 1 tablespoon fat. Sauté onion in fat until transparent. Add potato soup, milk, clams, and clam broth. Add reserved bacon. Heat, but do *not* boil. Season with butter, salt, and pepper.

Berkshire Seasonings

A Shaker Corn Chowder, ca. 1900

It was in the Shaker Village of Hancock, Massachusetts, that this straightforward, simple, but very good corn chowder was made. It will have more of a chowder consistency if the stock, milk, and cream are each reduced by about a fourth. Use white, rather than black pepper.

4 tablespoons diced salt
  pork
1 tablespoon butter
1 medium onion, sliced
3 potatoes, peeled and
  finely diced
2 cups chicken stock

2 cups corn scraped from the
  cob, or 2 cups home-canned
  corn (called homestyle)
4 cups whole milk
Salt and pepper
1 cup heavy cream
3 tablespoons butter

Fry the pork in butter; remove pieces when crispy and reserve. Add onions to fat and sauté until golden. Add potatoes and stock and cook slowly until soft. Add corn and milk, lower heat, and simmer until corn is tender. (Young corn takes 5 minutes. Dried corn which has been freshened will take longer.) Add salt and pepper. Bring to a boil and remove from heat. Add cream and butter. Stir up well and pour into soup plates or tureen. Float pork on top. Serves 6.

The Book of Chowder

Fresh Corn and She-Crab Chowder

10 ears fresh corn, husked
  and shucked (reserve cobs)
4 cups milk
2 bay leaves
¼ cup salt pork, diced
¼ cup hickory-smoked
  bacon, diced
½ pound butter
¼ cup onions, diced
¼ cup carrots, diced
¼ cup celery, diced
¼ cup each red, green, and
  yellow bell peppers, diced
½ cup flour

1 quart fresh or bottled
  clam juice
3 pounds fresh or frozen
  crab meat
½ cup white potato, blanched,
  peeled, and diced
1 (12–14-ounce) can creamed
  corn
2 tablespoons parsley,
  chopped
1 teaspoon fresh basil
1 teaspoon fresh thyme
Pinch dried oregano
Salt and white pepper to taste

Place the shucked corn cobs in a large pan and cover them with the milk. Add the bay leaves, bring to a boil, and reduce the heat to a simmer. Cook for 15 minutes, strain, and reserve the liquid.

In a large soup pot, render the diced salt pork and bacon over low heat until just crisp. Add the butter and diced onions, carrots, and celery. Sweat the vegetables over low heat for 5 minutes. Add the diced peppers and continue to sweat the mixture over low heat for 3 minutes. With the heat still low, dust the vegetables with the flour, stirring constantly, making a roux; cook for 15 minutes, stirring occasionally. Add clam juice, increase heat to medium, and continue to cook for 5-10 minutes.

Add the fresh corn kernels, cooked diced potatoes, and creamed corn, and continue to cook over moderate heat for 15 minutes, stirring occasionally. Add the strained reserved milk and the chopped crab meat. Cook the chowder for 5 minutes, adding the herbs, spices, salt and pepper to taste. Garnish with shreds of lobster meat. Serves 8-10.

The Regatta of Cotuit recipe, Cotuit, MA.

A Taste of Cape Cod

The Annual Head of the Charles Regatta in Boston, Massachusetts, is the world's largest regatta, with an average attendance of 500,000.

Oyster Bisque

1 dozen oysters
2 cups chicken stock
¾ cup soft bread crumbs
1 onion, sliced
2 stalks celery
1 sprig parsley
1 bay leaf
1 tablespoon butter or
  margarine

1 tablespoon flour
2 cups milk
Salt to taste
Pepper to taste
Whipped cream, lightly
  salted
Chopped parsley or dill

Clean and pick over the oysters, reserving their liquor. Cut firm part of oysters from soft part, and chop separately. Put chicken stock in a kettle and add bread crumbs, onion, celery, parsley, bay leaf, and chopped firm part of oysters. Simmer 3 minutes. Remove bay leaf and purée.

Melt butter, stir in flour, then add puréed mixture and oyster liquor. Bring to boil. Add milk, chopped soft part of oysters, and salt and pepper to taste. Warm through. If desired, purée soup again. Serve garnished with whipped cream and chopped parsley or dill. Yield: 4 servings.

Favorite New England Recipes

A Boston Fish Chowder, 1751

This is the earliest known recipe for chowder in North America. The lack of any definite measurements would make its testing a matter of individual preferences. An error in the recipe is the use of onions to protect the pork rather than the opposite.

Experimentation could transform this into an excellent dish, though only an immense chowder would be able to use an entire bottle of claret or any other wine. Much better, for a smaller chowder, would be a small amount of white wine.

Directions for making a Chouder—
First lay some Onions to keep the Pork from burning,
Because in Chouder there can be no turning;
Then lay some Pork in Slices very thin,
Thus you in Chouder always must begin.
Next lay some Fish cut crossways very nice
Then season well with Pepper, Salt and Spice;
Parsley, Sweet-Marjoram, Savory and Thyme,
Then Biscuit next which must be soak'd some Time.
Thus your Foundation laid, you will be able
To raise a Chouder, high as Tower of Babel;
For by repeating o're the Same again,
You may make Chouder for a thousand Men.
Last Bottle of Claret, with Water eno' to smother 'em,
You'll have a Mess which some call Omnium gather 'em.

From The Boston Evening Post, *September 23, 1751.*

The Book of Chowder

Clam Chowder

I think our clam chowder is the best in the business—and the public certainly agrees. We sell about 700 gallons of clam chowder each week at our restaurants and take-out counters. The reason for its popularity is simple. We use only the best ingredients and plenty of them. Don't try and economize by cutting back on the amount of clams or cream because the chowder will never taste as flavorful as ours.

4 quarts littleneck clams
 (about 1²/₃ cups, cooked
 and chopped)
1 clove garlic, chopped
1 cup water
2 ounces salt pork, finely
 chopped
2 cups chopped onions

3 tablespoons flour
4½ cups clam broth
3 cups fish stock
1½ pounds potatoes, peeled
 and diced into ½-inch cubes
2 cups light cream
Oyster crackers (optional)

Clean the clams and place them in a large pot along with the garlic and water. Steam the clams just until opened, about 6-10 minutes, depending upon their size. Drain and shell the clams, reserving the broth. Mince the clam flesh and set aside. Filter the clam broth either through coffee filters or cheesecloth and set aside.

In a large, heavy pot slowly render the salt pork. Remove the cracklings and set them aside. Slowly cook the onions in the fat for about 6 minutes, stirring frequently, or until cooked through but not browned. Stir in the flour and cook, stirring, for 3 minutes. Add the reserved clam broth and fish stock, and whisk to remove any flour lumps. Bring the liquid to a boil, add the potatoes, lower the heat, and simmer until the potatoes are cooked through, about 15 minutes.

Stir in the reserved clams, salt-pork cracklings, and light cream. Heat the chowder until it is the temperature you prefer. Serve in large soup bowls with oyster crackers on the side. Serves 8.

The Legal Sea Foods Cookbook

Oysters and clams take an average of four to five years to reach commercial size. A one-pound lobster is seven years old. Shell-fishermen can control the growth rate of clams and oysters by transferring their crop to deeper waters, which retards their growth. They can protect themselves from flooding the seafood market and thus lowering their profits.

Fish Chowder

½ pound salt pork
4 large potatoes
2 chopped onions
1 clove garlic, peeled and
  crushed
2 cups hot water
2 chicken bouillon cubes
1 handful of chopped
  celery leaves
1 bay leaf
2 teaspoons salt

¼ teaspoon pepper
¼ teaspoon dill weed or
  seed
1 teaspoon Worcestershire
  sauce
2 pounds haddock fillets
2 cups cream
½ cup dry white wine
¼ cup butter
Parsley

Fry up salt pork in a soup pot (or a few slices of chopped bacon). Add potatoes, peeled and cubed, onions, and garlic. Fry up 5 minutes or so and cover with hot water. Add chicken bouillon and celery leaves. Simmer until potatoes are tender. Then add bay, salt, pepper, dill, and Worcestershire. Break up fish, drop in, and simmer 5 minutes. Add cream, wine, and butter. Garnish with chopped parsley to serve. For a thicker soup, sprinkle in a little instant mashed potato. Serves 8-10.

Windjammer Cooking

Susie's Quahog Chowder

Leave quahogs in refrigerator overnight. Move very little—sneak up on them with a knife and open. Save juice.

24 large quahogs
¼ pound salt pork
3 large onions
7-8 medium potatoes

1½ cups water
¼ teaspoon pepper
1 can evaporated milk
2-3 cups whole milk

Grind up quahogs, salt pork, onions, and potatoes separately (coarse grind).

Sauté salt pork until crisp and then remove. Brown onions in pork fat. In separate kettle, add ground-up potatoes to 1½ cups water. Cook on low heat. Stir continually until tender. Add onions, quahogs, salt pork, and juice. Cook about 40 minutes on low heat. Add pepper, milk, and canned milk. Do not let boil after adding milk.

Note: Better if it stands overnight, but be sure to refrigerate. Don't forget Pilot crackers! Serves 6-8.

Come Savor Swansea

Connecticut Coastline Seafood Chowder

You can't beat the powerful aroma of this chowder simmering on the stove on a chilly afternoon.

CHOWDER BASE:

¼ pound diced salt pork
2 large onions, peeled and chopped
2 leeks, cleaned and sliced
1 rib celery, sliced
1 cup water
2 cups Doxie clam juice or fish stock

3 cups peeled and diced potatoes
1 tablespoon chopped parsley
½ teaspoon oregano
½ teaspoon thyme
1 bay leaf, broken in half
Freshly ground pepper

Cook the salt pork in a large soup kettle over medium heat until fat is rendered and pork is crisp. Add onions and leeks and sauté for 4 minutes. Add remaining chowder base ingredients to the pot, bring to the boil, reduce heat and simmer, covered, for about 15 minutes or until potatoes are tender. Cool base and chill overnight if possible.

INGREDIENTS TO FINISH CHOWDER:

½ pound bay scallops
½ pound firm white fish, cubed
3 dozen quahogs (or any kind of clams), coarsely chopped

4 cups light cream
Few drops Tabasco
2 tablespoons unsalted butter

Return pot to stove and bring base to a simmer. Add seafood, including any clam liquor, and simmer for 3 minutes. Add remaining ingredients and cook over low heat until just heated through. Serve chowder immediately. Yield: 8 servings.

Off the Hook

Seafood Chowder

May be prepared ahead and frozen.

WHAT YOU NEED:

¼ cup butter, melted
½ cup finely minced onion
2 cups chicken or fish stock
1 cup celery, chopped
1 cup thinly sliced carrots
1 teaspoon salt
⅛ teaspoon freshly ground
  pepper
½ bay leaf
½ teaspoon thyme
½ pound haddock fillets,
  bite-size pieces

3 cups milk
¼ cup flour
½ cup heavy cream, mixed with
  ½ cup milk
1 cup crab meat, flaked (fresh,
  frozen, or canned)
1 cup minced clams, (fresh or
  canned, drained)
3 tablespoons finely chopped
  parsley

WHAT YOU DO:

Sauté onion in melted butter until tender. Add stock, celery, carrots, salt, pepper, bay leaf, and thyme. Bring to a boil and simmer gently 10-15 minutes. Add haddock and simmer another 10 minutes, or until fish flakes away easily. Make a smooth paste by mixing 1 cup of the milk with flour. Add to hot mixture; cook and stir until mixture thickens. Add remaining milk, then stir in cream-milk, crab meat (if frozen, drain) and clams; reheat but do not allow to boil. Before serving, sprinkle with parsley.

Cape Collection–Simply Soup

Salads

The International Tennis Hall of Fame. Newport, Rhode Island.

Cranberry Aspic

1½ cups cranberry juice
cocktail
1 (3-ounce) package orange
gelatin

⅛ teaspoon ground cloves
½ cup apricot nectar

Heat 1 cup of the cranberry juice to boiling point, remove from heat; add orange gelatin and cloves. Stir to dissolve; stir in remaining half-cup cranberry juice and apricot nectar; pour into lightly oiled individual molds. Chill until firm. Serves 4-6.

Note: Can be made in 1 larger mold, and a small amount of unflavored gelatin can be added if you prefer it a bit firmer.

Come Savor Swansea

Baked Beets with Orange Vinaigrette

Beets that can't be beat!

8 medium beets, tops trimmed
to ⅛-inch long, roots
intact
1 tablespoon olive oil
1 crumbled bay leaf
2 teaspoons dried thyme
1 teaspoon dried marjoram
½ teaspoon dried rosemary
1 tablespoon balsamic
vinegar

¼ cup fresh orange juice
¼ teaspoon grated orange
zest
1 shallot, peeled and minced
Salt
Freshly ground black pepper
½ cup salad or vegetable
oil
Boston lettuce
Orange segments for garnish

Preheat oven to 400°. In a small bowl, toss beets with oil and herbs. Turn onto a wire rack on a cookie sheet and bake for 40 minutes to 1 hour or until beets are tender.

In a large mixing bowl, combine vinegar, orange juice, zest, shallot, salt, and pepper and let sit 30 minutes. Whisk in oil and adjust the seasonings.

Remove cooked beets from oven and let cool slightly. Slip off skins, cut into ¼-inch slices, stack, and cut into ¼-inch strips. Toss beets in vinaigrette to moisten and serve on 4 salad plates lined with Boston lettuce. Garnish with orange segments. Serves 4.

Fresh from Vermont

Gazpacho Mold

1 envelope Knox unflavored
   gelatine
1¾ cups V-8 juice
½ cup green pepper,
   chopped
½ cup cucumber, seeded and
   chopped

½ cup scallions, chopped
3 tablespoons lemon juice
1 teaspoon Worcestershire
   sauce
¼ teaspoon Tabasco (more,
   if desired)

Sprinkle gelatine on ½ cup of the V-8 juice to soften. Stir over low heat until dissolved. Remove from heat and stir in remaining juice, vegetables, and seasonings. Turn into individual molds or a small loaf pan and chill until firm. If doubling the recipe, a 9x5-inch loaf pan will be best. Garnish with green and red leaf lettuce, thin slices of scored cucumber, and parsley sprigs. Makes 4 servings.

The Chef's Palate Cookbook

Jellied Beet Salad

1 package lemon gelatin
   (low-calorie is fine)
1 cup boiling water
1 teaspoon salt
2 tablespoons horseradish

2 tablespoons vinegar
1 tablespoon chopped onion
½ cup beet liquid
1½ cups diced (cooked or
   canned) beets

Mix gelatin and boiling water and stir until gelatin is dissolved. Add all other ingredients except beets and chill until slightly thickened. Fold in beets and spoon mixture into a well-rinsed and lightly oiled mold. Chill thoroughly. At serving time, turn out on chilled plate and serve with a sauce of equal parts mayonnaise and sour cream or plain yogurt. Serves 4.

Vermont Kitchens Revisited

"The Archetypal Vermonter, that flannel-shirted fellow with the cow manure on his work boots, eats pots of baked beans laced with maple syrup and dishes of salt pork with milk gravy. The Sixties Vermonter, that young woman/man in Birkenstocks and natural fibers tending her/his organic garden, survives on granola, tofu, and sprouts. The Backwoods Vermonter, the one with the gun rack in his pickup and the deer slung over the fender, chows down on venison and beer. The Yuppie Vermonter? Sea urchins with papaya glaze and a glass of designer water, thank you."

—*Fresh From Vermont*

Easy Green Salad

So good!

2 (3¾-ounce) boxes instant
  pistachio pudding mix
1 (16-ounce) container sour
  cream

½ cup chopped nuts
1 (20-ounce) can crushed
  pineapple, drained
½ cup flaked coconut

Combine ingredients in mixing bowl; mix until thoroughly blended.
Pour into crystal serving dish, cover, and refrigerate until chilled.
Serves 8-10.

Connecticut Cooks III

Cheesy Cucumber Ring

1 envelope unflavored
  gelatin
½ cup cold water
½ teaspoon salt
1 medium cucumber, peeled,
  halved, and seeded
½ small onion, grated and
  drained
2 ribs celery, cut up

3 cups cream-style cottage
  cheese
1 (8-ounce) package cream
  cheese, softened
½ cup mayonnaise
²/₃ cup finely chopped
  celery
¹/₃ cup broken walnuts,
  toasted

Soak gelatin in water. Add salt. Heat until gelatin dissolves. Grate
by hand or in food processor cucumber, onion, and celery. Beat
cheeses until blended. Stir in gelatin. Add vegetables and remaining ingredients. Pour into 6-cup ring mold and chill until firm.

Unmold and serve with cucumber slices, radishes, tomatoes, and
cold cuts, or fill center with seafood. Makes 8 servings.

Merrymeeting Merry Eating

Gelatin Cottage Cheese Salad

3 cups cottage cheese
2 (8-ounce) containers
    frozen non-dairy whipped
    topping
1 (14-ounce) can mandarin
    oranges, drained

1 (16-ounce) can crushed
    pineapple, drained
2 (3-ounce) packages fruit-
    flavor gelatin

Mix cottage cheese and whipped topping; fold in fruit. Sprinkle gelatin over the mixture and blend well. Refrigerate until ready to serve. Serves 8-10.

Connecticut Cooks III

Cottage Cheese Molded Salad

Low in calories, high in nourishment—make it now, serve it later. Most attractive to look at and children like it, too.

1 tablespoon unflavored
    gelatin
¼ cup cold water
1 cup hot water
½ cup sugar
¼ teaspoon salt
½ cup lemon juice

1½ tablespoons vinegar
½ cup mayonnaise
⅛ teaspoon pepper
1 cup chopped raw spinach
¾ cup cottage cheese
⅓ cup diced celery
1 tablespoon chopped onion

Soak the gelatin in the ¼ cup of cold water. Dissolve it in the 1 cup hot water. Add the sugar and salt and stir until dissolved. Add the lemon juice, vinegar, mayonnaise, and pepper. Blend with a rotary beater. Pour into a refrigerator tray and chill until firm 1 inch from the edge (about 25 minutes).

Whip with the beater until fluffy. Fold in the spinach, cottage cheese, celery, and onion. Pour into individual molds and chill in the refrigerator for about 1 hour. Makes 6 servings.

The Country Innkeepers' Cookbook

York, Maine, first organized in 1641, is the first chartered city in America.

Sweetheart Salad

Everyone likes this!

2 cups crushed pineapple
 (undrained)
½ cup sugar
1½ tablespoons unflavored
 gelatin
½ cup cold water
2 tablespoons lemon juice

2 tablespoons maraschino
 cherry juice
2 (8-ounce) packages cream
 cheese, softened
12 maraschino cherries
1 cup whipping cream

Heat pineapple with sugar. Soften gelatin in ¼ cup of water and then stir into pineapple mixture. Add lemon and cherry juices. Cool.

Mash cream cheese and add finely cut cherries. Mix with pineapple mixture, adding a small amount of the pineapple mixture at a time. Chill until slightly thickened. Whip the cream and blend into pineapple mixture. Put into a heart-shaped mold and chill. Serves 10-12.

Tasty Temptations from the Village by the Sea

Seafoam Salad

1 large can pears, drained,
 juice reserved
1 package lime gelatin
1 (8-ounce) package cream
 cheese, softened

½ pint whipping cream,
 whipped
1 small bottle maraschino
 cherries, drained

Heat 1 cup of pear juice. Pour over gelatin and stir until dissolved. Mash drained pears with fork. Soften cream cheese with a little pear juice. Add mashed pears and cheese to gelatin; cool. Fold in whipped cream and cup of cherries. Mold as desired and chill until firm.

Cooking with H.E.L.P.

Boston's Freedom Trail is a three-mile walking tour marked by red bricks or a red-painted line that wanders among old streets and alleyways, following "the footsteps" of colonial Boston to 16 sites of freedom and independence.

Mandarin Salad

This salad has gotten rave reviews in many of my cooking classes and dinner parties!

SALAD:
½ cup sliced almonds
3 tablespoons sugar
½ head iceberg lettuce
½ head romaine lettuce

1 cup celery, chopped
2 scallions, chopped
1 (11-ounce) can mandarin
    oranges, drained

DRESSING:
½ teaspoon salt
¼ cup olive or canola oil
2 tablespoons sugar

2 tablespoons cider vinegar
Dash Tabasco sauce

In a small pan over medium heat, cook almonds and sugar; stir constantly until almonds are coated and sugar is dissolved. Cool and store in an airtight container. Combine all dressing ingredients and chill. Tear lettuce into bite-size pieces and place in a large bowl. Add celery, scallions, and oranges. Just before serving, add almonds and dressing and then toss.

Hint: When heating almonds and sugar, watch constantly so that they don't burn. The almonds may be glazed several days in advance and stored in a tin. The only problem is that they are so delicious that there may not be any left when you go to serve the salad!

From Ellie's Kitchen to Yours

Spinach-Strawberry Salad

It may sound strange, but you'll love it. And it is very pretty.

½ cup sugar
2 tablespoons sesame seeds
1 tablespoon poppy seeds
1½ teaspoons minced
   onions
¼ teaspoon Worcestershire
   sauce

¼ teaspoon paprika
½ cup vegetable oil
¼ cup cider vinegar
1 (10-ounce) bag fresh
   spinach
1 pint strawberries, sliced
   thin

In a blender mix sugar, sesame seeds, poppy seeds, onions, Worcestershire, paprika, oil, and vinegar for the dressing. Blend well. If too thick, add a few drops of water.

Remove stems from spinach and tear leaves into smaller pieces. Arrange them on individual salad plates. Place sliced strawberries on top. Drizzle a bit of dressing over each salad and serve. Serves 4-6.

The Lymes' Heritage Cookbook

Spinach Couscous Salad

A close friend and excellent cook shared this recipe with me when I was searching for no- and low-cholesterol dishes. It is particularly good served on a warm summer day.

1 cup chicken broth
¾ cup couscous
½ cup Italian salad
   dressing
2 cups shredded fresh
   spinach

12 cherry tomatoes
1 (6-ounce) can sliced water
   chestnuts

In a saucepan, bring the broth to a boil and stir in the couscous. Remove from the heat, cover, and let stand for 5 minutes. Transfer the couscous to a bowl and add the salad dressing. Cover and chill for 2-4 hours, or overnight. Before serving, toss the couscous mixture with the spinach, tomatoes, and water chestnuts. Serves 4.

As You Like It

Bildner's Famous Red Potato Salad

The quintessential picnic food, and our top-selling item at Bildner's. Since there's no mayonnaise in the dressing, it's a perfect outdoor food— no chance of spoiling in the sun.

1½ pounds medium new red potatoes
1 shallot
2 tablespoons Dijon mustard
1 tablespoon coarse mustard (with seeds), such as Pommery
¼ cup virgin olive oil
2 tablespoons red wine vinegar
2 tablespoons chopped fresh Italian parsley
Salt and freshly ground pepper to taste

Wash and boil the unpeeled potatoes until just tender (about 20 minutes). Drain and cool them completely. Cut into ½-inch slices. Place in a large serving bowl and set aside. Mince the shallot finely. In a small bowl, combine the mustards and olive oil. Add the red wine vinegar, minced shallot, chopped parsley, and salt and pepper. Mix to blend.

Pour the mustard mixture over the sliced potatoes and toss to coat. Serve or keep covered in the refrigerator. Return to room temperature before serving. Yield: 6 servings.

J. Bildner & Sons Cookbook

Broccoli and Raisin Salad

Very good, very crunchy, with a highly agreeable, sweet, and pungent flavor.

2 bunches broccoli
⅓ cup sugar
⅔ cup raisins
½ cup chopped onions

2 tablespoons vinegar
1 cup mayonnaise
4 bacon slices, cooked and crumbled

Blanch broccoli for 2 minutes if you wish. Cut off florets and cut into serving pieces, discard stems. Freshen florets in ice water for 5 minutes, drain, and dry. Put florets in a salad bowl. Mix together sugar, raisins, onions, vinegar, and mayonnaise. Pour dressing over broccoli and toss lightly. (Can be prepared an hour or so in advance; cover and refrigerate.) Just before serving, add crumbled bacon on top. Serves 8-10.

The Lymes' Heritage Cookbook

Crunchy Pea Salad

Add chicken to make a meal.

2 (10-ounce) packages frozen petite peas, thawed
1 cup chopped celery
¼ cup chopped green onion with 3-4 inches green tops
1 cup chopped cashews or macadamia nuts

½ cup crisp bacon bits
1 cup sour cream
½ teaspoon salt
¼ cup Garden Café Dressing

GARDEN CAFÉ DRESSING:
⅓ tablespoon lemon juice
½ cup red wine vinegar
½ tablespoon salt
½ teaspoon finely ground pepper
½ teaspoon sugar

½ teaspoon Dijon mustard
1 clove garlic, mashed
½ tablespoon Worcestershire sauce
1½ cups corn oil

Combine peas, celery, onion, nuts, and bacon.

To make dressing, combine all ingredients except oil in blender or food processor. While processing, gradually add oil. Mix together sour cream, salt, and dressing and fold gently into pea mixture. Chill and serve on a bed of lettuce. Serves 10.

The Cookbook II

Lemon-Ginger Chicken Salad

½ cup mayonnaise
¼ cup sour cream
1 tablespoon sugar
½ teaspoon lemon rind
1 tablespoon lemon juice
½ teaspoon ground ginger
½ teaspoon curry powder
2 cups cubed chicken
1 cup green grapes
1 cup sliced celery
¼ cup toasted almonds

In large bowl, mix together mayonnaise, sour cream, sugar, lemon rind, lemon juice, ginger, and curry powder. Fold in chicken, grapes, and celery. Toss to coat. Chill before serving. Serve on cantaloupe halves and sprinkle with toasted almonds.

What's Cooking at Moody's Diner

Bewitching Salad

2 (3-ounce) packages lemon
  gelatin
2 cups boiling water
1 (16-ounce) bottle ginger
  ale
Juice of 1 lemon
1 cup celery, finely diced
1 cup grapes, chopped
1 cup blanched nut meats,
  chopped
2 cups white chicken meat,
  diced
1 cup sweet pepper, finely
  shredded
Lettuce
Mayonnaise, to taste

Add gelatin to boiling water; cool and stir in ginger ale. Add lemon juice. When partially congealed, add celery, grapes, nuts, chicken, and pepper, and pour into mold rubbed with salad oil. Chill until firm. Serve on crisp lettuce with mayonnaise. Serves 8.

Seasoned with Grace

Chicken Avocado Salad

Created by a chef living aboard a 28-foot sailboat, this salad is as light and glorious as a perfect sail.

1 (11-ounce) can mandarin
  oranges
1 (3¼-ounce) can ripe
  pitted olives
¼ cup sliced water
  chestnuts
1½ cups cubed cooked
  chicken breast

¼ cup finely chopped
  celery
¼ small red onion, thinly
  sliced and separated into
  rings
1 medium ripe avocado
Lettuce leaves
Salt and freshly ground pepper

DRESSING:
1/3 cup mayonnaise
1/3 cup sour cream
2 teaspoons tarragon

Syrup reserved from mandarin
  oranges (about 3-4
  tablespoons)

Drain mandarin oranges and reserve syrup for dressing. Drain olives and water chestnuts, discarding liquid. Combine cubed chicken, celery, and onion. Add drained oranges, olives, and water chestnuts. Peel and cube avocado. Gently mix into salad.

Prepare dressing by mixing together mayonnaise, sour cream, and tarragon. Thin to desired consistency with mandarin orange syrup, about 3-4 tablespoons. Pour dressing over salad mixture; toss gently. Add salt to taste, if desired. Cover and refrigerate until needed. Serve on a bed of lettuce with freshly ground black pepper to taste. Yield: 4-6 servings.

All Seasons Cookbook

Honey-Mustard Dressing

¼ cup honey
½ cup applesauce
1 teaspoon spicy mustard
¼ cup lemon juice

1 teaspoon grated lemon peel
3 tablespoons vinegar
½ cup vegetable oil
Salt and pepper to taste

Mix all ingredients together well with a rotary beater or a wire whisk. Adjust seasonings. Chill.

Shake and serve with fresh mixed greens, orange and grapefruit segments, or fruit salad of your choice. Yield: About 1½ cups dressing.

Apple Orchard Cookbook

Curried Turkey Salad

This salad is standard fare at Falmouth Academy faculty luncheons. Do adjust ingredients according to supplies in your larder.

1½ pounds cooked turkey, cut up
½ cup raisins
½ cup toasted almonds, chopped
½ cup sliced celery

½ cup mayonnaise
1-2 tablespoons curry powder, or to taste
3 large Granny Smith apples, peeled and coarsely diced

Combine all ingredients, except apples, in a large bowl 1 day before serving. Stir once or twice. Just before serving, fold in apples. Serves 4 as salad, 6 as sandwiches.

The MBL Centennial Cookbook

Ducktrap Farm
Smoked Trout and Rice Salad

DRESSING:
3 cloves garlic
½ cup olive oil
½ lemon, juiced

1 teaspoon cider vinegar
1 teaspoon powdered mustard
Salt and pepper to taste

SALAD:
4 cups cooked rice
2 cups chopped cooked celery
2 cups finely chopped carrots

½ cup black olives, chopped
½ cup chopped parsley
1 medium onion, chopped
3–4 smoked trout fillets

Put all the dressing ingredients in a jar and shake. Set aside. Cook rice and allow to cool. Add celery, carrots, olives, parsley, and onions. Flake trout meat into the salad. Dress the salad at least 1 hour before serving and chill. Vegetables may be marinated in dressing beforehand. Serves 8.

The Maine Collection

Shrimp Salad with Snow Peas and Water Chestnuts

½ pound snow peas, strings
  removed
¾ pound cooked shrimp
1 cup sliced canned water
  chestnuts, drained

½ cup light vegetable oil
1 tablespoon rice vinegar
2 tablespoons honey
Juice of 1 lemon
2 tablespoons light soy sauce

Bring a large pot of water to the boil. Blanch the snow peas in rapidly boiling water for 30 seconds. Drain and refresh under cold water. Drain again.

    Arrange peeled shrimp, snow peas, and water chestnuts in a serving dish. Combine all remaining ingredients for the dressing and pour it over the salad. Toss well and serve. Yield: 4-6 servings for lunch.

Off the Hook

Crevettes et Avocats

The most delicious salad I've ever eaten! Served at one of our first gourmet dinners.

1 pound cooked shrimp
3 avocados
¼ teaspoon dry mustard
½ teaspoon salt
¼ teaspoon black pepper

⅓ cup olive oil
3 tablespoons wine vinegar
1 onion, chopped
1 clove garlic, minced

Shell shrimp and cut into small pieces. Cut the avocados in half and carefully scrape out meat, reserving shells. Cube the avocado meat and combine with shrimp.

    Mix mustard, salt, and pepper in a bowl. Gradually add the oil, mixing carefully until the spices are dissolved. Add the vinegar, onion, and garlic and beat well. Pour over shrimp and avocado mixture and mix carefully. Fill shells with mixture. Serves 6.

The Fine Arts Cookbook II

Spiced Coleslaw

4 cups finely grated red
  cabbage
6 shallots, chopped fine
1 cup golden raisins
¼ cup red wine vinegar
¾ cup vegetable oil
1 tablespoon poppy seeds
1 tablespoon celery seeds

1 teaspoon peeled and grated
  gingerroot
1 teaspoon Dijon mustard
½ teaspoon ground
  coriander
1 teaspoon ground black
  pepper
1 teaspoon salt

Combine all ingredients. Let the salad marinate in the refrigerator at least 2 hours. Adjust the seasonings and serve. Serves 6-8.

The Gardner Museum Café Cookbook

Three Week Coleslaw

The coleslaw recipe used by Women's Fellowship at their annual Winter Supper.

1 medium-large head cabbage
2 medium onions
1 green pepper
2 cups sugar

1 cup cooking oil
1 cup cider vinegar
2 teaspoons salt
Celery seed, to taste

Chop cabbage, onions, pepper and combine. In a saucepan combine remaining ingredients. Bring to a hard boil. Pour immediately over vegetables and stir to mix thoroughly.

Store in an airtight container for 3 days to 3 weeks. Keep refrigerated.

The Marlborough Meetinghouse Cookbook

Peerless Pasta Salad

This is the best pasta salad!

1 pound pasta, cooked and
  drained (I use rotini)
3 cups seedless grapes
¾ cup chopped scallions
1 (8-ounce) can pitted black
  olives, drained and halved

2-4 ounces bleu or
  Gorgonzola cheese
1 clove minced garlic
1 cup mayonnaise
3 tablespoons lemon juice

Combine pasta, grapes, scallions, black olives, cheese, and garlic. When cooled, add mayonnaise and lemon juice.

Heritage Fan-Fare

Pasta Salad

DRESSING:
¾ cup olive oil
2½ tablespoons red wine
  vinegar
Juice of 1 lemon
1 large garlic clove, minced
1 tablespoon fresh dill,
  minced
2 tablespoons honey

1 tablespoon fresh parsley,
  minced
2 tablespoons Dijon mustard
½ teaspoon salt
Freshly ground pepper
1 tablespoon fresh basil,
  minced

Blend all ingredients in food processor or blender. Let sit in refrigerator for at least several hours.

SALAD:
18 ounces of pasta shells,
  rotini, or whatever shape
  you like
4 scallions, chopped
1½ cups ham, cut in strips
¾ cup thawed peas

1 cup Swiss cheese, cut in
  strips
1 green bell pepper, cut in
  thin strips
½ red bell pepper, cut in
  strips

Cook pasta until "al dente" and cool. Add remaining ingredients and toss. Add dressing, mix in thoroughly (chill if desired) and serve.

A recipe from Bobby Orr, former hockey great and Hall of Famer.

Celebrities Serve

Hot Tortellini Salad

2 (6-ounce) jars marinated
  artichoke hearts
½ cup grated Parmesan
  cheese
1 tablespoon Dijon mustard
¼ teaspoon dill weed
1 (1-pound) package
  cheese-filled or spinach-
  filled tortellini

1 cup whole almonds
1 small head iceberg
  lettuce, about 4 cups, cut
  in chunks
1 cup sliced mushrooms
1 cup red pepper strips
½ cup sliced green onions

Drain artichoke hearts; reserving marinade. In small bowl, combine marinade with cheese, mustard, and dill weed; mix well and set aside.

Cook tortellini as directed on package, drain. In large bowl, combine hot tortellini with remaining ingredients. To serve, toss with artichokes and cheese dressing.

Home Cookin' is a Family Affair

Rice and Bean Salad

½ cup salad oil
½ cup wine vinegar
2 tablespoons sugar
1 teaspoon salt
½ teaspoon pepper
1 cup diced celery
½ green pepper, chopped
1 can red kidney beans,
  drained

1 can cut green beans,
  drained
1 medium red onion, thinly
  sliced
3 pimientos, diced
2 cups cooked cold rice

Blend oil, vinegar, sugar, salt, and pepper. In a bowl, mix celery, green pepper, kidney beans, green beans, onion, pimiento, and rice. Pour oil-vinegar mixture over vegetables and refrigerate a couple of hours before serving. Serves 6.

Windjammer Cooking

The first United States Open Golf Championship was played in Newport, Rhode Island, in 1885.

J & J's Basil Cream Dressing

Whenever possible, use fresh basil for this dressing. Dried basil works well, but is not nearly as pungent and aromatic.

1 clove garlic, minced	4-6 tablespoons fresh minced
2 tablespoons chopped	basil or 3-4 tablespoons
parsley	dried
¼ cup white wine vinegar	Dash of sugar
2 tablespoons Dijon mustard	Salt and freshly ground
1 egg	pepper to taste
⅔ cup vegetable oil	

Place garlic, parsley, vinegar, mustard, and the egg into the bowl of a food processor. Mix well. With the processor running, add the vegetable oil in a slow, steady stream and process until smooth and thickened.

Stop the machine for a minute to add the basil, sugar, salt, and pepper. Process briefly until blended. Taste and correct the seasoning as needed. To serve, spoon over a mixed garden salad and enjoy! Makes 1 cup.

Recipes from a New England Inn

Boothbay Harbor French Dressing

A zippy, easy dressing from Down East.

1½ cups oil	1 teaspoon grated onion
⅔ cup vinegar	½ teaspoon pepper
½ cup sugar	1 can tomato soup
1 teaspoon dry mustard	(undiluted)
1 teaspoon horseradish	Juice of 1 lemon

Mix well first 7 ingredients. Add can of soup and lemon juice. Mix well with egg-beater. I make this in the blender. Store in refrigerator and it will keep very well. It yields 1 quart.

Cooking with H.E.L.P.

Vegetables

The quiet beauty of a leaf-strewn country road in South Peacham, Vermont.

Harvard Beets

1 tablespoon cornstarch
⅓ cup sugar
¼ cup vinegar
¼ cup water

½ teaspoon salt
2 cups diced boiled beets
2 tablespoons melted butter

Mix cornstarch and sugar, add the water, vinegar, and salt, and bring to a boil, stirring until thick and smooth. Add beets, and cook over slow fire 15 minutes. When ready to serve, add butter and bring to a boil. Serves 4.

Good Maine Food

Roasted Broccoli with Sesame Dressing

1 pound large broccoli
   flowerets, including 3
   inches of stem
3 tablespoons olive oil
4 tablespoons fresh lemon
   juice
2 teaspoons oriental sesame
   oil

4 teaspoons soy sauce
3 tablespoons vegetable oil
4 teaspoons sesame seeds,
   toasted
1 teaspoon ground ginger
½ teaspoon minced garlic
Pinch sugar

In a bowl, toss the broccoli with the olive oil until it is coated well, and roast in a jelly roll pan in a preheated 500° oven, turning it occasionally with tongs, for 10-12 minutes, or until crisp-tender.

While the broccoli is roasting, in a blender or food processor, blend the lemon juice, the sesame oil, the soy sauce, the vegetable oil, the sesame seeds, the ginger, the garlic, and the sugar until the dressing is smooth. Transfer the broccoli to a serving dish and pour the dressing over it. Serves 4.

Hasbro Children's Hospital Cookbook

Born in a small room at the back of his father's store in Plymouth Notch, Vermont, Calvin Coolidge, the 30th President (1923) was the only president to have been born on the Fourth of July. Vermont's other president (1880-84), Chester Alan Arthur, the son of an Irish immigrant Baptist minister, was born in Fairfield.

Hot Broccoli Mold

2 (10-ounce) packages frozen
  chopped broccoli, cooked
  and drained well
¼ cup chicken broth
3 tablespoons butter
¼ cup chopped scallions
3 tablespoons flour
1 cup sour cream
3 eggs, lightly beaten

⅓ cup grated Swiss cheese
1 teaspoon salt
¼ teaspoon black pepper
½ teaspoon nutmeg
¼ cup finely chopped
  toasted almonds
3 tablespoons chopped
  pimento

Preheat oven to 350°. Grease well a 5-cup ring mold. Add chicken broth to well-drained, cooked broccoli; set aside. Melt the butter in large saucepan; add scallions and sauté until tender. Stir in flour and cook, stirring, about 1 minute. Blend sour cream into flour mixture; cook, stirring constantly, until thick, but do not boil. Remove from heat; stir in eggs. Stir in broccoli-broth mixture, cheese, seasonings, nuts, and pimento. Pour into mold. Set in a shallow pan of boiling water; bake 45 minutes or until knife inserted in center comes out clean. Let stand 5 minutes. Run knife around edges; unmold. Yield: 6-8 servings.

Christmas Memories Cookbook

Buttered Red Radishes

One of spring's earliest crops. If you cook red radishes quickly, they will not lose their color.

1 bunch red radishes
1 tablespoon butter,
  margarine, or Butter Buds

Salt to taste

Clean radishes and slice into thin rounds. Melt butter in skillet and sauté radishes briefly. Salt lightly and serve. Yield: 4 servings.

Favorite New England Recipes

Carrot Bake

For the many people who are shy about serving carrots to company.

9 or 10 large carrots	1 cup milk
¼ cup chopped green pepper	½ teaspoon salt
¼ cup chopped onion	2 tablespoons sugar
4 tablespoons butter or margarine	1 tablespoon butter or margarine
2 tablespoons flour	½ cup soft bread crumbs

Peel, slice, and steam the carrots until tender. Mash. Sauté the green pepper and onion in the 4 tablespoons butter or margarine. Stir in the flour, milk, salt, and sugar. Cook until thickened. Add the mashed carrots and put in a greased casserole.

Melt the 1 tablespoon butter or margarine and in this, toss the crumbs until golden. Spread over the carrots. Bake at 350° for 30 minutes. Serves 6.

The Country Innkeepers' Cookbook

Sister Mary's Zesty Carrots

6 carrots	1 teaspoon salt
Salt	¼ teaspoon pepper
Water to cover	¼ cup water
2 tablespoons grated onion	¼ cup buttered bread
2 tablespoons horseradish	crumbs
½ cup mayonnaise	

Preheat the oven to 375°.

Clean and cut the carrots into thin strips. Cook until tender in salted water. Drain the carrots and place them into a 6x10-inch baking dish.

Mix together the onion, horseradish, mayonnaise, salt, pepper, and water. Pour this over the carrots. Sprinkle the buttered bread crumbs over the top. Bake at 375° for about 15 minutes. Serves 4-6.

A recipe from Hancock Shaker Village, Pittsfield, MA.

Best Recipes of Berkshire Chefs

Boston Baked Beans

1 (2-quart) bean pot
2 pounds beans; pea beans,
  navy beans, or small white
1 pound salt pork
1 medium onion
8 tablespoons dark brown
  sugar

^{2}/$_3$ cup dark molasses
2 teaspoons dry mustard
^{2}/$_3$ teaspoon salt
½ teaspoon pepper

Soak beans overnight. In morning parboil them for 10 minutes with a teaspoon of baking soda. Run cold water through beans in a colander or strainer.

Dice salt pork and onion in small pieces. Put half of each on bottom of pot. Put in half of beans. Add rest of pork and onion, then rest of beans. Mix other ingredients with hot water (about 2 cups). Pour over beans to cover. Put in 300° oven for 6 hours.

Add water as necessary to keep beans moist—a little at a time. Don't flood the beans. Serves 10.

Come Savor Swansea

Tony's Baked Beans

½ pound bacon, fried crisp
  and crumbled
2 large onions, chopped
1 (16-ounce) can pork and
  beans, drained
1 (16-ounce) can red kidney
  beans, drained
1 (16-ounce) can baby lima
  beans, drained

½ cup firmly packed brown
  sugar
¼ cup vinegar
1 cup catsup
1 tablespoon mustard
  (prepared)
1 tablespoon Worcestershire
  sauce

Combine all ingredients in a large bowl and stir until mixed. Spoon into a lightly greased 2-quart casserole dish; cover and bake at 350° for 45 minutes. Makes 8-10 servings.

A Culinary Tour of the Gingerbread Cottages

"The Greatest Show on Earth" lives on at the P. T. Barnum Museum in Bridgeport, Connecticut, the city where P. T. Barnum was born.

Party Beans

2 pounds beans
Water
½ pound salt pork
2 chopped onions
2 cups molasses
¼ cup brown sugar
½ cup catsup

2 tablespoons dry mustard
1 cup dark beer
2 tablespoons vinegar
3 tablespoons Worcestershire
  sauce
1 pound bacon or chopped ham

After washing beans, cover them with water and let soak overnight. In the morning, change the water, add salt pork, and bring to a boil. Cover and simmer 1 hour.

Drain all but 2 cups of the broth from the beans (reserve), and add onions, molasses, brown sugar, catsup, dry mustard, dark beer, vinegar, Worcestershire sauce, and meat. Bake at 200° for 6-9 hours, adding more beer or bean broth as needed. Uncover the pot in the last hour. There are approximately 20 servings in this recipe.

Cuisine à la Mode

Casco Corn Pudding

2 cups milk
¼ cup sugar
6 eggs, well beaten
¼ cup minced onion
1 cup cracker crumbs

2 tablespoons flour
2 (16-ounce) cans creamed
  corn
½ cup butter

Mix milk, sugar, eggs, onion, crumbs, and flour. Beat well. Stir in corn. Melt ¼ cup butter and add. Pour into a buttered shallow baking dish. Dot with ¼ cup butter and bake at 350° 45 minutes. Allow to set a few minutes before serving. If you like, top with grated cheese and/or chopped parsley. Serves 6-8.

Windjammer Cooking

 Fiddleheads are the fronds of ostrich ferns. In the spring they are available fresh in many food stores. The young shoots of cinnamon and bracken ferns are also sometimes eaten as "fiddleheads." If you pick your own, gather them in very early spring before the veil covering the frond turns yellow. Snap off fronds that are about 6 inches high. Pick fronds from several plants if possible, so that the ferns remain in good health and can be picked next season.

Fiddleheads
(Microwave)

My first introduction to fiddleheads was in the early 1980s, when they suddenly became a "gourmet" treat, yet these fern sprouts have been eaten as a vegetable since Colonial times. They have a delicate flavor, similar to asparagus, and should be cooked as soon as possible after picking.

1 pound fresh or frozen
  fiddleheads
¼ cup water
2 tablespoons butter or
  margarine

1 tablespoon cider vinegar
1 teaspoon salt
⅛ teaspoon ground black
  pepper

If the fiddleheads are frozen, unwrap and put in a 1-quart casserole. Heat at DEFROST or LOW (30%) power for 3–4 minutes or just until almost completely thawed. Stir once while heating. Let stand for 5 minutes. Drain off any liquid.

If the fiddleheads are fresh, rinse well and drain. Remove any bruised parts and veils (thin covering over the curl). Put in a 1-quart casserole. Add ¼ cup water to the thawed or fresh fiddleheads. Cover with vented plastic wrap. Heat at HIGH (100%) power for 3–5 minutes, or until just tender. Stir once while heating. Drain.

Add the butter, vinegar, salt, and pepper. Stir gently to melt the butter. Serve hot. Makes 6 servings.

Classic New England Dishes from Your Microwave

Green Beans with Basil

3 tablespoons butter
½ cup chopped onion
¼ cup chopped celery
1 clove garlic, minced

½ teaspoon dried rosemary
½ teaspoon dried basil (if
  fresh, use 2 teaspoons)
1 pound green beans

Melt butter. Add all remaining ingredients except beans and cook until onions and celery are clear. Cook beans in separate pan until crunchy. Drain. Toss in the basil sauce and serve. Serves 5-6.

The Maine Collection

Peas Pernod

2 (10-ounce) packages
  frozen peas
1 cup sour cream
1 teaspoon bottled
  horseradish
1 teaspoon salt
1 red apple, cored and chopped

½ teaspoon Pernod or
  anisette liqueur
3 scallions, chopped
  (with green tops)
¼ teaspoon dried mint (or
  1 tablespoon chopped
  fresh mint)

Thaw the peas and pat dry on paper towels. Place the peas in a large bowl and combine with the other ingredients. Serve chilled. Serves 8.

As You Like It

Sweet and Sour Red Cabbage

3 slices bacon, finely
  chopped
1 large onion, chopped
1 medium-sized red cabbage,
  shredded
4 whole cloves

1 bay leaf
2 tablespoons sugar
½ cup vinegar mixed with
  ¾ cup water
Salt and pepper to taste

Sauté finely chopped bacon in kettle. Add chopped onion. Cook until onion is soft but not browned. Add shredded cabbage, cloves, bay leaf, sugar, vinegar-water, salt and pepper. Mix well and cook very slowly for 1 hour. Stir occasionally.

Great Island Cook Book

Red Cabbage with Cranberries

A baked sweet 'n' sour accompaniment—outstanding with pork or duck.

2 apples, grated
2 cups cranberries, washed
and picked over
8 cups finely shredded red
cabbage
½ cup brown sugar

1 teaspoon salt (or less to
taste)
¼ cup (½ stick) butter
1 cup apple cider or apple
juice
Freshly ground black pepper

Preheat oven to 350°. Butter large casserole with lid. Combine grated apple, cranberries and shredded cabbage with remaining ingredients. Place in buttered casserole; dot with butter. Cover and bake for 1 hour until cabbage is tender. Serve hot. Yield: 6 servings.

All Seasons Cookbook

Potatoes

The poor, misused, misunderstood, taken-for-granted potato. I am astonished to think of how often it is simply boiled, baked, fried, or mashed with no imagination whatsoever. To boil a potato and then mash it is insultingly mundane; but who doesn't like mashed potatoes?

The next time you make them, bake the potatoes in their skins until soft, then scoop the meat out of the skins, add milk and butter and salt and pepper, and mash them that way. Much more taste and much better for you. And mashed potatoes are the ideal food for trying out a spice that you haven't used before. Add it to the potato when you are mashing it. Try caraway seeds, or basil, or saffron. And if you have no gravy, use a little butter and sour cream and chives—these things don't always have to fall upon the center of the potato.

Or, after you've mashed the potatoes, add a couple of egg yolks to them, whip until smooth, then whip the egg whites until stiff and blend the potatoes into that and bake them for another 15 minutes. Sprinkle a little white wine across them, or lemon-flavored bread crumbs, or Parmesan cheese, or grated Swiss or Muenster cheese, or a combination of grated cheese and chopped onions and chives or scallions.

The Blue Strawbery

Mashed Potato Casserole

A very tasty dish that you can do ahead of time and pop into the oven at the last minute. Good for a buffet.

10 medium-size potatoes, peeled	½ cup butter or margarine
1 cup sour cream	¼ teaspoon pepper
1 cup cottage cheese	1 teaspoon salt
1 tablespoon grated onion	¼ cup grated Parmesan cheese

Boil the potatoes in salted water to cover until tender. Mash or rice. While still hot, add the sour cream, cottage cheese, onion, butter or margarine, pepper, and salt. Mix well.

Place in a casserole. Sprinkle Parmesan on top. Bake in a 325° oven for 30 minutes. Serves 8-10.

The Country Innkeepers' Cookbook

Block Island Potatoes

3 pounds small new or red potatoes	1½ teaspoons fresh or dried rosemary, crushed
6 tablespoons unsalted butter	1½ teaspoons paprika
3 tablespoons olive oil	Dash of cayenne pepper
3 large garlic cloves, crushed (I prefer to mince)	½ teaspoon salt
1 tablespoon fresh thyme, crushed, or ½ teaspoon dried	¼ teaspoon fresh ground pepper
	½ cup chopped fresh parsley

Preheat oven to 375°. Scrub and dry potatoes. Melt butter in oil over moderate heat in roasting pan or casserole. Add the next 8 ingredients. Stir to mix. Add potatoes and roll them in butter mix to coat well. Bake, basting potatoes occasionally, for about 40 minutes or until tender.

A Taste of Salt Air & Island Kitchens

Potatoes Appleyard

7 good-sized potatoes
¼ pound butter
¼ pound mild Cheddar
  cheese, crumbled
1 large onion, minced

½ teaspoon pepper
1 teaspoon paprika
Salt to taste
½ cup milk
½ cup cream

Peel potatoes. Slice them thin. Melt 2 tablespoons butter in a large iron frying pan. Put a layer of potatoes into pan. Dot with butter, sprinkle with cheese, onion, and seasonings. Repeat until you have 4 layers. Put extra butter on top layer. Now pour milk and cream into pan. The liquid should come up to the top layer but not cover it. It is somewhat difficult to give precise amounts of ingredients because size of potatoes and pans vary. If you're in doubt, be generous.

Bake all in a preheated 450° oven for 10 minutes. Reduce heat to 350° and bake 35-40 minutes longer. The potatoes should absorb all the liquid and be brown on top and a glazed brown underneath. Cut into pie-shaped wedges on a hot platter. If the pan is thoroughly buttered to begin with, the wedges will come out with no trouble. Serves 6.

Mrs. Appleyard's Family Kitchen

Golden Parmesan Potatoes

6 large potatoes
¼ cup sifted flour
¼ cup grated Parmesan
  cheese

¾ teaspoon salt
⅛ teapoon pepper
⅓ cup butter
Chopped fresh parsley

Pare potatoes; cut into quarters. Combine flour, cheese, salt, and pepper in a bag. Moisten potatoes with water and shake a few at a time in a bag, coating potatoes well with cheese mixture. Melt butter in 13x9x2-inch baking pan. Place potatoes in a layer in pan. Bake at 375° for 1 hour, turning once during baking. When golden, sprinkle with parsley. Makes 6-8 servings.

Home Cookin' is a Family Affair

Red Lion Inn Home Fries

Chef Mongeon uses this seasoning mix for a variety of dishes. He sprinkles it over roasted potatoes, or rubs it into the skin of a chicken before roasting it, as well as using it as a seasoning for Red Lion Inn Home Fries.

2 pounds potatoes, peeled and diced into ¼-inch cubes
1 cup butter
¾ cup onions, diced

2 tablespoons Home Fries Seasoning Mix
Butter, for serving (optional)

Cook the potatoes in a vegetable steamer over simmering water for 20-30 minutes, until just tender.

Melt the butter in a heavy skillet, and add the onions and 1 tablespoon of the seasoning mix. Sauté over medium heat until the onions are limp and translucent, about 10 minutes. Do not let them brown. Add the potatoes, and sprinkle with the remaining 1 tablespoon seasoning mix. Sauté over medium heat until golden brown and crisp, about 15 minutes. Dot with more butter for added flavor. Serves 8.

HOME FRIES SEASONING MIX:
1 cup salt
½ cup paprika
¼ cup ground black pepper

¼ cup ground white pepper
½ cup onion powder
½ cup garlic salt

Combine all the ingredients in a large jar or other covered container. Shake to mix well. This will last up to 6 months. Yields 3 cups.

The Red Lion Inn Cookbook

Nacho Potato Slices
(Microwave)

2 medium potatoes (about 12
  ounces total)
2 tablespoons thinly sliced
  green onion
2 tablespoons finely chopped
  green pepper

¼ cup bottle taco,
  barbecue, or spaghetti sauce
⅓ cup shredded Cheddar
  cheese

Scrub potatoes. Trim ends. Cut potatoes into ⅜-inch thick slices. In an 8x8x2-inch microwave-safe baking dish, arrange potato slices, putting smaller slices in the center. Sprinkle with green onion and green pepper.

Cover with vented clear plastic wrap. Cook on 100% power (HIGH) for 7-10 minutes or until tender, giving the dish a half-turn once. Drizzle sauce over slices. Sprinkle with shredded cheese. Cook uncovered, for 30-60 seconds more or until cheese is melted. Makes 4 servings.

Visions of Home Cook Book

Potatoes Au Gratin Kaleel

The best scalloped potatoes you'll ever make!

6-8 cloves garlic
1½ teaspoons salt
1 tablespoon butter
6 small shallots, finely
  minced
5-6 large potatoes, peeled
  and thinly sliced

¾ teaspoon pepper
¾ pound freshly grated
  Parmesan cheese, divided
2 cups heavy cream, divided
½ pound Swiss cheese,
  grated

Chop garlic; add salt and pulverize using a mortar and pestle until no garlic is visible. Generously grease a 2-quart casserole with 1 tablespoon butter. Sprinkle ⅓ shallots and ⅓ garlic-salt mixture into the bottom of the casserole. Add a layer of potato slices ½ to ¾-inch thick. Sprinkle with ½ teaspoon pepper, and ⅓ of Parmesan cheese and cover with ⅓ cup cream. Sprinkle with shallots and garlic-salt mixture. Continue 2 more layers in same order until pan is nearly full. Add remaining Parmesan cheese, gently mixing throughout casserole. Top with grated Swiss cheese. Cover with foil and bake at 350° for 45 minutes or until potatoes are tender.

Connecticut Cooks III

Sweet Potato Turnovers

These "trutas" are as much of a favorite with the non-Portuguese of Provincetown as they are with the Portuguese.

PASTRY:

1 pound butter	1 cup sugar
1 pound lard (do not use vegetable shortening)	1½ cups warm orange juice, more if needed
4 pounds flour (not self-rising)	2 jiggers whisky or red wine mixed in 1 cup warm water

Melt butter and lard together. Put flour in a deep pan—I use a white enameled dish pan. Make a well in the flour with your hands and place all the other ingredients in this well. Work dough with hands until it feels soft and leaves the side of the pan.

Roll out the dough on a pastry board, a bit on the thin side. Cut out circles with a 3-inch pastry cutter and place a tablespoon of Sweet Potato Filling in the dough circles. Fold the dough over like a turnover. Use a pastry wheel to close each one, pressing down so truta won't open when it is being fried.

Fry trutas in deep fat, drain, and let cool. When cool, shake turnovers lightly in a bag of powdered sugar.

You may prefer to use honey instead of sugar—warm some honey mixed with a little water and lemon juice and place in a pan. Dip the trutas in the mixture so they are coated, and eat them at once or they will become very sticky and hard to take off the serving dish.

SWEET POTATO FILLING:

4 pounds sweet potatoes, cooked and peeled	1 teaspoon grated lemon peel
1½ teaspoons lemon extract or fresh lemon juice, or concentrated juice	1½ teaspoons cinnamon
	1 cup sugar

Mash sweet potatoes. Mix potatoes and all other ingredients in a pan. Stir over a low fire until the sugar has dissolved. Taste to see if more sugar is needed. The mixture should be a dark color when it is cooked—be sure to stir constantly so potato won't stick or burn. Makes approximately 10 dozen.

Traditional Portuguese Recipes from Provincetown

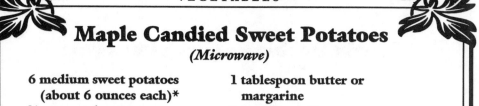

Maple Candied Sweet Potatoes
(Microwave)

6 medium sweet potatoes
(about 6 ounces each)*
½ cup maple syrup
½ cup apple cider (or
unsweetened apple juice)

1 tablespoon butter or
margarine
1 teaspoon salt

Wash and dry the potatoes. Prick each potato twice with a fork to allow steam to escape. Arrange them in a circle on the microwave oven floor at least 1 inch apart. Heat at HIGH (100%) power for 5 minutes. Turn the potatoes over. Heat at HIGH for 4–6 minutes, or until the potatoes just yield when squeezed gently. Roll in a dish towel and let stand for 5 minutes.

Peel and slice the potatoes. Put in a shallow baking dish. Put the maple syrup, cider, butter, and salt in a 2-cup glass measure. Heat at HIGH (100%) power for 3 minutes, or until boiling. Pour over the potatoes and mix gently. Heat at MEDIUM (50%) power for 6–8 minutes, or until heated through. Makes 6 servings.

*Two 1-pound cans of sweet potatoes or yams may be substituted. Slice the potatoes and proceed as above. Canned sweet potatoes need no precooking.

Classic New England Dishes from Your Microwave

New England Autumn Casserole

2½ cups sliced pumpkin or
winter squash, peeled and
seeded
1½ cups sliced apples
¼ cup butter, melted
3-4 tablespoons brown sugar

1 teaspoon cinnamon
½ cup walnuts or almonds,
broken up
Salt to taste
Butter

Place a layer of pumpkin, then a layer of apples, in a 2-quart casserole. (The pumpkin or squash will not cook as quickly, so slice it more thinly than the apples.)

Combine ¼ cup melted butter, sugar, cinnamon, nuts, and salt; drizzle some over apples and pumpkin. Continue alternating layers and drizzling with butter-and-sugar mixture until all ingredients have been used. Dot with a bit more butter.

Cover casserole and bake at 350° for 45-60 minutes or until pumpkin and apples are tender. Yield: 4 servings.

Apple Orchard Cookbook

Cousin Debbie's Squash Casserole

2 pounds yellow summer
   squash, sliced
¼ cup chopped onion
1 can cream of chicken or
   celery soup
1 cup sour cream
1 cup shredded carrot
1 cup butter, melted
1 (8-ounce) package
   herb-seasoned stuffing mix

Cook squash and onion 5 minutes and drain. Combine soup and sour cream. Stir in carrots. Then, fold in squash mixture. Combine stuffing and butter. Layer squash and stuffing mixtures. Bake at 350° for 30 minutes.

Berkshire Seasonings

Stuffed Acorn Squash

4 medium acorn squashes
1 pound mushrooms, chopped
2 cups onion, chopped
2 garlic cloves, mashed
½ cup fresh parsley,
   minced
1 teaspoon dried basil
4 tablespoons dry white wine
1½ cups wild brown rice
   blend, cooked

Cut squashes in half lengthwise. Remove seeds and bake for 30-35 minutes at 350°. Meanwhile, sauté mushrooms, onion, and garlic in a lightly oiled skillet until ingredients are lightly browned. Combine with herbs, wine, and cooked rice. Set aside.

Remove pulp from cooked squash and transfer to a large mixing bowl. Blend in the vegetable-rice mixture and spoon into each squash shell. Sprinkle with freshly ground pepper, paprika, and a little more parsley. Bake at 350° for 25-30 minutes, or until heated through. Makes 8 servings.

The Chef's Palate Cookbook

Vegetable Cheese Cake

3 tablespoons oil
¾ cup sweet red pepper, chopped
1½ cups mushrooms, chopped
1½ cups zucchini, chopped
¾ cup onion, chopped
1 large clove garlic, minced

6 eggs
¼ cup heavy cream
1 pound cream cheese, diced
1½ cups Cheddar cheese, shredded
2 cups one-day-old bread, cubed
Salt and pepper

Sauté vegetables in oil until zucchini is crisp-tender; remove from heat and cool. Beat together the eggs and heavy cream in a large bowl and add the cooked vegetable mixture. Combine cream cheese, Cheddar cheese, bread cubes, and salt and pepper to taste, and add to the eggs-vegetable mixture. Pour everything into a well-greased 10-inch springform pan; seal bottom of pan with foil, as eggs run a bit until set. Bake at 350° for 1 hour. Makes 1 (10-inch) cake.

The MBL Centennial Cookbook

Vegetable-Cheese Casserole
(Microwave)

2 zucchini squash, ¼-inch slices
1 yellow summer squash, ¼-inch slices
1 green sweet pepper, strips
1 stalk celery, 1-inch slices
1 carrot, sliced
1 cup fresh mushrooms or canned
¼ cup water

1 tablespoon olive oil
2 cloves of garlic
1 large onion, cut in thin slices
½ teaspoon thyme
⅛ teaspoon oregano
Salt
Freshly ground pepper
1 cup mozzarella cheese, shredded

Place zucchini, squash, green pepper, celery, carrot, and fresh mushrooms in a casserole dish with ¼ cup cold water and cook in the microwave for 2 minutes. Stir. Cook for 2 minutes longer. Drain water and set aside.

In a frying pan, heat oil and sauté garlic and onion slices. Add microwave vegetables and spices. Stir gently and simmer for 5-7 minutes. Remove from heat and place vegetables in casserole dish. Top with shredded mozzarella cheese and place under broiler until cheese melts. Serves 4.

Heritage Cooking

Zucchini Squares

1 cup Bisquick
½ cup chopped onion
½ cup grated Parmesan
  cheese
3 tablespoons chopped
  parsley
½ teaspoon salt
½ teaspoon crumbled dried
  marjoram

Pinch freshly ground black
  pepper
1 clove garlic, finely
  chopped
½ cup vegetable oil
4 eggs, slightly beaten
3 cups thinly sliced
  zucchini

Preheat oven to 350°. Grease a 13x9x2-inch pan. In a large mixing bowl, combine all ingredients, adding zucchini last. Transfer to prepared pan. Bake 30 minutes or until golden brown. When cool, cut into 2x1-inch squares. Yield: 12 squares.

May also be cut into smaller squares and served as an appetizer.
A recipe from the Waterford Inne, East Waterford, ME.

Country Inns and Back Roads Cookbook

Spinach-Stuffed Zucchini Boats

4 medium zucchini
Salt to taste
1 pound fresh spinach,
  rinsed, trimmed
1 egg
½ cup crumbled feta cheese

Garlic powder, nutmeg, and
  freshly ground pepper to
  taste
½ cup grated Parmesan
  cheese

Cut zucchini into halves lengthwise. Cook in salted water in saucepan for 5 minutes. Drain, reserving cooking liquid; remove and discard seeds. Steam spinach in saucepan until wilted. Drain and chop spinach, pressing out excess moisture. Combine spinach with egg, feta cheese, garlic powder, nutmeg, and pepper in bowl; mix well. Spoon into squash. Arrange in nonstick baking pan. Sprinkle with Parmesan cheese. Pour reserved cooking liquid into pan. Bake, covered with foil, at 350° for 10 minutes. Bake, uncovered, until tops are brown. Yield: 8 servings.

Approximately Per Serving: Cal 74; Prot 6 g; Carbo 4 g; Fiber 3 g; T Fat 4 g; 46% Calories from Fat; Chol 37 mg; Sod 228 mg.

Rhode Island Cooks

Italian Zucchini Casserole

2-2½ pounds zucchini	½ cup shredded Cheddar
½ cup chopped onion	cheese
½ cup chopped green pepper	1 (4-ounce) can mushrooms
4 tablespoons oleo	1 (6-ounce) can tomato paste
1 package spaghetti sauce	1 cup water
mix	Grated Parmesan cheese

Slice zucchini into ½-inch pieces and drop into boiling water. Cook 4-5 minutes and drain. Place zucchini in casserole dish. Sauté onion and green pepper in oleo. Add sauce mix, Cheddar cheese, mushrooms, tomato paste, and water. Mix well and pour over zucchini. Sprinkle top with Parmesan cheese. Bake 25-30 minutes at 350°, or microwave 13 minutes on HIGH; turn once. Let stand 5-10 minutes before serving.

What's Cooking at Moody's Diner

Sautéed Spinach with Garlic

It amazes me how often guests comment when we serve this spinach—they just love it, especially because of all the garlic. Many of us tend to use spinach mostly in salads, but try this dish and you'll be a fan of cooked spinach.

Pinch salt	2 tablespoons olive oil
1½ pounds fresh spinach,	4 garlic cloves, sliced
leaves only, washed and	Salt and fresh-ground pepper
drained	to taste

In a saucepan, heat 2 cups water with a pinch of salt. When the water comes to a boil, add the spinach leaves. Stir to immerse all the leaves. Bring the water to a second boil, and simmer the spinach for 5 minutes. Immediately place the pan in the sink and run cold water into it.

Transfer the spinach to a strainer. Press the spinach with the back of a spoon to extract as much of the liquid as possible. Chop the spinach coarsely.

Heat the olive oil in a skillet. Add the garlic slices, and sauté them just until they begin to brown. Add the spinach, and sauté for 4 minutes, stirring frequently. Season the spinach with salt and pepper, and serve it immediately. Serves 4.

Chris Sprague's Newcastle Inn Cookbook

Spinach Hau Pia

The best spinach dish you've ever tasted.

3 (10-ounce) packages frozen
  chopped spinach, thawed
  and drained
3 cups dry cottage cheese
3 cups flaked coconut

4 eggs
1½ cups sour cream
⅓ cup flour
⅓ cup soy sauce

Place spinach on paper towels and squeeze out as much liquid as possible. Combine spinach, cottage cheese, and coconut. In blender, combine eggs, sour cream, flour, and soy sauce. Blend until smooth. Fold into spinach mixture. Spoon into ungreased 2½-quart casserole. Refrigerate, covered, up to 2 days.

Bake, uncovered at 350° for 40-45 minutes. Allow to stand 10 minutes before serving. Serves 12.

Connecticut Cooks

Tomatoes with Spinach Mornay

3 (10-ounce) packages frozen
  chopped spinach
Salt and pepper
4 tablespoons butter
3 tablespoons flour
Dash salt
Dash cayenne pepper
1 teaspoon Dijon mustard
1 teaspoon dry mustard

1 cup milk
4 tablespoons shredded Swiss
  cheese
4 tablespoons grated
  Parmesan cheese
4 tablespoons half-and-half
8-10 medium tomatoes
Grated Parmesan cheese

Cook spinach slowly, without any additional water. Drain thoroughly. Season with salt and pepper. Melt butter in separate pan. Remove from heat and add flour. Season with salt, cayenne, mustards, and blend in milk. Stir over heat until it boils, then add cheeses and light cream. Simmer 5 minutes, then combine with spinach mixture. Cut tops off tomatoes and remove seeds and center membranes. Pile spinach into tomato cases and sprinkle with Parmesan cheese. Bake at 350° for 20 minutes. Serves 8-10.

RSVP

Spinach-Artichoke Casserole

2 boxes spinach
1 pound mushrooms, sliced
1 medium onion, chopped
2 jars marinated artichoke
   hearts with liquid
5 eggs

1 clove garlic, crushed
¾ cup Parmesan cheese
¾ cup shredded Cheddar
   cheese
Dash of thyme

Defrost and drain spinach. Sauté mushrooms and onion. Drain one jar artichoke hearts. Slightly beat eggs. Combine all ingredients. Heat covered at 350° for 30-40 minutes.

Home Cookin' is a Family Affair

Spinach Timbales

Popeye wears his tuxedo for this!

3 eggs
½ cup shredded Cheddar
   cheese
¼ cup half-and-half
½ teaspoon prepared
   horseradish
¼ teaspoon salt
Dash pepper

Dash Tabasco sauce
1½ cups well-drained
   cooked, chopped spinach
   (about 2 [10-ounce] packages
   frozen)
Fresh spinach leaves for
   garnish, if desired

Preheat oven to 325°. Butter well 6 (6-ounce) custard cups, ramekins, or molds. Beat eggs slightly in mixing bowl; add cheese, cream, horseradish, and seasonings. Stir in spinach.

Spoon mixture equally into custard cups. Place cups in a 13x9x2-inch baking pan and add 1 inch hot water to pan. Bake uncovered 20-30 minutes or until set. Unmold and serve immediately, garnished with fresh spinach leaves. Yield: 6 servings.

All Seasons Cookbook

Oven Vegetables

The Italians make a dish similar to this called Vegetable al Forno; loosely translated, this means "oven vegetables." I try to bake as many vegetables as I can and the only ones that I usually do on top of the stove are green vegetables or those that I happen to be deep-frying.

For this dish you need a nice-sized baking dish—preferably one you might also serve in. Place on the bottom a layer of thin-sliced eggplant, on top of that a layer of thin-sliced zucchini, then a layer of sliced tomatoes, then sliced peppers.

Then take a cup of red wine, mix it with half a cup of melted butter or margarine, about 4 tablespoons of tamari or soy sauce, some pepper, garlic, oregano, and basil. Pour it over the vegetables, lay slices of Swiss or mozzarella cheese across the top, and bake it uncovered in a 400° oven for 45 minutes to an hour, depending on the size of the dish. The cheese should be crusty on top. Makes a terrific one-dish meal, or a hot salad (a hot salad!?), a side dish with meat, or just a nice late, light supper with some rosé wine.

The Blue Strawbery Cookbook

Pasta, Etc.

A hillside shrine in Lower Shaker Village. Enfield, New Hampshire.

Quiche Cargo Boat

This luscious "boat" will please every crew member.

1 loaf French bread,
    unsliced
2 tablespoons butter
½ cup scallions, chopped
1½ teaspoons flour
1 cup Swiss or Cheddar
    cheese, shredded
½ cup light cream

2 teaspoons cornstarch
2 eggs, lightly beaten
¼ teaspoon dry mustard
¼ teaspoon salt
¼ teaspoon pepper
1 tablespoon Parmesan
    cheese, grated

Preheat oven to 425°.

Cut off top of bread and hollow out, leaving about 1 inch of bread on bottom. Cover with foil. Place on baking sheet and bake 5 minutes. While bread is in oven, melt butter in saucepan and sauté scallions until tender. Mix in flour and set aside. Layer shredded cheese and any cooked meats or vegetables you might want to add in the bottom of the bread shell.

In a medium bowl, stir small amount of the cream into cornstarch, blending until smooth. Add remaining cream, eggs, and seasonings. Mix well and add to the onion mixture. Pour cream mixture over cheese in bread shell. Sprinkle with Parmesan. Bake 40 minutes or until inserted knife comes out clean. Let stand 10 minutes before slicing. Serve or wrap to go. Serves 8-10.

Variations: Crumbled bacon, ham, basil, mushrooms, cooked shrimp, broccoli, or spinach may be added to the egg mixture.

Moveable Feasts Cookbook

Vegetable Sandwiches

This filling for sandwiches also may be used as a salad if desired. It uses varied amounts; if you do not have enough of one vegetable, another may be substituted.

2 large carrots, shredded	1 small cucumber, grated
3 cups cabbage, shredded	1 (3-ounce) package cream
½ cup chopped celery	cheese and chives, beaten
1 green pepper, chopped	2 or 3 tablespoons
1 small onion, grated	mayonnaise
2 tablespoons chopped	Salt and pepper to taste
chives, if available	

Prepare vegetables. In beater bowl, beat the cream cheese until fluffy. Stir in mayonnaise. Place in salad bowl. Add prepared vegetables. When ready to serve, toss all together. You may like more salt and pepper or mayonnaise. Butter bread slices and spread filling. Cut in desired shapes.

Memories from Brownie's Kitchen

Two-and-a-Half-Minute Skillet Pizza

No one should have to wait to eat a pizza like you do when you call up for one to go—"That'll be twenty minutes, please." This one's gone by then.

Start with a low, round loaf of bread. Its diameter should closely match the frying pan you'll use. Cut the bread in half so that you have two round loaves (you'll love this pizza so much that you'll want to make another right away). Heat ¼ inch of olive oil in the frying pan until it just begins to smoke. Quickly sprinkle in a healthy mixture of herbs—I use 2 tablespoons each of basil, black pepper, garlic, marjoram, oregano, and rosemary; also 1 tablespoon of beef bouillon. Add 1 cup of tomato sauce; stir a few times as it begins to bubble. Then sprinkle 2 cups of mixed grated provolone and Jarlsberg cheese and ½ cup of grated Parmesan evenly across the sauce. Lay the bread, cut-side-down, into the sauce. Let it simmer for about 30 seconds. Turn it upside down onto a plate and cut into wedges to serve. It goes without saying that you can add whatever you want to that sauce—mushrooms, pepperoni, and so on.

Another Blue Strawbery

Crabmeat Quiche

1 (9-inch) unbaked pie shell
½ pound Swiss cheese, cut
  in strips
1 cup crabmeat
½ cup small shrimp
2 cups light cream
4 eggs, beaten

1 tablespoon flour
½ teaspoon salt
Dash of pepper
Dash of cayenne
¼ teaspoon nutmeg
2 tablespoons melted butter
2 tablespoons sherry wine

Line pie shell with cheese. Cover with a layer of crabmeat and shrimp. Combine cream, eggs, flour, salt, pepper, cayenne, and nutmeg. Stir in melted butter and sherry. Beat well and pour over seafood. Refrigerate or freeze. When ready to serve, bake at 375° for 40 minutes or until golden brown. Let stand 20 minutes before serving.

Sandy Hook Volunteer Fire Co. Ladies Aux. Cookbook

Reuben-in-the-Round

Great for late-night snack or as a party appetizer.

1 (8-ounce) package
  refrigerated crescent rolls
1 (12-ounce) can corned
  beef, shredded
¼ cup chopped green pepper
2 tablespoons catsup

1 teaspoon horseradish
1 (8-ounce) can sauerkraut,
  well drained
½ teaspoon caraway seed
1 cup shredded Swiss cheese

Separate chilled dough into 8 triangles. Place 6 triangles in ungreased 8-inch pie pan, pressing edges together to form crust. Combine beef, pepper, catsup, and horseradish; mix well. Spoon into crust. Spread sauerkraut over mixture. Sprinkle with caraway. Top with cheese. Cut remaining triangles into ½-inch strips. Stretch strips over filling to form lattice top. Bake at 350° for 20 minutes. Place aluminum foil strip around rim and bake for 15-20 minutes. Yields 8 servings.

Connecticut Cooks II

Lobster Quiche

CRUST:

1½ cups flour
1 teaspoon salt
6 tablespoons butter or
  shortening

3-5 tablespoons ice water

Mix together the flour and salt. Using a pastry fork or food processor, cut in the shortening until the mixture resembles coarse sand. Mix in just enough ice water to form a ball. Wrap the pastry in plastic wrap and refrigerate for 1 hour. Roll out the chilled dough on a lightly floured board to ⅛-inch to ¼-inch thickness. Line a 9-inch quiche pan with the pastry, cover with plastic wrap, and refrigerate until ready to use.

FILLING:

3 eggs
1½ cups half-and-half
1 tablespoon butter, melted
1½ cups cooked lobster
  meat, chopped coarsely
¾ cup grated Swiss cheese
¾ cup grated Cheddar
  cheese

1 small onion
1 clove garlic
¼ teaspoon dry mustard
½ teaspoon tarragon
1 teaspoon parsley
Salt and pepper to taste

Preheat oven to 350°. In a large bowl, beat the eggs well. Add the half-and-half and beat again. Stir in the lobster meat and cheeses. Set aside. Chop the onion fine and sauté in a little butter. When the onion is almost done, crush the garlic and stir in: remove from heat. Add the onion and garlic, dry mustard, herbs, salt, and pepper to the lobster mixture and combine well. Pour into the quiche crust and bake at 350° for 45 minutes. Cool on a rack for 5 minutes before slicing.

A recipe from Murphy's Bed & Breakfast, Narragansett, RI.

The Bed & Breakfast Cookbook

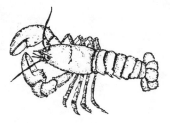

Portuguese Quiche
(Linguica-Cheese Pie)

½ cup heavy cream
½ pound bacon, cooked, drained, and chopped
½ pound grated Sierra da Estrella cheese (Swiss cheese may be substituted)
1 tablespoon chopped chives
2 slightly beaten egg yolks

1 cup light cream
2 tablespoons parsley, chopped
1 tablespoon onion, chopped
¼ pound linguica, thinly sliced
1 (9-inch) pastry shell, unbaked

Preheat oven to 350°. Combine all the ingredients except the linguica and fill the pastry shell with the mixture. Sprinkle the slices of linguica over the top.

Bake in oven for 20-30 minutes, or until center of quiche is firm. Serves 4-6.

A recipe from The Moors, Provincetown, MA.

A Taste of Provincetown

Onion, Walnut, and Swiss Quiche

3 tablespoons butter
2 large white onions, diced
2 cloves garlic, minced
¾ cup chopped walnuts
6 eggs
1¼ cups light cream

1 teaspoon salt
1 teaspoon ground black pepper
1 teaspoon ground nutmeg
1 cup grated Swiss cheese
1 unbaked pie shell

Heat the butter in a frying pan over low to medium heat. Sauté the onions and garlic until the onions are soft and clear. Add the walnuts, and toast for about 5 minutes. Remove from the heat and set aside.

Combine the eggs, cream, salt, pepper, and nutmeg in a large mixing bowl. Beat well with an electric mixer or by hand with a wire whisk. Lightly stir the walnut and onion mixture and the Swiss cheese into the egg mixture.

Pour the filling into the pie shell. Bake at 425° for 10 minutes, then reduce the heat to 300° and bake for 25-30 minutes, until a knife inserted in the center comes out clean. Cover the quiche with buttered aluminum foil if it browns too quickly. Serves 6.

The Gardner Museum Café Cookbook

Spinach Pie

1 pound frozen chopped
  spinach
¼ cup chopped onion
4 eggs
1 teaspoon lemon juice
¼ teaspoon pepper
¼ teaspoon salt

1 (8-ounce) package cream
  cheese
¾ cup milk
8 ounces grated Cheddar
  cheese
1 unbaked pie shell

Cook and drain spinach. (Squeeze out water well.) Blend in other ingredients except half of Cheddar cheese. Mix well with spinach and pour into pie shell. Bake at 375° for 25 minutes. Then sprinkle rest of cheese on top and bake until cheese melts, approximately 5 minutes. Makes 6-8 slices. A Dianne Lowe specialty.

A Culinary Tour of the Gingerbread Cottages

Ham & Spinach Quiche

5-6 ounces spinach (about
  ½ bag)
¼ teaspoon salt
⅛ teaspoon pepper
1 tablespoon horseradish
4 tablespoons sour cream
4-6 ounces Swiss cheese,
  grated (part sharp cheese
  may be used)

⅓ cup minced onion
4-6 ounces ham, cubed or cut
  into small pieces
4 eggs
1½-2 cups half-and-half
¼ teaspoon sugar
⅛ teaspoon cayenne pepper
⅛ teaspoon nutmeg
1 unbaked pastry shell

Cook spinach. Drain thoroughly, pressing out the water. Add salt, pepper, horseradish, and sour cream. Spread on pastry in 9-inch pie plate or regular quiche dish. Sprinkle with cheese and onion. Add ham.

Beat eggs with a whisk; add half-and-half, sugar, cayenne, and nutmeg. Mix well. Pour into pie shell. Bake at 425° for 15 minutes. Reduce heat to 300° for 30 minutes more or until a knife comes out clean. Cool on a rack 5-10 minutes before serving.

Homespun Cookery

Burlington is the largest city in Vermont (1991 population 39,127); Montpelier (population 8,247) is the smallest state capital in the U.S.; and Vermont's Vergennes is the smallest city (1.8 square miles) in America.

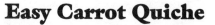

Easy Carrot Quiche

3 large potatoes, shredded
½ teaspoon salt
½ teaspoon pepper
2 tablespoons vegetable oil
2 cups shredded carrots
1 medium onion, chopped
1 clove garlic, minced
3 eggs

1 cup cottage cheese
½ cup shredded Swiss
   cheese
¾ cup milk
1 tablespoon parsley
3 tablespoons grated
   Parmesan cheese

Preheat oven to 425°. Grease quiche pan or pie plate. Mix grated potato with half the salt, pepper, and oil and spread on bottom of the greased dish. Bake 20 minutes or until lightly browned. Remove and reduce oven to 375°.

Sauté carrots, onion, and garlic in remaining tablespoon oil over medium heat until softened.

Whisk together the eggs, cheeses, milk, parsley, and remaining salt and pepper. Stir in carrot mixture and pour over potato crust. Sprinkle with Parmesan and bake for 30 minutes, or until lightly browned. Serves 6.

Vermont Kitchens Revisited

Broccoli Rice Bake

1 cup brown rice
½ teaspoon salt
2 tablespoons oil
1 large onion, chopped
2 cloves garlic, minced
1 teaspoon each: dill,
   thyme, oregano
4 tablespoons parsley,
   chopped

½ pound mushrooms, sliced
1 green pepper, diced
2 pounds broccoli, stalks
   peeled and all thinly sliced
½ cup cashews, broken
1 cup grated Gruyère cheese
¼ cup grated Parmesan
   cheese
1 cup sour cream

Cook rice in salted water until barely done; sauté onion, garlic, seasonings, parsley, mushrooms, and green pepper in oil briefly. Add broccoli; cook and stir until crisp-tender; add nuts. Spread cooked rice in a greased 9x13-inch baking dish; cover with vegetable mixture, sprinkle with cheeses, and put sour cream on top. Bake in a 350° oven for 20 minutes or until bubbling. Serves 8.

The MBL Centennial Cookbook

Sausage-Broccoli Bake

1 pound bulk sausage
1 cup sliced celery
1 (6-ounce) package long
  grain and wild rice mix
1 (10-ounce) package frozen
  broccoli spears, thawed

1 can cream of mushroom soup
2/3 cup milk
4 tablespoons grated
  Parmesan cheese

Break up sausage and combine with celery in large skillet. Cook over medium-high heat until sausage is lightly browned. Remove from skillet, draining any fat, and place in a shallow round 2-quart baking dish. Preheat oven to 350°. Prepare rice mix with water as package directs, omitting butter or margarine in skillet. Stir into sausage mixture. Arrange thawed broccoli on top. Mix soup, milk, and half of cheese. Pour over broccoli. Sprinkle remaining cheese on top. Bake 30 minutes or until bubbly.

A Hancock Community Collection

Hot Chicken Salad

3 cups cooked chicken, diced
1½ cups noodles
  (uncooked)
3 cups celery, chopped
2 tablespoons lemon juice
1 teaspoon salt
¾ cup slivered water
  chestnuts

2 (4-ounce) cans mushrooms
  and juice
1 tablespoon grated onion
1½ cups mayonnaise
¾ cup grated Cheddar
  cheese
Crushed potato chips

Heat oven to 450°. Mix all ingredients, except cheese and chips. Pile lightly in 9x13-inch casserole. Sprinkle with chips and cheese. Bake 15-20 minutes.

Perennials

Oriental Rice
(Indonesia)

1 tablespoon vegetable oil	½ cup water chestnuts
2 cups cooked rice, chilled	¼ cup soy sauce
½ cup raisins	

Heat oil in a wok or skillet; add rice, stirring and tossing until grains are coated with oil. Add raisins and water chestnuts; stir until mixture is heated through. Add soy sauce and blend. Yield: 4 servings.

Variation: Cooked, diced beef or chicken may be added.

The Art of Asian Cooking

Wild Rice Chicken Casserole

May be made ahead, frozen, thawed, and baked. Easy—tossed salad and hot bread—yum!

1 (6-ounce) package wild rice mix	1 (5-ounce) can water chestnuts, sliced
1 (10¾-ounce) can condensed cream of chicken soup	1 (4-ounce) can mushrooms, drained
4 cups cooked chicken, cubed	3 tablespoons soy sauce
1 cup chopped celery	1 cup chicken broth
¼ cup chopped onions	Topping

Cook rice according to package directions. Blend in soup and next 6 ingredients; mix gently. Add broth and mix. Spread in a 13x9x2-inch dish. Sprinkle with topping; bake at 350° for 1 hour.

TOPPING:

1½ cups seasoned stuffing mix	½ cup butter or margarine, melted

Toss together and sprinkle on top of casserole. Serves 8.

Connecticut Cooks III

Connecticut, the third smallest state in the nation, is officially called the Constitution State, but most people call it the Nutmeg State, and its residents, "Nutmeggers." Indians called it Quinnehtukut, or "beside the long tidal river" (the Connecticut River). Its 60-100-year-old northern hardwood trees that cover six-tenths of the state are glorious in the fall.

Cider Rice Pilaf

This is especially good with pork or lamb.

3 tablespoons butter
1 cup white or brown rice
Salt and pepper, to taste
½ cup chopped onion
¾ cup chopped celery
1 teaspoon grated orange
  peel

¼ cup minced parsley
¼ teaspoon dried rosemary
  or ¾ teaspoon fresh
1¾ cups apple cider

Melt butter in a skillet. Add rice and stir until golden. Add salt, pepper, onion, celery, and orange peel. Sauté 5 minutes more. Add half the parsley and all the rosemary.

In a separate pan bring the cider to a boil, then stir into rice. Cover the skillet and cook over low heat about ½ hour for white rice, or an hour for brown rice. Serve sprinkled with remaining parsley. Serves 4.

Vermont Kitchens Revisited

Vegetable Pie with Rice Crust

1 cup carrots, sliced
¼ cup onion, chopped
1 green pepper, chopped
1 cup turnips, cubed
1½ cups celery, chopped

2 cups potatoes, cubed
4 tablespoons butter
4 tablespoons flour
1 teaspoon salt
1 cup milk

Cook all vegetables except potatoes in salted water for 15 minutes. Add potatoes. Cook until tender. Drain. Melt butter, and add flour, salt, milk, and vegetables. Put in casserole and cover with rice crust. Bake at 400° for 20 minutes.

RICE CRUST:
1 cup rice, boiled
⅓ cup milk
2 eggs, separated
1½ cups flour

1 tablespoon sugar
1 teaspoon baking powder
½ teaspoon salt
1 tablespoon butter, melted

Mix rice and milk. Beat yolks and add to rice mixture. Sift dry ingredients and add to mixture with butter. Beat well and fold in beaten egg whites. Serves 4.

Seasoned with Grace

Spring Vegetable Tart

1 sheet frozen puff pastry
2 pounds ricotta cheese
½ cup grated Parmesan
  cheese
½ cup sour cream
½ teaspoon oregano
½ teaspoon garlic salt

Salt to taste
½ teaspoon pepper
2 tomatoes, sliced
1 zucchini, sliced
1 yellow squash, sliced
16 asparagus spears
8 mushrooms, sliced

Thaw pastry at room temperature for 10-15 minutes. Press into greased and floured 10-inch tart pan with removable side. Combine ricotta cheese, Parmesan cheese, sour cream, oregano, garlic salt, salt, and pepper in bowl; mix well. Spread evenly in prepared tart pan. Arrange vegetables over top. Bake at 350° for 30 minutes or until pastry is golden brown. Place on serving plate; remove side of pan. Yield: 8 servings.

Approximately Per Serving: Cal 405; Prot 19 g; Carbo 20g; Fiber 2 g; T Fat 28 g; 62% Calories from Fat; Chol 68 mg; Sod 477 mg.

Rhode Island Cooks

Vermont Turkey and Broccoli Puff

SHERRY CHEDDAR SAUCE:

¼ cup butter
¼ cup flour
1 cup light cream
½ cup sherry

1 teaspoon salt
½ teaspoon basil
1 cup Vermont sharp Cheddar
  cheese

Melt butter in saucepan, add flour, and stir to combine. Stir in the cream, sherry, salt, and basil and cook over low heat, stirring, until thick. Stir in 1 cup Cheddar cheese until melted.

1 head broccoli, flowerets
  and stems
6 baked puff pastry squares
Fresh spinach leaves

Sliced turkey
Vermont sharp Cheddar
  cheese, sliced

Steam broccoli flowerets and stems; cut into diagonal slices ¼-inch thick, until tender. Mix the broccoli into the sauce and keep warm over low heat.

Split baked puff pastry squares and layer on the bottom half of each, in order: fresh spinach leaves, sliced turkey, ½ cup broccoli in sauce, 2 slices Vermont sharp Cheddar cheese. Heat under a broiler or in a hot oven to melt cheese. Cover with top of puff and serve immediately. Serves 6.

Peter Christian's Favorites

Zucchini Pancakes

Nutritious and delicious.

3 cups grated zucchini
½ cup flour
1 teaspoon baking powder

½ teaspoon salt
2 tablespoons dried onion
2 eggs

Combine all ingredients. Mix well. Pour batter by ¼ cupfuls onto hot, well-greased griddle. Mixture will be thick; spread slightly. Brown lightly, turn. Cheese may be grated directly on finished side. Cheese will melt while cooking. Brown second side. Add butter each time batter is placed on the griddle. These make a full meal when served with a salad. Serves 4.

Connecticut Cooks

Linguine with Tomatoes and Basil

Perfect for those hot, lazy days of summer when ripe tomatoes and basil are abundant. The heat of the pasta warms and brings out the flavors of the sauce in a wonderfully subtle way. Delicious and easy.

4 large ripe tomatoes (1 pound) cut into ½-inch cubes
1 pound Brie cheese, rind removed, torn into irregular pieces
1 cup cleaned fresh basil leaves, cut into strips
3 garlic cloves, peeled and finely minced

1 cup plus 1 tablespoon best quality olive oil
2½ teaspoons salt
½ teaspoon freshly ground black pepper
1½ pounds linguine
Freshly grated imported Parmesan cheese (optional)

Combine tomatoes, Brie, basil, garlic, 1 cup olive oil, ½ teaspoon salt, and pepper in a large serving bowl. Prepare at least 2 hours before serving and set aside, covered, at room temperature.

Bring 6 quarts water to boil in large pot. Add 1 tablespoon olive oil and remaining salt. Add the linguine and boil until tender, but still firm, 8-10 minutes. Drain pasta and immediately toss with tomato sauce. Serve at once, passing the pepper mill and grated Parmesan cheese. Serves 4-6.

Tasty Temptations from the Village by the Sea

Spaghetti Sauce

2 tablespoons olive oil
1½ cups onion, finely
  chopped
1 green pepper, finely
  chopped
2 cloves garlic, minced
6 cups crushed or stewed
  tomatoes

1 cup tomato sauce or purée
¼ cup red wine
2 teaspoons basil
2 teaspoons oregano
1 teaspoon sugar
½ teaspoon chili powder
⅛ teaspoon cayenne pepper
1 teaspoon salt or to taste

Sauté in 2 tablespoons olive oil the onion, green pepper, and garlic in a heavy soup kettle, over medium high heat, for 10–15 minutes, until tender. Add the remaining ingredients and simmer, covered, over medium-low heat, stirring occasionally, for 2 hours.

Peter Christian's Favorites

Peter's Sweet Italian

½ recipe Spaghetti Sauce
1 pound sweet Italian
  sausage
2 tablespoons oil
1 large Spanish onion,
  coarsely chopped
1 large green pepper,
  coarsely chopped

1 clove garlic, minced
4–6 small loaves French
  bread
½ pound sliced mozzarella
  cheese

Make one-half recipe of Spaghetti Sauce and keep it hot. Fry or bake Italian sausage until browned and cooked through; drain on paper towels and cool slightly.

In frying pan add 2 tablespoons oil and sauté Spanish onion, green pepper, and garlic until tender, but still a little crisp. Slice the sausages in fourths lengthwise and then in half widthwise. Add sausage and onions and peppers to the Spaghetti Sauce and mix well.

Cut a wedge lengthwise out of the tops of 4–6 small loaves of French bread and fill the cavities with the sausage and tomato mixture, dividing it evenly. Cover each sandwich with sliced mozzarella cheese. Broil or heat the sandwiches in a microwave to melt the cheese and serve immediately. Serves 4–6.

Peter Christian's Favorites

Vegetarian Lasagna

2 cups chopped onions (2 large)

2-4 cloves garlic, finely minced

½ pound fresh mushrooms, sliced

1 tablespoon oil or margarine

1 bunch broccoli, chopped (about 4 cups)

½ pound fresh spinach, washed, stemmed, and chopped (about 2 cups)

½ teaspoon any low-salt seasoning of your choice

2 cups lowfat cottage cheese

8 ounces part-skim mozzarella, shredded

Parmesan cheese

¼ cup chopped parsley

2 eggs

Salt and pepper, if desired

Oregano, basil, dill (dried) for sprinkling

3-5 cups ready-made spaghetti sauce

9 lasagna noodles, cooked al dente and spread on aluminum foil until needed

In a large skillet (electric fry pan is perfect) sauté the onion, garlic, and mushrooms in the oil until they are soft. Add broccoli, spinach, and low-salt seasoning. Stir to combine, reduce heat, cover and simmer for about 5 minutes, or until broccoli is almost tender. In a bowl, combine the cottage cheese, mozzarella, 3 tablespoons Parmesan, parsley, eggs, and salt and pepper if desired.

In a 9-x13-inch baking dish spread ½-1 cup spaghetti sauce. Then layer the lasagna as follows: 3 lasagna noodles, half egg-cheese mixture, half vegetable mixture, spaghetti sauce to cover, generous sprinkling of oregano, basil, dill, Parmesan cheese.

Repeat, ending with last 3 noodles covered with spaghetti sauce and sprinkled with more herbs and Parmesan. Bake, covered with foil, for about 30 minutes at 375°. Remove foil and bake 5-10 minutes more until lasagna bubbles. Let stand 10 minutes before cutting. Makes 12 servings.

Note: Preparation time can be simplified by using frozen broccoli and spinach, and canned mushrooms, but the result is not as good. Freeze any extra in individual servings, ready to microwave whenever you want a quick healthy, delicious meal.

Vermont Kitchens Revisited

The name "Vermont" is itself derived from the French, *les monts verts*, "the green mountains."

Seafood Lasagna

This dish was created for seafood, and is an especially good choice for a festive buffet. But it also works with cooked turkey or chicken—a great addition to your basic repertoire of reliable recipes.

1 pound lasagna noodles	6 tablespoons butter
¾ pound peeled, deveined shrimp	½ cup flour
¾ pound scallops	Salt, pepper
2 cups white wine	Paprika
2 cups stock (fish or chicken depending on what you're making)	Sherry, to taste
	2 pounds sharp Cheddar cheese, grated

Cook lasagna noodles al dente according to package directions and cool on sheets of aluminum foil.

In a large saucepan, cook seafood in wine and stock for 3-5 minutes. Save the stock for the sauce. Remove seafood to food processor and chop coarsely. In saucepan, melt butter, add flour and seasonings, and cook, stirring, for a few minutes. Stir in 2 cups of the wine-stock mixture and cook until thickened. Add seafood mixture and set aside.

Layer noodles, cheese, and seafood mixture, in that order, in a greased lasagna pan, finishing with a layer of cheese. Bake at 375° for 45 minutes, or until bubbly. Let stand 10 minutes before serving. Serves 10-12 and freezes well.

Vermont Kitchens Revisited

Short Cut Spinach Lasagna

This is a wonderful low-cholesterol, low-fat pasta dish that appeals to people of all ages. It is especially appealing to the cook, because it is so quick and easy to make! You don't even have to cook the lasagna first, which saves both time and mess.

1 (10-ounce) package frozen
  chopped spinach
2 cups (1 pound) low-fat or
  non-fat cottage cheese
2 cups (½ pound) part-skim
  shredded mozzarella cheese,
  divided
1 egg or egg substitute

1 teaspoon oregano
Salt and pepper, to taste
29-32 ounces spaghetti
  sauce
9 lasagna noodles (½ pound),
  uncooked
1 cup water

Thaw and drain spinach. In large bowl combine cottage cheese, 1 cup of mozzarella, egg, spinach, oregano, salt, and pepper. In greased 9x13-inch baking dish, layer 1 cup sauce, ⅓ of noodles and half the cheese mixture. Repeat. Top with remaining noodles, then remaining sauce. Sprinkle with remaining 1 cup mozzarella. Pour water around edges. Cover tightly with foil. Bake at 350° for 1 hour and 15 minutes or until bubbly. Let stand 15 minutes before serving.

Hint: This may be made up to 2 days in advance. It also freezes very well.

From Ellie's Kitchen to Yours

Pesto Chicken with Bow Tie Pasta

2 whole chicken breasts,
  boned, skinned
2 tablespoons olive oil
Garlic powder, salt, and
  pepper to taste
12 ounces uncooked bow tie
  pasta

8 ounces prepared pesto
½ cup grated Parmesan
  cheese
½ cup grated Romano cheese

Rinse chicken and pat dry. Rub with olive oil; sprinkle with garlic powder, salt, and pepper. Place in baking dish. Bake at 350° for 20 minutes or until tender. Cut into bite-sized pieces. Cook pasta using package directions; drain. Toss with chicken, pesto, and cheeses in bowl. Yield: 6 servings.

Approximately Per Serving: Cal 620; Prot 49 g; Carbo 47 g: Fiber 2 g: T Fat 31 g: 45% Calories from Fat; Chol 66 mg; Sod 596 mg.

Rhode Island Cooks

Chicken with Fine Herbs and Sundried Tomatoes

10 sun-dried tomatoes, cut
  julienne
2 tablespoons shallots,
  chopped
2 (8-ounce) boneless chicken
  breasts, cut into julienne
  strips
¼ cup white wine

½ teaspoon each, freshly-
  chopped basil, thyme, and
  tarragon
¼ cup heavy cream
½ pound fettucine, cooked
  al dente
Salt and white pepper to taste
¼ cup Parmesan cheese

Sauté sundried tomatoes and shallots in olive oil in a skillet for a few minutes. Add chicken, cook on both sides until almost done, then deglaze the pan with white wine. Add the fresh herbs, heavy cream and pasta. Reduce the heavy cream over medium heat while tossing the pasta gently. Season with salt and white pepper. Garnish with chopped parsley and Parmesan cheese. Serves 2.

A recipe from Café Zelda, Newport, RI.

A Taste of Newport

Pasta Gorgonzola Miraculous

Chef Edmond Grosso tells this story about the origin of this recipe's name. "Some time ago an elderly woman using two crutches entered the Springs for lunch. She and her party ate on the day this dish was introduced. Two hours later, when I went back into the dining room, she had departed, but her two crutches still rested against the back of her chair. So we christened the recipe after her: Pasta Gorgonzola Miraculous."

GORGONZOLA SAUCE:

1 beef bouillon cube
2 cups hot water
1 onion, chopped
1 cup skim milk
3 tablespoons corn oil
2 tablespoons vodka
¼ cup Triple Sec or
  Cointreau

2 thin slices ham, chopped
3 ounces Gorgonzola cheese,
  crumbled
8 ounces frozen chopped
  spinach
3 ounces low-fat ricotta
  cheese

In a saucepan, dissolve the beef bouillon cube in the hot water. Add the rest of the ingredients and boil, while stirring, until the onions are cooked through.

CONTINUED

PASTA:

1 pound rotelle   Grated cheese on the side
Freshly ground pepper

Boil the rotelle according to the package directions and drain thoroughly.

Combine the pasta and the sauce and add ground pepper to taste. Serve with grated cheese on the side. Serves 6.

A recipe from The Springs Restaurant, New Ashford, MA.

Best Recipes of Berkshire Chefs

Masi's Manicotti

One of the easiest pastas to make. Kathi used this one when teaching home economics and the kids loved doing it.

2 cups flour   2 eggs
¼ teaspoon salt   Margarine
1 cup water

Mix flour, salt, water, and eggs until smooth. Melt ¼ teaspoon margarine in a 6-inch skillet. Add about ¼ cup batter and roll liquid in pan, so entire bottom of pan is covered; cook until just firm. Do not brown. Turn, let cook only 10-20 seconds on other side. Cook much the same as crêpes. Set aside to cool on a cookie sheet. Repeat with remaining batter.

Fill and roll like a jelly roll, but be sure and turn in ends first. Lay side by side in a buttered 9x13-inch baking dish. Cover with tomato sauce of your choice. Bake at 350° for 30-40 minutes.

SPINACH FILLING:

1 (10½-ounce) package   1 egg, beaten
   frozen chopped spinach   ½ cup Parmesan cheese
½ pound freshly grated   1 tablespoon chopped parsley
   mozzarella cheese   ¼ teaspoon nutmeg
2 cups ricotta cheese   Salt and pepper

Thaw and drain spinach. Place all ingredients in bowl; mix well. Place about 1 tablespoon filling on each shell and roll to enclose.

The Island Cookbook

Angel Hair Pasta Primavera

1 (16-ounce) package angel
  hair pasta or vermicelli
¼ cup vegetable oil
1 medium-sized yellow
  squash, sliced (about 1 cup)
1 medium-sized onion, diced
1 cup sliced fresh mushrooms
4 ounces fresh or 6 ounces
  frozen Chinese pea pods,
  thawed

1 large clove garlic
2 large ripe tomatoes,
  chopped
1½ teaspoons salt (optional)
1 teaspoon dried basil
¼ cup grated Parmesan
  cheese

In a deep 4-quart saucepan bring 2 quarts of water to a boil. Cook angel hair pasta according to package directions. In a 12-inch skillet over medium heat, heat oil, adding squash, onion, mushrooms, pea pods, and garlic. Cook 5 minutes, stirring occasionally until vegetables are crisp-tender. Add tomatoes, salt, and basil to vegetables; cook 2 minutes until heated through. Drain pasta. Add vegetables to pasta in saucepan along with ¼ cup Parmesan cheese. Stir to mix. Serve with additional cheese. Serves 6.

The Parkview Way to Vegetarian Cooking

Vermicelli Anita

6 ounces vermicelli
1 tablespoon butter
1 medium onion, minced
1 cup crushed tomatoes
1 (7-ounce) can white tuna
  in oil

1 cup frozen peas, thawed
¼ cup chopped fresh
  parsley

In a large saucepan cook vermicelli al dente, according to directions on package. While pasta is cooking, sauté onion in butter until soft in a saucepan, over medium-low heat. Stir in tomatoes and cook for 5 minutes. Break tuna into pieces, add to sauce, simmer for 5 minutes. Add peas, stir, and cook for about 2 minutes. Place drained vermicelli on heated plates and spoon sauce over each portion. Garnish with chopped parsley. Serves 2.

Note: One-half pound of peeled, deveined shrimp can be used instead of tuna. Serve with a green salad and crusty French bread.

Seafood Expressions

Zucchini with Noodles & Basil

4 ounces (¼-pound box)
    egg noodles
1 clove garlic
2 medium zucchini, thinly
    sliced

2 tablespoons margarine or
    butter
1 teaspoon leaf basil, crushed
¼ teaspoon pepper (optional)

Cook noodles. Sauté garlic and zucchini in butter or margarine until zucchini is tender, about 5 minutes. Stir in basil and pepper. Drain noodles and toss with zucchini. Serve immediately.

The Parkview Way to Vegetarian Cooking

Spinach Pasta with Scallops

The boursin cheese adds a savory flavor to the tender scallops in this recipe.

2 tablespoons butter
2 tablespoons olive oil
¾ pound bay or sea
    scallops
½ green bell pepper,
    seeded and diced
1 large tomato, seeded and
    diced
4 green onions, chopped
10 mushrooms, sliced

2 cups heavy cream
½ cup freshly grated
    Parmesan cheese
1 (5-ounce) package boursin
    garlic cheese
9 ounces spinach fettucine,
    cooked al dente and drained
Salt and freshly ground
    black pepper to taste

In a large skillet over moderate heat, melt butter with olive oil. Add scallops and sauté 1-2 minutes. Stir in green pepper, tomato, green onions, and mushrooms. Sauté for 4 minutes. Add cream and Parmesan cheese and stir until well blended. Reduce heat and simmer until sauce thickens, about 8 minutes. Add boursin cheese and stir until blended. In heated serving dish, toss warm fettucine with scallop mixture. Add salt and pepper to taste. Serve immediately. Makes 4-6 main dish servings or 8-10 side dish servings.

More Than Sandwiches

Robert Frost Farm, Derry, New Hampshire, was built in the 1880s. The poet's house is a simple two-story, white clapboard structure typical of New England at that time.

Noodles Romano

It's rich and delicious.

½ cup butter, softened
2 tablespoons parsley,
  finely chopped
1 teaspoon crushed basil
1 (8-ounce) package
  cream cheese, softened
Dash pepper

²/₃ cup boiling water
8 ounces fettuccine noodles
1 large clove garlic,
  finely minced
¾ cup freshly shredded
  or grated Romano or
  Cheddar cheese

In saucepan, combine ¼ cup butter with parsley and basil. Blend in cream cheese and pepper. Stir in boiling water and blend well. Keep warm on stove. Cook noodles according to package directions, 8-10 minutes. Drain. Sauté garlic in remaining butter, 1-2 minutes. Pour over noodles. Toss lightly and quickly to coat. Sprinkle with remaining cheese, tossing lightly to blend. Serve immediately. Serves 4.

The Cookbook II

Harvest Relish

Good with baked beans.

4 onions, ground
4 cups chopped cabbage
4 cups chopped green
  tomatoes
12 green peppers, chopped
6 red peppers, chopped
½ cup salt

6 cups sugar
1 tablespoon celery seed
2 tablespoons mustard seed
2 teaspoons turmeric
4 cups vinegar
2 cups water

Combine vegetables and salt and let set overnight. In morning, rinse vegetables and drain. Combine remaining ingredients and pour over vegetables. Bring to a boil. Simmer 3 minutes, stirring frequently. Pack into hot sterilized pint jars and process in boiling water 10 minutes. Makes 8-10 pints.

Merrymeeting Merry Eating

The cranberry is one of only three fruits native to America, the others being the Concord grape and the blueberry.

Apple Relish

1 cup finely chopped apples
  (unpeeled)
1 cup finely shredded
  cabbage
½ cup finely chopped
  celery
1 tablespoon chopped green
  pepper

1 tablespoon chopped pimento
⅓ cup sugar
3 tablespoons cider vinegar
½ teaspoon salt
¼ teaspoon ginger
¼ teaspoon dry mustard
Dash of cayenne pepper

Combine all ingredients and mix thoroughly. Store in refrigerator.

Recipes from Smith-Appleby House

Spiced Cranberry Sauce

Spicy and not too sweet.

1½ cups sugar
¾ cup water
¼ cup lemon juice
½ teaspoon grated lemon
  rind

½ teaspoon ginger
½ teaspoon nutmeg
3 cloves
1 stick cinnamon
1 pound cranberries

In saucepan, combine sugar, water, lemon juice, rind, and spices. Boil for 5 minutes. Remove cinnamon and cloves. Add cranberries. Boil 5 minutes or until skins pop open. Cool. Refrigerate until served. Yield: 1 quart.

The Cookbook II

Cranberry Chutney

1 cup water
1 cup sugar
2 tablespoons vinegar
½ cup raisins
½ cup nuts (almonds or
  walnuts)

1 tablespoon brown sugar
¼ teaspoon cayenne pepper
¼ teaspoon ground ginger
¼ teaspoon garlic salt
2 cups cranberries

Combine all ingredients in a saucepan and cook on low heat for ½ hour or until thick. Pour into fancy jars and cover with wax to give as a gift. Great with poultry. Keep in the refrigerator. Will keep for several weeks.

More Than Sandwiches

Apricot Ginger Chutney

A wonderful accompaniment for freshly grilled fish, meat, or poultry.

2 cups dried apricots
1½ tablespoons chopped
  candied ginger
1 cup dark raisins
½ lime, thinly sliced
1 large onion, thinly sliced
1½ cups packed dark brown
  sugar

½-1 cup orange juice
½ cup wine vinegar
3 cloves garlic, minced
1 teaspoon dried mustard
½ cup tomato sauce
½ teaspoon cinnamon
½ teaspoon allspice
½ teaspoon cloves

Wash and chop apricots. Combine all ingredients in a medium saucepan and simmer 20 minutes, stirring often until slightly thickened. Pour cool chutney into a covered container and refrigerate. May be served cold or at room temperature. Serves 10-12 or more.

The Maine Collection

Southward Inn Cranberry Relish

3 cups fresh cranberries
1 orange, seeds removed

1 apple, peeled and cored
2 cups sugar

Wash cranberries well; put through meat grinder along with entire orange and apple. Stir in sugar and set aside (cold) for several weeks before serving. Improves with storage.

Recipes from a Cape Cod Kitchen

Zucchini Pickles

4 quarts sliced zucchini
1 quart sliced onions
2 cloves garlic, crushed
¼ cup salt
4 cups sugar

½ cup water
4½ cups vinegar
1 tablespoon dill
2 teaspoons turmeric

Mix vegetables with salt. Cover with cold water. Let stand at least 3 hours. Drain well. Bring sugar, water, vinegar, and spices to a boil and add veggies. Heat to boiling. Pack in hot jars and seal. Yield: 6 pints.

A Taste of Hallowell

Seafood

Lobster traps along the shorelines in coastal Maine.

Cape Shore Lobster Bake

6-8 pounds clams	½ dozen eggs, optional
6-8 lobsters (1¼ pounds each)	Seaweed
6-8 ears of corn	Butter, melted (for dunking lobster meat and clams)
1 pound hot dogs, optional	Asbestos gloves (optional)

Prepare fireplace using cement blocks or rocks. A metal trash can with cover, lined with approximately 2 inches of stone, provides for a simple and convenient means of preparing a small, 6-8-person Downeast Bake. With an abundant supply of dry wood, start the fire and establish a good base of hot coals. Cover stones in bottom of container with salt water (sea water or salted fresh water). Cover with about 3 inches of fresh seaweed. Cover with fresh clams, which have been washed in cold water and wrapped in cheesecloth in individual portions. Allow 1 pound of clams per person. Cover with seaweed. Add 6-8 lobsters and cover with seaweed. Before adding corn, carefully pull back husk and remove silk! Fold back a couple of layers of husk. Add to bake and cover with seaweed. Hot dogs and eggs may be added if desired. Place cover on container; weight with rock if loose fitting. Place container over fire and cook for 50 minutes after steam starts coming out from under the cover. Have melted butter, lemon, salt, chips, beer, and appetite ready when bake is opened up. A pair of asbestos gloves is handy at this point. Serves: 6-8.

Comments: Do not pack any of the layers tightly as this will prevent the steam from circulating freely. For larger bakes, a 3-foot to 4-foot square steel plate (⅜-inch to ½-inch thick) would be required. This is set on cement blocks and food added before starting the fire. Layering of food should be accomplished as described above, and then covered with a tarp or aluminum foil to contain the steam. Cooking time is, again, 50 minutes after steam is up.

Caution: If additional water is needed, pour in along side of container or directly onto the steel plate. Do not pour over top of bake as this will cause "cool down" and prevent or delay cooking.

RSVP

 Maine catches nearly 90 percent of the nation's lobster supply, over 26.8 million pounds in 1992.

Steamed Lobsters

2 lobsters (1¼-1½ pounds
  each)
2 cups water

1 teaspoon sea salt
¼ pound melted butter
Lemon wedges

Select a pot with a tight-sealing lid large enough to hold the 2 lobsters. Put water and salt in the pot and bring to a boil. Set live lobsters in the pot, and cover. Cook lobsters 12 minutes. Add 5 minutes for each additional ½ pound of lobster.

Remove cover, (be careful as the steam will be hot) and remove lobsters to heated plates. Serve with individual nut crackers and a bowl for the shells. Serve immediately with warm melted butter and lemon wedges.

Seafood Expressions

Lobster Thermidor

2 boiled lobsters
¼ pound fresh mushrooms
2 tablespoons butter
Salt and pepper, to taste
2 ounces sherry or cooking
  wine (optional)

2 tablespoons flour
1 cup milk or cream
¼ cup diced Cheddar cheese
Paprika
2 egg yolks

Boil lobsters and remove meat. Reserve shells. Sauté lobster meat and sliced mushrooms in butter for 5 minutes. Add salt and pepper to taste. Add sherry and braise for 2 minutes. Blend flour into mixture, then slowly stir in milk. Add cheese and stir until it melts. Sprinkle with paprika. Remove from heat and blend in egg yolks. Fill lobster shells. Sprinkle with Parmesan cheese and a dash of paprika. Place under broiler to brown.

A recipe from Ron Machtley, Congressman from Rhode Island.

Celebrities Serve

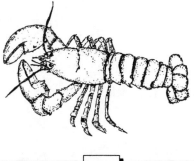

Lobster à la Newburg

½ pint of cream
1 tablespoon butter
1 tablespoon flour
Yolks of 2 eggs
Salt and cayenne pepper (few grains)

1 large lobster, cooked, cut in pieces
Juice of half a lemon
Wine glass of sherry

Make a cream of the cream, butter, flour, and egg yolks; season with salt and very little cayenne. Put the lobster meat in a double boiler and when hot, add the creamed mixture, allowing it to come just to a boil, then add the juice of half a lemon and a wine glass of sherry.

All-Maine Cooking

Individual Baked Lobster Pie

2 tablespoons butter
¼ cup sherry with 1 tablespoon lemon juice
1 cup well-packed lobster meat

3 tablespoons butter
1 tablespoon flour
¾ cup thin cream
2 egg yolks

Melt 2 tablespoons butter; add sherry and boil 1 minute. Add lobster and let stand. Melt 3 tablespoons butter; add flour. Stir 1 minute until bubbles. Remove. Slowly stir in cream and wine, drained from lobster. Return to heat until smooth and thick. Remove. Beat egg yolks very well. Stir into yolks 4 tablespoons of sauce, 1 tablespoon at a time. Add to sauce. Mix well. Heat over hot water in top of double boiler. Do not let water boil or sauce may curdle. It takes about 3 minutes. Remove from heat. Add lobster. Turn into small deep dish pie plate. Sprinkle with topping. Bake slow in 300° oven for 10 minutes. Serves 2.

TOPPING:

¼ cup cracker meal
¼ teaspoon paprika
1 tablespoon finely crushed potato chips

1½ teaspoons Parmesan cheese
2 tablespoons melted butter

Mix first 4 ingredients. Add melted butter and blend well. Sprinkle on lobster pie.

More Than Sandwiches

Merrymount Lobster

Can be prepared ahead of time. Excellent for large buffets.

3 cups cut-up lobster, crab, shrimp, or sea legs
1 tablespoon lemon juice
2 eggs, slightly beaten
2 cups light cream
2 tablespoons butter
1 cup soft bread crumbs
1 cup buttered cracker crumbs (saltines may be used)

1 heaping teaspoon prepared mustard
Dash of cayenne pepper
Black pepper, freshly ground (about ¼ teaspoon)
Salt to taste

Lobster may be frozen, canned, or fresh. Sprinkle lemon juice and beaten eggs over lobster. Bring cream, butter, and bread crumbs just to a boil; stir well together and pour over lobster. Stir mustard, cayenne pepper, black pepper, and salt carefully into lobster mixture. Pour into a buttered casserole dish and top with 1 cup buttered cracker crumbs. Bake, uncovered, in a preheated oven at 350° until crumbs are brown and lobster is bubbly--no more. Serves 8.

Sandy Hook Volunteer Fire Co. Ladies Aux. Cookbook

Garlic Broiled Shrimp

2 pounds large fresh shrimp,
  peeled and deveined
½ cup (8 tablespoons)
  butter, melted
½ cup olive oil
¼ cup fresh parsley,
  chopped

1 tablespoon chopped green
  onion
3 cloves garlic, minced
1½ tablespoons fresh
  lemon juice
Freshly ground black pepper

Combine butter, olive oil, parsley, green onion, garlic, and lemon juice in a large shallow dish. Add shrimp, tossing to coat. Cover and marinate at least 30 minutes, stirring occasionally. Set oven to broil.

Place shrimp on broiler pan and broil 4 inches from the heat source for 3-4 minutes. Turn and broil for another 3 minutes or until done. Top with a few turns of the peppermill and serve with the pan drippings with pasta or rice. Yield: 4-6 servings.

Note: I prefer to use shrimp that have been peeled but with the tails left on and split (or "butterflied") up the back. You can ask your fish market to do this for you.

Off the Hook

New England Shrimp Creole

1 small onion, minced
1 green pepper, chopped
½ cup chopped celery
¼ cup butter, melted
½ cup chopped pimento
1 (27-ounce) can stewed
  tomatoes

1 tablespoon cornstarch
2 tablespoons water
Salt and pepper to taste
1 tablespoon parsley
1 pound cooked shrimp

Add onion, green pepper, and celery to melted butter. Cook until tender. Add pimento and tomatoes. Bring to boil and simmer until well blended. Mix cornstarch with water and add to mixture. Season to taste. Add parsley and cooked shrimp. Serve over hot rice.

A Taste of New England

Shrimp Versailles

2 tablespoons sliced green
onions
3 tablespoons margarine
1½ pounds medium shrimp,
shelled and deveined
1 (8-ounce) package cream
cheese, cubed
3 tablespoons milk
½ cup shredded Swiss
cheese

2 tablespoons dry white wine
Dash of red pepper
¼ cup fine dry bread
crumbs
2 tablespoons margarine,
melted
Hot cooked rice or pasta of
choice

Sauté onions in margarine in large skillet until tender. Add shrimp. Cook over medium heat, stirring occasionally, until pink. Remove shrimp with slotted spoon and set aside.

Add cream cheese and milk to skillet, stirring constantly until cheese melts. Stir in Swiss cheese and wine. Add shrimp and pepper. Cook just until heated. Pour into lightly greased casserole. Combine bread crumbs and margarine. Sprinkle over casserole. Broil 1-2 minutes, until golden. Serve over rice or pasta. Serves 4.

More Than Sandwiches

Shrimp Stir-Fry with Lemon

½ pound peeled raw shrimp
¾ cup thin sliced celery
½ medium green pepper, cut
in strips
2 scallions, sliced,
including tops
½ cup bamboo shoots
1 (4-ounce) can sliced
mushrooms (drained,
reserve liquor)

2 or 3 pimentos, cut in
strips
1 tablespoon oil
1½ tablespoons cornstarch
1½ teaspoons soy sauce
1 tablespoon lemon juice
1 chicken bouillon cube
Salt and pepper to taste
½ teaspoon grated lemon
peel

Stir-fry the shrimp, celery, green pepper, scallions, bamboo shoots, mushrooms, and pimentos in oil for 3 minutes in a 10-inch skillet. Add enough water to mushroom liquid to make 1 cup. Combine liquid with cornstarch, soy sauce, lemon juice, bouillon cube, and seasonings. Cook until sauce is clear and thickened, 1-3 minutes. Stir sauce into shrimp mixture. Serve over hot rice.

Heritage Fan-Fare

Sweet-Sour Shrimp

8 uncooked large shrimp, shelled, deveined, and tails removed
¼ cup peanut oil or vegetable oil
1 medium onion, chopped
1 stalk celery, sliced thin
1 green pepper, seeded and cut into bite-size chunks
1 sweet red pepper, seeded and cut into bite-size chunks

1 tablespoon cornstarch
1 tablespoon lemon juice
1 (13-ounce) can pineapple tidbits, not drained
1 tablespoon brown sugar
1 tablespoon soy sauce
1 cup chicken stock
2 cups cooked rice
Watercress for garnish

Melt oil in a large skillet or wok. Add onion and celery and sauté slowly 3 minutes. Add shrimp, green, and red pepper and sauté 3 minutes. Mix cornstarch with lemon juice. To shrimp mixture add pineapple, brown sugar, soy sauce. Stir in cornstarch mixture, then chicken stock. Simmer until thickened. Add rice, and heat until hot. Spoon shrimp mixture onto heated plates.

Seafood Expressions

Shrimp Cakes

½ pound Italian bread crumbs
1¼ pounds cooked shrimp, chopped
5 eggs, beaten
½ cup chopped parsley
½ cup mayonnaise
3 tablespoons Dijon mustard
1 teaspoon salt

1½ teaspoons Worcestershire sauce
½ teaspoon cayenne pepper
½ teaspoon Tabasco sauce
Additional beaten egg and bread crumbs for dipping
Oil for frying
Lemon wedges for garnish

Mix all ingredients to blend thoroughly. For each cake, shape ¼ cup of batter into a patty 1 inch thick. Dip into additional beaten eggs and coat with additional bread crumbs. Deep fry at 350° until golden and crisp, about 3 minutes for each. Garnish with lemon wedges. Serve with coleslaw or a lemon saffron aioli [garlic mayonnaise]. Serves 6 (makes 12 cakes).

Note: You may substitute crab or lobster meat in place of shrimp.
A recipe from Gallerani's Cafe, Provincetown, MA.

Cape Cod's Night at the Chef's Table

Grilled Shrimp in Lemon Butter Sauce

1 pound large raw shrimp
¼ pound butter
¼ cup olive oil
1 tablespoon parsley, chopped

½ teaspoon garlic, minced
¼ teaspoon oregano
¾ teaspoon salt
½ of 1 lemon

Preheat oven to 450°. Peel, devein, and slice shrimp halfway through from head portion to tail. Place in a baking dish. Melt butter and combine with oil, herbs, salt, and juice of lemon (can be made ahead to this point). Pour over shrimp and broil for 5 minutes at 450°. Serve with brown rice.

BROWN RICE:
1 cup brown rice

3 cups chicken broth

Cook rice in chicken broth over low heat until rice is tender and absorbs all the liquid, about 45 minutes. Serves 4-6.

A recipe from tennis pro, Mats Wilander.

Celebrities Serve

Shrimp and Artichoke Casserole

Shrimply delicious!

6½ tablespoons butter
4½ tablespoons flour
¾ cup milk
¾ cup heavy cream
½ teaspoon salt and pepper
  to taste
½ pound fresh mushrooms,
  sliced
1 (20-ounce) can artichoke
  hearts, drained

1½ pounds large shrimp,
  cooked
½ cup dry sherry
1 tablespoon Worcestershire
  sauce
½ cup freshly grated
  Parmesan cheese
Paprika

Preheat oven to 375°. Butter an oblong baking dish. Melt 4½ tablespoons of the butter; blend in flour; add milk and cream, and cook stirring constantly, until thickened. Add salt and pepper to taste; set aside.

In remaining 2 tablespoons of butter, sauté mushrooms gently for about 5 minutes. Arrange artichokes in a single layer on the bottom of prepared baking dish; scatter shrimp over artichokes; cover shrimp with a layer of mushrooms. Stir sherry and Worcestershire sauce into cream sauce and pour over contents of baking dish; sprinkle with cheese and paprika. Bake 20-30 minutes, or until bubbly. (Or refrigerate several hours; bake 45 minutes.) Yield: 6 servings.

Christmas Memories Cookbook

Alice's Special Shrimp

This dish was created for visual as well as culinary effect, with different shapes and colors, all retaining their own individuality. It turned out to be an all-time favorite at Alice's Restaurant, the famous Berkshire eatery immortalized by the '60s movie of that name, starring Arlo Guthrie and a contingent of Berkshire locals.

1 or more tablespoons butter
5 raw jumbo shrimp, shelled
  and deveined
4 black olives, pitted
4 green olives, pitted
4 ripe cherry tomatoes
3-4 artichoke hearts (packed
  in oil, lightly drained)

1 handful freshly chopped
  scallions and parsley
1 tablespoon sherry
Generous pinch of crumbled
  dried tarragon
One portion of cooked orzo

Melt the butter in a sauté pan over fairly high heat. Toss in the remaining ingredients, except the orzo, all at once. Let it all sizzle up, turning the shrimp once, and immediately serve over the orzo the moment the shrimp are cooked. It takes just minutes.

In the restaurant, each portion was cooked to order in its own little pan. Four or so portions can be prepared at a time in a 12-inch or larger pan. The ingredients should not be crowded. Serves 1.

Best Recipes of Berkshire Chefs

Scampi Sauté

A quick delicious dish.

10 large shrimp
Salt and pepper to taste
¼ cup butter
3 large mushrooms, thinly
  sliced
2 shallots, minced
2 cloves garlic, minced

3 tablespoons diced green
  onion
1 tablespoon sherry
¼ cup whipping cream or
  half-and-half
1 teaspoon chopped parsley

Season shrimp with salt and pepper. Sauté in butter, heating to about 350°; turn shrimp when pink. Add mushrooms, shallots, garlic, and green onion; sauté about 4 minutes. Add sherry and simmer 1 minute. Add cream; shake pan until sauce is thickened. Garnish with parsley. Yields 2 servings.

Connecticut Cooks II

Seafood In A Wok

Quick and easy!

1/3 cup teriyaki sauce
1/3 cup white wine or sherry
Dash of ground ginger
1/2 pound shrimp, cleaned
and deveined
1/4 pound bay scallops
2 tablespoons peanut oil
1/4 pound snow peas, sliced
on the diagonal

1/2 green pepper, chopped
6-8 scallions, sliced
6-8 mushrooms, sliced
2 teaspoons arrowroot or
cornstarch
Cashew nuts

Mix together teriyaki sauce, wine, and ginger. Marinate seafood in sauce for 1-2 hours. Sauté seafood in peanut oil in wok; set aside. Sauté vegetables in remaining oil until tender-crisp; return seafood to wok. Add marinade with arrowroot or cornstarch. Heat until thickened. Add cashews. Serve over hot rice or chow mein noodles. Serves 2-3.

Connecticut Cooks III

Seafood Bisque Casserole

1/2 pound each: shrimp,
crabmeat, fresh scallops
1 tablespoon chopped
shallots
7 tablespoons butter
10 tablespoons sherry

1/2 teaspoon salt
1/4 teaspoon pepper
3 tablespoons flour
1 1/2 cups milk
Bread crumbs
Parmesan cheese

Sauté seafood and shallots in 4 tablespoons of the butter. Cook 5 minutes. Sprinkle with 6 tablespoons of sherry; salt and pepper. In another pan melt the remaining 3 tablespoons butter and add flour to make paste. Add milk and remaining 4 tablespoons sherry; stir until smooth. Combine sauce and seafood mixture and place in a casserole or individual ramekins. Top with bread crumbs and Parmesan. Bake at 400° for 30 minutes. Serves 4.

More Than Sandwiches

Shrimp and Crabmeat Casserole

We can't explain why, exactly, but this is the most popular dish we've ever served. Nobody has ever failed to ask for the recipe. It's also easy to make and can be put together in advance, then baked at the last minute.

½ pound macaroni
1 tablespoon salt
1 tablespoon vegetable oil
4 tablespoons butter or
  margarine
½ pound fresh mushrooms,
  sliced
2 tablespoons butter or
  margarine
1 cup light cream

1 (10-ounce) can cream of
  mushroom soup
¾ cup grated sharp Cheddar
  cheese
1 pound cooked shrimp,
  shelled and deveined
1 cup cooked crabmeat
1 cup soft bread crumbs
1 tablespoon butter or
  margarine

Add the salt and vegetable oil to 3 quarts boiling water. Add the macaroni and boil rapidly for 10 minutes. Drain and toss with 4 tablespoons butter or margarine.

Sauté the mushrooms in 2 tablespoons butter or margarine for about 5 minutes, shaking the pan frequently. Mix the cream, mushroom soup, and Cheddar cheese together and add to the macaroni. Add the mushrooms, shrimp, and crabmeat, which have been cut into bite-size pieces.

Place in a buttered casserole, top with soft bread crumbs which have been tossed with the 1 tablespoon melted butter or margarine. Bake in a 350° oven for 25 minutes. Serves 6.

The Country Innkeepers' Cookbook

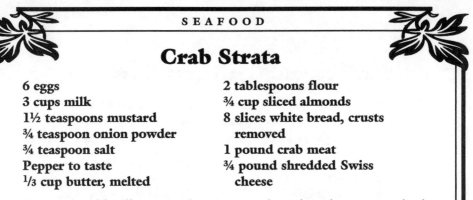

Crab Strata

6 eggs	2 tablespoons flour
3 cups milk	¾ cup sliced almonds
1½ teaspoons mustard	8 slices white bread, crusts
¾ teaspoon onion powder	removed
¾ teaspoon salt	1 pound crab meat
Pepper to taste	¾ pound shredded Swiss
⅓ cup butter, melted	cheese

Beat eggs; add milk, mustard, onion powder, salt and pepper, melted butter, and flour. Toast almonds in 350° oven for 15 minutes. Line a buttered 3-quart dish with 4 of the slices of bread that have been cut into 6 squares each. Layer half the crab meat, half the cheese, half the almonds, and repeat, finishing with the almonds. Top with 1-inch bread cubes cut from remaining bread slices. This preparation can be done ahead and all refrigerated until ready to cook. At that time, pour egg mixture over the layered ingredients. Bake at 350° for 50–60 minutes or until an inserted knife comes out clean. Serves 8.

All-Maine Seafood Cookbook

Poor Man's Crab Casserole

1 pound cod fillets, frozen,
  thawed and drained

Place cod in casserole dish. Combine all Crab Mixture ingredients and sprinkle on top. Combine Topping Mix and spread over all. Bake in 350° oven for 30-35 minutes. Serves 4, double for 6.

CRAB MIXTURE:

⅔ cup butter, melted	1 egg
1 cup crushed herb seasoned	2 tablespoons fresh parsley,
stuffing mix	chopped
1 (6-ounce) package frozen	¼ teaspoon salt
crab meat, thawed and	2 tablespoons lemon juice
drained	¼ teaspoon hot pepper
1 (4-ounce) can mushroom	sauce
stems and pieces, drained	

TOPPING MIX:

½ cup stuffing mix	2 tablespoons melted butter

Anita Welles served this one Christmas Eve for 9 guests. "Not one snip left!"

A Culinary Tour of the Gingerbread Cottages

Scallop Stuffed Shrooms

40 good fresh mushrooms
(large, approximately
1¾-2 inches in diameter)
40 good fresh sea scallops
(approximately 2 pounds)
20 slices bacon, cut in halves
to make 40 short slices
(should be about 1 pound)

⅓ stick of butter or
margarine
5 tablespoons Italian bread
crumbs
40 toothpicks

Wash mushrooms and pat dry. Remove stems with a sharp paring knife, hollowing out each mushroom slightly. Save the stems for soup, stews, steaks, or omelets. Melt butter in small saucepan and mix in the bread crumbs. Remove from heat. Take each mushroom cap, place a small amount of bread crumbs mix in the bottom of the hollow. Take the raw scallops and fit each one inside a mushroom cap. Large scallops go into large mushrooms; small scallops go into small mushrooms and so on. Fill in any gaps and top scallops with small amount of bread crumbs mix. Wrap each piece with bacon and secure with toothpick.

Place in a shallow baking dish and bake at 350° for 10-15 minutes. Remove from oven and place dish in broiler. Broil mushrooms, turning them over once or twice until bacon reaches desired doneness, approximately 5 minutes.

A Taste of Salt Air & Island Kitchens

Scallops en Casserole

If you have scallop-shaped individual shells or casseroles, use them for this recipe. Fresh or frozen peas cooked with sliced water chestnuts, steamed acorn squash, peach and cottage cheese salad on lettuce, and apple sauce with cookies could complete the menu.

4 tablespoons butter or
  margarine
½ pound fresh mushrooms,
  sliced
1 green onion, chopped
2 tablespoons flour
1 cup dry white wine
1 tablespoon lemon juice

½ teaspoon salt
Freshly ground pepper to
  taste
1½ pounds bay or ocean
  scallops
2 tablespoons chopped fresh
  parsley
1 cup buttered crumbs

Heat butter in skillet and sauté mushrooms and onion until tender. Stir in flour and cook 2 minutes. Add wine and cook and stir until mixture boils and is thickened. Add lemon juice, salt, and pepper. Stir in scallops (if ocean scallops are used, cut in half) and parsley. Spoon into a buttered shallow casserole or individual casseroles and sprinkle with crumbs. Bake at 400° for 25 minutes. Makes 6 servings.

A Cape Cod Seafood Cookbook

Cuttyhunk Paprika Scallops

With summertime memories of sunsets across Vineyard Sound.

¾ cup seasoned bread
  crumbs
1 tablespoon paprika
¼ cup flour
1¾ pounds scallops

4 tablespoons butter
½ cup scallions, chopped
2 tablespoons parsley,
  chopped

Combine bread crumbs, paprika, and flour in a mixing bowl. Add the scallops and toss thoroughly to coat. Melt the butter over medium-high heat in a large frying pan. If you do not have a pan large enough to hold scallops in 1 layer, cook them in 2 batches.

Add the scallops and cook for 5 minutes, stirring gently. Let them brown nicely, then add the scallions and parsley. Cook for 3 more minutes and serve on hot plates, garnished with lemon slices. The nutty flavor of short grain brown rice is perfect with this scallop dish. Serves 4.

Seafood Secrets Cookbook

Dill Sauce with Scallops Over Angel Hair Pasta

1¼ tablespoons chopped shallots	⅓ teaspoon salt
1½ tablespoons butter	¼ teaspoon freshly ground white pepper
2 tablespoons flour	1¼ pounds bay scallops
1 cup heavy cream	1 tablespoon butter
1¼ cups half-and-half	½ cup dry white wine
6 drops of Tabasco sauce	1½ pounds angel hair pasta, cooked
2½ tablespoons chopped fresh dill	

Sauté shallots in 1½ tablespoons butter in 1½-quart saucepan until translucent. Stir in flour. Cook for 5 minutes to make roux, stirring frequently. Bring cream and half-and-half to the simmering point in saucepan. Whisk into roux. Cook for 5-10 minutes or until thickened to desired consistency, stirring frequently. Stir in Tabasco sauce, dill, salt and white pepper; keep warm. Sauté scallops in 1 tablespoon butter in skillet for 2-3 minutes. Stir in wine. Add to cream sauce. Serve over pasta. Yield: 6 servings.

Approximately Per Serving: Cal 780; Prot 34 g; Carbo 93 g; Fiber <1 g; T Fat 28 g; 33% Calories from Fat; Chol 119 mg; Sod 343 mg.

Rhode Island Cooks

Steamed Clams

Clams for steaming should be bought in the shell and always alive. The old-fashioned rule for steaming is to let the clams boil up and lift the cover 3 times. Then they are done. Save clam liquor, as it is delicious to drink. Liquor should be drained and clear. Serve clams with individual dishes of melted butter. Some prefer a few drops of vinegar or lemon juice added to the butter. Also, serve clam liquor with the clams.

4 quarts clams	Melted butter
½ cup hot water	

Wash clams thoroughly. Scrub with a brush and change water several times.

Put into a large kettle. Allow ½ cup hot water for 4 quarts of clams; cover closely, and steam until shells partially open, care being taken that they are not overdone. Serves 4-6.

Come Savor Swansea

Clam Pot

¼ cup butter
1 medium onion, chopped
1 mashed clove garlic
½ cup chopped green pepper
1 teaspoon minced parsley
Dash Tabasco
1 teaspoon oregano

Dash cayenne
1 teaspoon lemon juice
2 cups chopped clams, with
   juice
½ cup dry bread crumbs
Grated cheese
Parmesan cheese

Mince and simmer the onion, garlic, green pepper and parsley in ¼ cup butter. Add Tabasco, oregano, cayenne, lemon juice, and clams with juice and simmer for 5 minutes. Add bread crumbs. Place mixture in a buttered 9-inch square pan. Top with grated Swiss or American cheese and sprinkle with Parmesan cheese. Bake at 350° for 30 minutes. Serve hot or cold with crackers.

Note: You may use 2 cans of chopped clams in place of the fresh.

Windjammer Cooking

Clam Fritters
(Fritura de Marisco)

1 cup flour
½ teaspoon pepper
½ teaspoon chopped parsley
½ teaspoon baking powder
2 cups ground sea clams

1 onion, ground with the
   clams
2 eggs, beaten
Olive oil or other
   shortening for frying

Mix flour, pepper, chopped parsley, and baking powder together. Add ground clams and onion and mix well. Add beaten eggs and mix well again.

Drop teaspoonsful of the mixture into hot fat. Fry until fritters are lightly browned on one side. Turn them and brown the other side. Drain and serve. Always taste the first fritter to see if they need more seasoning.

Note: These clam fritters make a good meal accompanied with home-made baked beans and a green salad. They may also be served as an appetizer at parties, either hot or cold.

Traditional Portuguese Recipes from Provincetown

Clams have been around for 400 million years—more or less.

Stuffed Quahaugs

4 cups chopped quahaugs with
  juice (save their shells)
1 red pepper, chopped
1 green pepper, chopped
1 medium onion, chopped
2 cloves garlic, minced
½ cup Parmesan cheese
⅛ cup safflower oil

1 teaspoon parsley
1 teaspoon basil
1 teaspoon oregano
1 egg, beaten
2 cups bread crumbs
  (preferably unseasoned)
4 dashes black pepper
Tabasco sauce (optional)

Mix all ingredients. Lightly oil cleaned quahaug shells and fill with stuffing mixture. These can be packaged and frozen at this point. Bake in oven approximately 20 minutes at 425°, or until heated through. This favorite of Larry and Judy Stearns makes 25-30 stuffers.

A Culinary Tour of the Gingerbread Cottages

Quahog is derived from "poquahock," a Wampanoag Indian word. The Indians used the purple part of the linings of quahaug shells to make "suckanhock" beads which was money, or "wampum."

Baked Flounder
with Scallop Stuffing

SCALLOP STUFFING:

½ cup butter
1 clove garlic, minced
1 small onion, finely
  chopped
½ pound scallops, chopped
Salt
Freshly ground black pepper

Dry white wine
Fine bread crumbs
6 (5-7-ounce) flounder
  fillets (2-2½ pounds)
¼ cup butter, melted
½ cup hot water

In a 10-inch skillet, melt the ½ cup butter. Add garlic and onion and sauté until onions are translucent. Add scallops and cook 2 or 3 minutes. Season with salt, pepper, and white wine to taste. Add sufficient bread crumbs to prepare a moist stuffing.

Place each flounder fillet dark-side-up on a flat surface. Placing the scallop stuffing in the center of each fillet, divide evenly among the fillets. Fold both ends of each fillet over the stuffing, overlapping the ends. Pour melted butter and the hot water into a 9x12-inch baking dish. Transfer the stuffed fillets to the baking dish and bake 20 minutes while you prepare a white sauce.

WHITE SAUCE:

2 tablespoons butter
2 tablespoons flour
1 cup milk

Salt
Freshly ground black pepper
Dry white wine

In a small saucepan, melt butter, then whisk in flour. Cook over low heat 2-3 minutes, whisking constantly. Then add milk, and salt, pepper, and white wine to taste. Increase heat to medium, whisking constantly until the sauce is thickened. Cook several minutes over low heat, stirring.

When the flounder has baked 20 minutes, pour the white sauce over the stuffed fillets. Return the baking dish to the oven briefly and heat until the sauce begins to bubble. Serves 6.

Country Inns and Back Roads Cookbook

Baked Bluefish
Stuffed with Wellfleet Oysters

1 (5-pound) bluefish

Take a whole 5-pound bluefish and stuff it with a Wellfleet oyster dressing made as follows:

OYSTER DRESSING:

3 dozen oysters with liquor   **3-4 slices French bread**
1 cup white wine   **Melted butter for brushing**
Fresh ground pepper to taste

Place oysters and their liquor and a cup of white wine in a pan, and add a little fresh ground black pepper (the liquor furnishes the salt); poach the oysters gently until their edges curl. Drain off the broth and use it to wet down and knead 3 or 4 slices of French bread into a paste. Mix this paste with the oysters and stuff the bluefish with it.

Sew the fish up, lay it on greased aluminum foil in a baking pan, and bake in a preheated oven at 350° for 30 minutes or until it is browned and cooked through. Brush it a couple of times with melted butter during the baking to keep it from drying out. Lay the whole fish out on a platter on a bed of lettuce leaves. Serve a tomato sauce on the side and a bottle of white wine moderately chilled.

Provincetown Seafood Cookbook

Oyster Cocktail Sauce

½ cup tomato ketchup   **2 teaspoons horseradish**
1 teaspoon celery salt   **¼ cup lemon juice**
Dash of pepper   **2 drops Tabasco sauce**

Mix ingredients together and chill. Serve chilled with oysters on the half shell.

Good Maine Food

One of the laws regulating oysters prohibited their taking during the months without an "R". Although this was done as a conservation measure during spawning, people erroneously came to believe that oysters were inedible in May, June, July, and August.

Bluefish Grilled in Foil

This recipe comes from Fishers Island and is a DuPont family favorite. The packet can be prepared ahead and stored for up to 12 hours before grilling.

2 large bluefish fillets
  (about 1 pound each)
1 medium onion, thinly
  sliced
1 green pepper, seeded and
  thinly sliced
1 large firm tomato, thinly
  sliced

1 cup bottled Italian salad
  dressing
Lemon wedges for garnish
Large pieces of aluminum
  foil

Prepare a barbecue fire. Coals should burn down until they are covered with a white ash.

Rinse and dry the bluefish. Tear off 2 pieces of aluminum foil large enough to wrap around the fish and seal it tightly. On 1 sheet of foil, place 1 of the bluefish fillets, skin-side-down. Layer sliced onion, green pepper, and tomato on top. Top with the second fillet, skin-side-up.

Raise the sides of the foil and pour the salad dressing over the fish. Seal foil by crimping the edges together and wrap again with the second sheet of foil. Place the packet on the grill and cook for 20 minutes, turning once. Poke holes in foil with fork to let liquid escape and grill for another 5 minutes or so per side or until fish tests done. Remove from grill, open foil, and serve with lemon wedges. Yield: 4-6 servings.

Off the Hook

Baked Bluefish

Fresh bluefish
Mayonnaise
Salt and pepper

Fresh dill weed
1 small onion, sliced

Clean, rinse well, and dry bluefish. Lay in a buttered baking dish (flesh-side-up if halved). Coat fish generously with mayonnaise; sprinkle with salt and pepper and fresh dill weed. Slice onion thinly and lay over fish. Bake in 350° oven, 15 minutes per pound.

Savory Cape Cod Recipes & Sketches

Stonington Baked Fish Fillets

We love this with fresh peas and red potatoes.

2 pounds fish fillets (a
   thick fish, haddock or
   cod, is best)

¼ teaspoon paprika
3 tablespoons lemon juice

Cut fish fillets into serving pieces. Place in a buttered shallow baking dish. Sprinkle with paprika and lemon juice.

WHITE SAUCE:

2 tablespoons butter
3 tablespoons flour
1 tablespoon dry mustard
1¼ cups milk

Salt and pepper
½ cup bread crumbs,
   buttered
1 tablespoon parsley, minced

In a small saucepan, melt butter over medium heat. Whisk in flour quickly and add dry mustard and milk. Salt and pepper to taste. Cook, stirring constantly for 3 or 4 minutes until thickened. Pour the sauce over the fish, sprinkle with crumbs and parsley. Bake at 350° for 35 minutes until browned. Serves 6.

Seafood Secrets Cookbook

Home-Fried Fish

1-1½ pounds white fillets
   (scrod, haddock, sole, cod)
1 egg, beaten

2-3 tablespoons milk
Cornflake crumbs

Cut fish into serving size. Dip in egg wash of egg and milk. Coat with crushed cornflakes on both sides. Fry in a thin layer of hot corn oil in a skillet until brown on both sides. Or put in a metal fish platter which has just a little oil on bottom and bake at 350° until coating is brown and fish is flaky.

Note: May use an egg substitute for egg wash.

The Island Cookbook

 Eastport, Maine, is the most easterly city in the U.S. The residents of Washington County are usually the very first Americans to greet the sun each morning when it rises. On approximately 200,000 acres of open land in this county, 80% of the nation's wild blueberry crop is raised.

Baked Boston Scrod

Scrod, a young cod, is strictly a New England dish, and abundantly available. It is firm, tender, and moist—a delightful fish.

4 pieces scrod fillet (6-8
  ounces each)
Salt and pepper to taste
2 tablespoons lemon juice

1½ cups white wine
½ cup butter, melted
1 cup dried bread crumbs

Preheat the oven to 350°. Butter a baking pan large enough to hold the scrod in a single layer. Place the scrod in the prepared baking pan, and add the salt, pepper, lemon juice, and wine. Drizzle ¼ cup of the melted butter over the fish. Bake at 350° for approximately 20 minutes, or until the fish flakes but is still moist. Remove the pan from the oven and preheat the broiler. Scatter the bread crumbs over the fish, and drizzle with the remaining ¼ cup butter. Brown under the broiler for 2-5 minutes only, until lightly browned, and serve. Serves 4.

The Red Lion Inn Cookbook

Fried Sesame Scrod

1½ pound scrod cut into 6
  serving pieces
2 tablespoons soy sauce
2 tablespoons toasted sesame
  seeds

⅛ teaspoon black pepper
2 tablespoons minced
  scallions
2 tablespoons sesame oil
2 tablespoons vegetable oil

Rinse and pat scrod dry. Combine soy sauce, sesame seeds, pepper, and minced scallions in a shallow dish. Heat the 2 oils in a large skillet. Dip fish in sesame-soy mixture and fry in the skillet over medium heat until fish is nicely browned and cooked through, 6-8 minutes. Yield: 4-6 servings.

Off the Hook

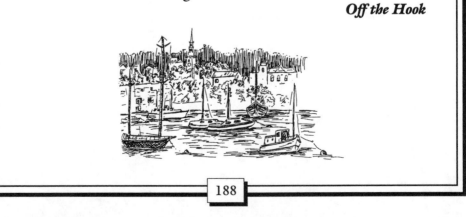

Marinated Cod

This is a good all-purpose seafood marinade and excellent for other fish such as red snapper, swordfish, or any fairly thick, firm fleshed fish.

1 pound cod
¼ cup corn oil
1 tablespoon Dijon mustard
1 tablespoon Na Soy Sauce
⅛ cup lemon juice

1 tablespoon chopped onion
1 garlic clove, minced
1½ teaspoons
   Worcestershire sauce
½ teaspoon pepper

Blend in blender or food processor all of the above ingredients except the cod. Pour over cod and marinate for several hours. Place on greased broiling pan, pouring extra marinade on top of fish. Broil until fish flakes easily, about 7-10 minutes. Serves 2-3.

Hasbro Children's Hospital Cookbook

Salmon or Rainbow Trout in Foil

I have made this recipe in many cooking classes and demonstrations and people who have never tasted salmon before, or those who never liked it before, always rave about it. Cooked this way, the fish has a very delicate flavor. The added bonus is that it is a very healthy recipe!

1½ tablespoons olive oil
1½ tablespoons fresh
   lemon juice
1½ teaspoons Dijon
   mustard

1 pound salmon or rainbow
   trout fillets
1½ tablespoons parsley,
   chopped

Whisk oil, lemon juice, and mustard together. Cut fillets in half and place each half on a piece of foil approximately 12 inches square. Pour half of the lemon-oil mixture on top of each portion of fish. Sprinkle half the parsley on top of that. "Drugstore wrap"* fish in foil and place on a baking sheet. Bake at 450° for 15-18 minutes, or until salmon is cooked completely. Serve 1 packet per person. To prepare in advance, assemble packets several hours earlier in the day and refrigerate. Remove from refrigerator a half hour before placing them in the oven.

*Bring 2 opposite ends of foil together and fold over tightly. Then seal the other 2 ends.

From Ellie's Kitchen to Yours

Dilled Haddock Parmesan

1 cup sour cream
¼ cup freshly grated
  Parmesan
¼ cup grated Swiss cheese
1 teaspoon fresh minced dill
  (or ½ teaspoon dried)
¼ cup very soft butter

Salt and pepper to taste
3 pounds haddock fillets
Sprinkle of sweet Hungarian
  paprika
6 sprigs of dill for garnish
6 lemon wedges

In a small bowl, mix the sour cream, cheeses, minced dill, and butter. Add salt and pepper to taste. Set aside.

Preheat oven to 375°.

Cut fillets into 6 individual servings and place them on a buttered baking sheet. Top each piece with cheese mixture and bake for 15-20 minutes. Sprinkle lightly with paprika, garnish with dill sprig, and serve with a lemon wedge. Serves 6.

Recipes from a New England Inn

Finnan Haddie Casserole

Holler loud just once and your guests will come running...serve old-fashioned gingerbread and whipped cream for dessert.

1½–3 pounds finnan
  haddie
6 medium-sized potatoes,
  sliced
2 medium-sized onions,
  sliced

3 slices salt pork (not too
  fat)
2 cups water
Shake of salt and pepper
Milk, cream, butter
Paprika

In a 3-quart casserole put the finnan haddie, sliced potato, and onion with slices of pork on top. Add 2 cups of water with the salt and pepper. Put cover on casserole and place in a 300° oven. Cook until ingredients are tender. Remove cover, put back in oven, and cook until liquid is nearly cooked away. Take from oven and remove pork slices. Cover fish with milk, a bit of cream added if desired, and ⅛ pound of butter. Return to the oven until milk is hot and butter melted. Shake paprika over top sparingly, for color. Three pounds of finnan haddie cooked this way will serve 6 people.

All-Maine Seafood Cookbook

Poor Man's Lobster

This is delicious—I serve it with rice.

**1 pound haddock, skinned
    and boned**
½ cup butter, melted

**1 stack-pack round buttery
    crackers, crushed**

Cut haddock into bite-size pieces. Dip in melted butter, then dredge in cracker crumbs. Place in a lightly greased 1½-quart shallow baking dish. Cover.

Bake at 350° for 10 minutes. Uncover. Bake 10 minutes longer. Serves 4.

Note: Do not substitute any other fish for haddock.

Cuisine à la Mode

Woods Hole Seafood Strudel

1 tablespoon unsalted butter
1 medium onion, chopped
½ pound mushrooms, sliced
**2 pounds cooked shrimp,
    crabmeat, scallops or
    lobster, or combination,
    cut up**
**1 pound white, non-oily
    fish, sautéed in butter and
    flaked**

**1 tablespoon parsley,
    chopped**
1 cup ricotta
2 eggs, beaten
Salt and pepper to taste
8 sheets phyllo pastry
**8 tablespoons melted sweet
    butter (1 stick)**

Melt butter in a Dutch oven and sauté onion and mushrooms until all liquid is gone. The final mixture should not be runny. Add shellfish and fish and stir. Remove from heat and add parsley, ricotta, eggs, salt, and pepper and mix well. Preheat oven to 400°.

Butter a large baking sheet or use a nonstick one. Place 2 sheets of phyllo pastry on sheet and cover the rest with a damp cloth to prevent drying. Brush the pastry lightly with melted butter out to edges and repeat with remaining sheets, brushing every second 1 with butter. Spoon fish mixture in a long even shape down center of pastry; carefully fold pastry and roll into a strudel. Tuck ends under and brush with butter.

Reduce oven heat to 375° and bake strudel 30 minutes, until top is browned. Brush top with butter twice during baking. Cool slightly, slice, and serve. Serves 6-8.

The MBL Centennial Cookbook

Provincetown Boiled Haddock

Such good Provincetown eatin'!

1 (6-pound) haddock (leave
  the head and tail on for
  good looks)
1 large onion, sliced
2 pieces celery, chopped
2 bay leaves
½ lemon, sliced

1 teaspoon mixed pickling
  spices
2 cloves garlic, crushed
1 cup white wine
Salt and fresh ground black
  pepper

In old Provincetown they used to boil a whole haddock, and to keep it from falling apart, they would sew it up tightly in a clean piece of linen with a strap at each end for lifting it. (Rub it first with flour to keep the skin from sticking to the cloth.) The fish was lifted in its shroud into the pan of gently boiling water, which was flavored with the vegetables, spices, and wine. Then when it was done (approximately 30 minutes), it was lifted out, and the shroud cut away, and the fish would be lying there as pristinely beautiful as the moment it was caught. Serves 4.

THE MODERN METHOD:

You can do this more simply nowadays by wrapping the floured fish in a double layer of foil and rolling and crimping the edges tightly together. Punch lots of small holes in the foil so the cooking liquid will be in free contact with the fish. Take a turkey roasting pan and place it in enough water to cover the fish; bring to a boil and add the onion slices, celery, bay leaves, lemon slices, pickling spices, garlic, wine, salt, and fresh ground black pepper. Boil vigorously for 15 minutes to make a good liquor. Lower the heat to a slow boil, place the shrouded fish in the pan, cover and boil gently for 30 minutes. Remove the fish and de-shroud it on a bed of parsley on a platter; make it look alive! And make it look even purtier by decorating with lemon slices, parsley, watercress, radish roses, sliced rings of green pepper, cape jasmine, gardenias, morning glories, etc., etc., etc.

Provincetown Seafood Cookbook

Provincetown, Massachusetts, the birthplace of the commercial fishing industry of the U.S, was the wealthiest town per capita in New England in the 1840s and '50s. It is still considered the gourmet seafood capital of the Atlantic seaboard, supplying fresh fish for the tables of gourmets everywhere.

Friday Night Fish

1½ pounds fish fillets,
saltwater fish recommended

3 tablespoons butter,
softened

1 tablespoon lemon juice

1 teaspoon dried tarragon

½ teaspoon grated lemon
peel or lemon-pepper

⅓ cup dry white wine or
vermouth

3 tablespoons minced fresh
parsley

1 teaspoon dried chives, or 1
tablespoon minced fresh

½ cup round, buttery
cracker crumbs, optional

Preheat oven to 425°. Place fish in lightly buttered baking dish.
Mix together butter, lemon juice, tarragon, and lemon peel or
lemon-pepper. Spread on top of fish fillets. Pour wine over fish.
Sprinkle parsley, chives, and crumbs over fish. Cover dish with foil
and bake for 15-20 minutes until fish flakes with a fork. Transfer to
a serving platter and pour pan juices over fish. Yield: 4 portions.

Hospitality

Erdine's Fish Pie

2 cups flaked fish (haddock,
pollock, etc.)

2 tablespoons butter or
margarine

2 tablespoons flour

1 cup milk or milk and fish
water

1 teaspoon salt

1 cup cooked peas (canned or
frozen)

1 tablespoon grated onion

1 tablespoon chopped green
pepper

2 cups mashed potato,
seasoned

Steam or cook the fish in water until it flakes. Prepare a white
sauce with butter, flour, milk, and ½ teaspoon salt. (Part of the
white sauce liquid may be the water from the cooked fish.) To the
white sauce add peas, grated onion, green pepper, and ½ teaspoon
salt. Place the cooked fish in a buttered casserole; pour the sauce
over it. Top with well-seasoned mashed potato. (To freshly cooked
and mashed potato, add 1 tablespoon butter, ½ cup milk, and salt
and pepper to taste.) Bake in a hot oven 400° for 12 minutes or
until hot and bubbly.

All-Maine Seafood Cookbook

Fish Florentine

A luscious and very easy way to serve bland fish. Give it to the family in a baking dish or to your luncheon guests in ramekins.

1 (12-ounce) package frozen
   spinach soufflé
1-1½ pounds fish fillets
   (cod, flounder, ocean
   perch, etc.)

½ cup sour cream
½ cup mayonnaise
¼ cup freshly grated
   Parmesan cheese

Defrost spinach soufflé 5-6 hours at room temperature or until soft. Push into a 9-inch pie pan. Cut fillets and arrange on top of soufflé. Mix together sour cream, mayonnaise, and Parmesan and spread over fish. (Can be prepared in advance; cover and refrigerate.) Bake in a preheated 350° oven for 30 minutes. Serves 4.

Variation: Divide soufflé, fillets, and sour cream mixture between 4 ramekins. Bake at 350° for about 25 minutes.

The Lymes' Heritage Cookbook

Perch with Creamy Garlic Sauce

2 pounds perch or other
   fish fillets
2 (10-ounce) packages frozen
   broccoli spears or
   equivalent fresh
¾ cup dry white wine or
   water
1 small onion, sliced
1 small bay leaf
1¼ teaspoons salt

½ teaspoon tarragon
   (measure carefully, a little
   goes a long way)
1 clove garlic, minced
½ teaspoon dry mustard
¼ teaspoon black pepper
1 cup salad dressing or
   mayonnaise
1 tablespoon lemon juice
Paprika or chopped parsley

Thaw fish if frozen. Cook and drain the frozen broccoli spears. Combine water or wine, onion, bay leaf, 1 teaspoon salt, and tarragon in a skillet. Bring to a boil and simmer for 5 minutes. Add fillets; cover and simmer for 8 minutes or until fish flakes easily. Drain and save liquid. To prepare sauce: Combine garlic, mustard, pepper, and ¼ teaspoon salt. Mash together until smooth. Stir in salad dressing or mayonnaise and lemon juice. Strain the fish liquid and stir ¼–½ cup into the sauce until desired consistency. Arrange hot cooked, drained broccoli spears on heated platter and place hot drained fillets on top of spears. Spoon sauce over top of fish and broccoli. Sprinkle with paprika or parsley. Serves 6.

All-Maine Seafood Cookbook

Grilled Salmon with Garlic Cream and Tomato Butter

4 fillets of salmon, 6 ounces each
Salt and white pepper to taste

4 basil leaves for garnish

TOMATO BUTTER:

2 large tomatoes, quartered
1 clove garlic
1 branch basil leaves
2 sprigs parsley
2 shallots, sliced
½ small carrot, cooked

1 cup dry white wine
2 tablespoons very good sherry or red wine vinegar
6 ounces unsalted butter, softened
Salt and pepper to taste

Purée tomatoes, garlic, basil leaves, parsley, 1 shallot and carrot and reserve. Chop remaining shallot and place in a large saucepan with the white wine and vinegar. Reduce over medium heat until 1 tablespoon remains. Pour in reserved tomato purée and cook over medium heat until it is thick. Reduce more if necessary (most of the liquid should evaporate, making the flavor intense). Whisk in butter, a little at a time, over low heat. Strain into a clean saucepan and season with salt and pepper. Add more vinegar if necessary. Keep warm.

GARLIC CREAM:

1 medium-sized baking potato, peeled and sliced
6 large garlic cloves, peeled and thinly sliced

Approximately ½ cup milk
Approximately ½ cup heavy cream
Salt to taste

Cook potato and garlic in milk and cream (equal amounts to cover) until potato is tender. Purée in a food processor and strain mixture into a pan. Thin with cream if necessary. Add salt to taste.

Season both sides of salmon fillets with salt and pepper. Grill for 3 or 4 minutes each side over a hot grill, or until just cooked. Spoon Garlic Cream into the center of each plate and surround with Tomato Butter. Top Garlic Cream with a salmon fillet and garnish with a basil leaf. Serves 4.

A recipe from Angels, Providence, RI.

A Taste of Providence

Grilled Lime Salmon Steaks

4 salmon steaks
¼ cup lime juice
½ cup oil

1 teaspoon dried tarragon
Salt and pepper

Whisk lime juice together with oil. Add tarragon, salt, and pepper. Place salmon steaks in a shallow dish. Pour marinade over salmon. Refrigerate 4 hours or overnight.

Grill over hot coals until cooked to desired degree of doneness, approximately 5 minutes per side.

Dining on Deck

Grilled Salmon

This goes well with baked sweet potatoes and any green vegetable in season. It also goes well with bagels and cream cheese for breakfast.

Soy sauce or teriyaki sauce
   (enough to cover the surface
   of a shallow baking pan)
½ teaspoon garlic, minced

Salmon steaks
Ginger and black pepper
Butter
Any other favorite spices

Blend garlic with sauce. Place steaks in the pan and marinate on each side for 5 minutes. Remove from the pan and place on a large piece of foil. The foil will protect the steaks while they are cooking and prevent them from breaking apart on the grill.

Sprinkle ginger, black pepper, and any other favorite spices on the steaks. Place a small piece of butter on top of the fish and close foil. Use a fork to make small holes on top of the foil for heat to come through. Place on a hot grill and cook until the meat is a light pink color. It does not need to be turned during cooking. When salmon is almost done, pour some of the sauce over the fish, reclose the foil, and finish cooking.

A recipe submitted by Rich Kaufman, ATP chair umpire.

Celebrities Serve

Salmon Cakes with Fresh Pea Sauce

There is a long-standing tradition of serving salmon and peas together on the Fourth of July.

FRESH PEA SAUCE:

2 tablespoons minced shallots

3 tablespoons unsalted butter

1 cup dry white wine

2½ cups heavy cream

3 cups fresh peas, coarsely chopped

1 teaspoon lemon juice

Salt and pepper to taste

Crushed mint (optional)

Sauté the shallots in the butter in a large saucepan. Add the wine and reduce by half over medium-high heat. Add the heavy cream and continue cooking until slightly thickened, about 15 minutes. Add the chopped peas and simmer another 5-7 minutes until thickened to desired consistency. Add lemon, salt and pepper to taste, and the optional mint. To serve, spoon sauce over the cakes on the platter or transfer to individual heated dinner plates.

SALMON CAKES:

1½ pounds salmon fillet, skinned

6 scallions, chopped fine

2 tablespoons fresh ginger, minced

1 egg, lightly beaten

1 tablespoon fresh lemon juice

1 teaspoon soy sauce

Salt and pepper to taste

¼ cup vegetable oil or more if necessary

Preheat oven to 200°. Chop the salmon coarsely with a knife (using a food processor for this will give the cakes a mealy texture). In a large bowl, mix the salmon with the remaining ingredients except the oil. Shape into 12 patties and set aside. When ready to cook them, heat 1 tablespoon of vegetable oil in a large nonstick pan. Working in batches, sauté the cakes until lightly browned on both sides, about 3 minutes. Add oil to pan as needed. Drain cakes on paper towels. Transfer to a heat-proof platter and keep warm in the oven for up to 30 minutes. Serves 6.

The Maine Collection

The International Tennis Hall of Fame opened in Newport, Rhode Island, in 1880. Features include changing exhibits on tennis, and the history of the game and its players. Major professional tennis tournaments are played there during the summer months.

Baked Swordfish Steak

Swordfish is the king of the fish that cut well into steaks. It is a toss-up whether my off-Cape friends prefer swordfish or lobster when they visit here.

Swordfish can be baked (as in this recipe), charcoal-broiled, or broiled in the range broiler. It is one fish that I would not pan-fry if facilities for the other cooking methods were available. All swordfish recipes can also be prepared with Mako shark or salmon.

2 pounds swordfish steak, 1-inch thick	½ cup finely chopped onion
Cooking oil	2 tablespoons chopped fresh dill (or more to taste)
Flour seasoned with salt, pepper, and paprika	4 tablespoons melted butter
	½ cup dry white wine

Dip steaks in cooking oil and then in seasoned flour. Place steaks in 1 layer in an oiled flat baking pan. Sprinkle with onion, dill, and melted butter. Pour wine around fish.

Bake at 400° for 20-25 minutes or until fish flakes easily, basting twice with wine. Serve fish with pan sauce. Makes 4 servings.

Note: With Baked Swordfish Steak, put 4 potatoes in the oven to bake about 35 minutes before the fish. Steamed broccoli, watercress salad, and fresh or frozen sliced peaches can complete the dinner.

A Cape Cod Seafood Cookbook

 The first-in-the-nation Presidential primary election is held in the Granite State every four years. Until the 1992 elections, no candidate had ever won the Presidency without first winning in New Hampshire.

Poultry

A typical farm in Keene, New Hampshire. In autumn, the leaves set the countryside afire with natural brilliance.

Fall Apples and Chicken

2 large onions
5 tablespoons butter or
  margarine
1 teaspoon salt
½ teaspoon pepper
3 boneless chicken breasts,
  halved (approximately 2
  pounds)

3 medium apples, sliced
1¼ cups shredded Cheddar
  or Swiss cheese
½ cup Parmesan cheese
½ cup unflavored bread-
  crumbs
2 tablespoons cider or apple
  jack

Preheat oven to 350°. Coat a baking dish with spray or margarine. Sauté onions in margarine. Do not brown. Sprinkle salt and pepper on chicken breasts. Arrange over apple slices. Combine cheeses with crumbs. Sprinkle over chicken and apples. Drizzle with cider. Bake 35 minutes at 350°.

A Taste of New England

Tomato Cheese Chicken

2 whole chicken breasts,
  skinned, boned, halved and
  flattened, with excess fat
  removed
½ cup flavored bread
  crumbs
2 teaspoons olive oil

2 tomatoes, sliced
¼ teaspoon dried basil or
  fresh basil leaves
4 slices provolone cheese
Sprig of fresh chopped
  parsley

In a flat dish, press crumbs into chicken on both sides; reserve. Oil 1 ovenproof casserole dish large enough to contain the 4 breaded chicken breasts.

Lay out chicken in oiled casserole. Top chicken with tomato slices. Sprinkle tomato slices with basil or basil leaves. Top with provolone cheese and garnish with chopped parsley. Bake in a preheated 400° oven for 20 minutes. Remove from oven with a spatula. Serve on heated plates.

Chicken Expressions

The Hyde Log Cabin of Grand Isle, Vermont, built in 1783, is considered the nation's oldest log cabin still standing in its original condition.

Five-Minute Breast of Chicken in a Sour Cream Sauce with Fried Peaches and Zucchini

Melt enough butter to cover the bottom of a frying pan and heat it until it begins to simmer. Flatten a boned chicken breast with the side of a cleaver, or something flat and heavy, and lay it in the simmering butter. Salt and pepper the breast and sprinkle it with thyme. Slice the zucchini into long quarters, lay them in the pan, and sprinkle with salt, pepper, and basil. Then cut a peach in half, remove pit, and lay the two halves in the simmering butter. Sprinkle with salt, pepper, cinnamon, and sugar; cook everything over a medium-high flame for about 2 minutes on each side, spicing the peaches, zucchini, and chicken again after they have been turned.

As soon as the chicken is done, remove it and lay it on the dinner plate, then surround it with the zucchini and peaches. Sprinkle about a handful of flour into the frying pan with the greases and drippings, turn the fire to a moderate heat, and stir the flour until it takes up the juices and becomes pasty. Then add a splash of white wine, half a pint of sour cream, and some salt and pepper. Stir until the sauce gets hot, then pour it over the chicken and you're ready to eat.

The Blue Strawbery Cookbook

Chicken with Peaches (or Pears) and Ginger

2 medium peaches or pears	2 tablespoons oil
2 tablespoons cider vinegar or lemon juice	2 tablespoons honey
4 boneless chicken breasts	1 knob fresh ginger, grated
Salt and pepper to taste	¼ teaspoon curry powder

Peel peaches and sprinkle 1 tablespoon lemon juice over them. On medium heat fry seasoned chicken in oil until golden. Reduce heat and cook until just about done. Add honey. Cook on medium-high heat until caramelized, about 2 minutes. Pour 1 tablespoon lemon juice over chicken to thin caramel. Sprinkle grated ginger and curry powder. Turn chicken to coat evenly. Remove chicken and place on warm platter. Put peach quarters or thick slices into skillet to glaze with pan juices. Place around chicken. Serves 4.

The Hammersmith Farm Cookbook

Chicken Breasts in Champagne

1 carrot, finely chopped
1 small onion, finely
    chopped
3 large mushrooms, finely
    chopped
2 tablespoons butter

1 cup champagne or dry white
    wine
2 chicken breasts (halved,
    boned, and skinned)
Salt and pepper to taste

SAUCE:
½ cup heavy cream
¼ cup champagne or white
    wine

Salt and pepper to taste
Parsley, finely chopped

In a heatproof casserole, make a bed of carrot, onion, and mushrooms. Add butter cut into thin slices and add champagne or wine.

Place chicken breasts on top of the mixture. Sprinkle the chicken with salt and pepper, cover the casserole, and bake chicken in a moderate oven (325°) basting it frequently with the liquid from the casserole for 50-60 minutes or until it is tender.

Remove chicken to a platter and keep warm. Cook sauce uncovered over moderate heat until it is reduced by half.

Stir in heavy cream and champagne or wine and pour sauce through a sieve. Season with salt and pepper and a little finely chopped parsley. Pour sauce over the chicken breasts and garnish the platter with braised celery and sautéed pimentos. Serves 2.

The Hammersmith Farm Cookbook

Baked Chicken Breasts

1 jar apricot preserves
1 bottle creamy French
    dressing

1 package dried onion soup
Chicken breasts

Mix together preserves, dressing, and onion soup mix. Spread over chicken breasts which skin has been removed from. (Can be prepared the day before if desired, but not necessary.) Bake approximately 1 hour at 350°, uncovered.

Berkshire Seasonings

Cheesy Chicken Florentine

Always requested for a repeat performance.

3 packages frozen chopped
  spinach, thawed and
  squeezed dry
3 whole chicken breasts,
  cooked and cut into pieces
2 (8-ounce) packages cream
  cheese
14 ounces extra-sharp
  Cheddar cheese, grated
2 cups milk

¼ teaspoon salt
¼ teaspoon pepper
½ teaspoon dill
½ teaspoon garlic
1 tablespoon parsley flakes
1 cup Parmesan cheese
1 cup bread crumbs
¼ cup (½ stick) butter,
  melted

Preheat oven to 375°.

Lightly butter a 13x9-inch casserole. Line with uncooked spinach. Add chicken. Set aside.

Make sauce by melting cream cheese, Cheddar cheese, milk, seasonings, and ⅔ cup Parmesan cheese. (Reserve ⅓ cup of Parmesan cheese for bread crumb mixture .) Blend over low heat until smooth. Pour cheese sauce over spinach and chicken. Combine bread crumbs with melted butter. Add ⅓ cup Parmesan cheese. Sprinkle mixture on top of mixture. Bake uncovered for 30 minutes. Serves 4-6.

Moveable Feasts Cookbook

Chicken Clayton

2 whole chicken breasts, skinned, boned, halved, and flattened, with excess fat removed
½ cup flavored bread crumbs
2 tablespoons butter
1 small finely chopped onion
1 clove chopped garlic
½ cup cooked rice
¼ cup white raisins
Sprig chopped parsley
½ teaspoon curry powder
¼ teaspoon poultry seasoning
½ teaspoon brown sugar
2 teaspoons olive oil
4 slices Monterey Jack cheese

In a flat dish, press bread crumbs into chicken on both sides; reserve. Make stuffing by melting butter in fry pan. Cook onion until yellow. Add garlic, rice, raisins, parsley, curry, poultry seasoning, and brown sugar. Mix well; reserve and cool. Oil an oven-proof casserole dish large enough to contain the 4 chicken breasts. Lay breaded chicken in oiled casserole dish. On each breast, spoon prepared stuffing. Top each portion with Monterey Jack cheese. Bake in a preheated 400° oven for 20 minutes. Remove from oven with a spatula. Serve on heated plates.

Chicken Expressions

Chicken Pillows

1 whole chicken breast, halved, skinned, boned
1 clove garlic, halved
2 slices ham (1 ounce)
2 slices mozzarella cheese (1 ounce)
2 tablespoons seasoned bread crumbs
2 tablespoons medium-dry sherry
2 tablespoons clarified butter
1 tablespoon chopped parsley

Pound chicken breasts to ¼ inch. Rub each with garlic. Place ham and cheese over chicken. Sprinkle with crumbs. Roll up and secure with wooden picks; place in lightly greased pan.

Combine sherry and butter; heat briefly. Pour over chicken. Bake at 350° for 20-25 minutes. Sprinkle with parsley. Serves 2.

The Marlborough Meetinghouse Cookbook

Chicken Breast Baked in a Crust with Ham and Swiss Cheese

2 whole chicken breasts,
skinned, boned, halved,
and flattened with excess
fat removed
½ cup flavored bread
crumbs
2 teaspoons olive oil
2 Pepperidge Farm Patty
Shells, thawed (available
at most markets)

2 slices of ham
2 slices Swiss cheese
2 large mushroom caps
without stems
Sprig of fresh chopped
parsley
1 egg
½ teaspoon milk

In a flat dish, press bread crumbs into chicken on both sides. In a sauté pan using half the oil, lightly sauté the breaded chicken breasts; reserve and cool. On a floured board, roll thawed patty shells about 8x8-inches round; reserve and keep cool.

On a flat surface, lay out pastry. Top successively with 1 cooked chicken breast, slice of ham, other chicken breast, Swiss cheese, mushroom cap, and parsley. Do this with each portion. Wrap chicken like a package, sealing seams with water.

In a cup, beat egg and milk with fork. Spread egg mixture on crust with fingers or pastry brush. Put chicken package on oiled and floured cookie sheet. Bake on top shelf of a preheated 400° oven for 20 minutes. Remove from oven with a spatula; serve on heated plates.

Chicken Expressions

Breast of Chicken
Le Petit Chef

Many years ago Maurice Champagne, owner-chef of The Mill on the Floss in New Ashford, Massachusetts, shared his recipe with me for Chicken Amandine. The batter marinade is particularly good for moistening chicken and holding the crust. My daughter, Betty, combined that technique with pine nuts (pignoli) and grapes instead of almonds. It has been a favorite at her Wilmington, Vermont, restaurant, Le Petit Chef.

6 halves of chicken breasts, skinned and boned
½ cup flour
¼ teaspoon salt
⅛ teaspoon pepper
1 egg (or 2 egg whites)
⅔ cup milk (or light cream)
⅔ cup plain bread crumbs

⅓ cup ground pine nuts (pignoli)
2 tablespoons each oil and butter
½ cup sweet vermouth
¼ cup whole pine nuts (pignoli)
1 cup seedless grapes

Cover each chicken breast with wax paper or aluminum foil, and pound to flatten if the thickness is uneven.

Mix flour with salt and pepper. Add egg and milk or cream. This can be done in the food processor. Marinate the chicken in this batter for at least 30 minutes, or marinate refrigerated for up to 2 days.

When ready to cook, heat a 10-12-inch skillet over low heat. Preheat the oven to 300°.

Combine bread crumbs and ground pine nuts on a sheet of wax paper. Use a pair of tongs to coat each chicken breast with the crumbs and pine nuts. Set aside until all are completed.

Add oil and butter to the heated skillet. The butter will sizzle and foam but should stay golden and not turn brown. Fry 2 or 3 pieces of chicken at a time so as not to crowd the skillet. Lightly brown chicken on both sides and then remove to a shallow baking dish. Sprinkle vermouth, whole pine nuts, and grapes over all. Bake in the oven for 15-18 minutes. Serve immediately. Serves 6.

The Best from Libby Hillman's Kitchen

Sauté of Chicken Breasts Primavera

4 tablespoons unsalted
butter
6 large mushrooms, stemmed
and thinly sliced
Salt and freshly ground
white pepper to taste
3 whole chicken breasts,
skinless, boned and cut in
half
All-purpose flour for
dredging
2 teaspoons peanut oil

½-¾ cup chicken stock or
bouillon
1 cup heavy cream
Juice of 1 large lemon
1½ teaspoons beurre manie
(made by rolling 1
tablespoon soft butter with
a tablespoon flour in a
ball)
½ cup fresh peas, cooked
2-3 tablespoons finely
minced fresh dill or chives

In a small skillet, melt 2 tablespoons of the butter over medium-high heat. Add the mushrooms and sauté quickly until they are lightly browned. Season with salt and pepper and set aside. Dry chicken breasts thoroughly on paper towels and season with salt and pepper. Dredge lightly in flour, shaking off the excess. Reserve.

Melt the remaining butter in a 12-inch iron skillet, together with the oil, over high heat. Add the chicken breasts and sauté until nicely browned on both sides. Add about a quarter cup of stock, reduce the heat to medium-low and simmer, covered, for 5 minutes, adding a little more stock if it has evaporated significantly, until the chicken is done. The juices should run pale yellow. Remove the chicken breasts from the skillet and set aside.

Add a quarter cup of stock to the skillet, bring to a boil, whisking, and reduce by a quarter. Add cream, lemon juice, and bits of beurre manie, and whisk until the sauce lightly coats the spoon. Taste and correct the seasoning.

Return the chicken breasts to the skillet together with the mushrooms and peas and just heat through. Transfer the chicken to a serving dish, spoon the sauce over, and garnish with the dill or chives. Serve at once with a crusty loaf of French bread. Yield: 6 servings.

Recipe from Intl. Tennis Hall of Famer, Joseph F. Cullman 3rd.

Celebrities Serve

Chicken Breasts Durant

4 boned chicken breasts
2 teaspoons minced chives
2 tablespoons snipped
  parsley
½ teaspoon salt

4 tablespoons margarine
2 eggs
¾ cup dry bread crumbs
1 chicken bouillon cube*

Lay breasts flat (do not pound) and sprinkle each with equal amounts of herbs and salt. Starting at a long side, roll and fasten securely with 3 or 4 toothpicks. Melt margarine in a shallow baking dish. Beat eggs with a fork. Roll each breast in egg, then in bread crumbs, then in egg again. Place in baking pan. Pour any leftover egg over chicken. Bake 20 minutes in 400° oven. Dissolve a chicken bouillon cube in 1 cup boiling water and pour into pan. Reduce heat to 350° and bake 40 minutes more.

*Instead of bouillon cube in water, white wine or dry sherry may be used.

Homespun Cookery

Lemony Chicken

Easy and always good.

3 whole boneless, skinless
  chicken breasts (6 halves)
¼ cup flour
½ teaspoon salt
⅛ teaspoon pepper

3 tablespoons butter or
  margarine
1 chicken bouillon cube
1 cup water
1 large lemon, halved

Pound chicken to ⅛-inch thick. Mix flour, salt, and pepper; pat onto both sides of chicken. Reserve remaining flour mixture.

In large skillet over medium-high heat in 3 tablespoons margarine, cook 3 chicken pieces at a time until lightly browned on both sides. Remove chicken to a plate.

Reduce heat to low. Into drippings in skillet, stir reserved flour mixture; add bouillon, water, and juice of half lemon, stirring to loosen bits.

Return chicken to skillet. Thinly slice lemon half and top chicken with slices; cover and simmer 5 minutes.

The Marlborough Meetinghouse Cookbook

Chicken with Artichokes and Mushrooms

4 boned and skinned chicken breasts
4 large shallots, sliced thinly
1 garlic clove, mashed
1 teaspoon dried tarragon
4 medium mushrooms, sliced thinly
4-6 canned artichokes, drained dry and sliced
½ cup dry red wine

Sauté chicken breasts for 2-3 minutes on each side, along with the scallions, garlic and tarragon. Remove from skillet. Sauté mushrooms and artichokes until lightly browned and remove. Add wine to skillet; bring to a boil over high heat until liquid has been reduced to ¼ cup. Reduce heat to low, add chicken and vegetables, and baste thoroughly. Cover until ready to serve. Serves 4.

The Chef's Palate Cookbook

Sweet-N-Sour Chicken

Chicken breasts (uncooked)
½ tablespoon salt
1 tablespoon cornstarch
⅓ cup cooking oil
2 cloves garlic, crushed
1 (8-ounce) can pineapple chunks, drained
1 (4-ounce) jar sweet mixed pickles, drained
2 teaspoons soy sauce
½ cup green pepper strips
2 teaspoon cornstarch
1 teaspoon water
1 medium tomato, cut in wedges

Cut uncooked chicken breasts into thin strips and mix with salt and cornstarch. Heat cooking oil in fry pan. Sauté garlic 1 minute in hot oil. Remove garlic from pan. Add seasoned chicken to pan and stir constantly, about 2 minutes, over high heat. Add pineapple juice, liquid from pickles, and soy sauce. Bring to boil. Add pickles, pineapples, and green pepper strips. Bring to boil again. Blend in cornstarch which has been dissolved in water. Add tomato wedges. Stir and serve.

Cooking with H.E.L.P.

Cranberried Chicken

This recipe is especially nice to serve during the cranberry season.

4 tablespoons soy sauce
4 tablespoons fresh lemon
  juice
½ teaspoon garlic powder
3 tablespoons margarine

1 (1-pound) can whole
  cranberry sauce or homemade
  sauce
6 chicken breasts, split

Combine all ingredients, except chicken, in a saucepan and bring to a boil. Place chicken in a baking pan, skin-side-down. Cover with sauce and bake at 425° for 30 minutes. Turn chicken, reduce oven to 350°, and bake for 30 minutes more, basting about 4 times.

Hint: Use low sodium soy sauce, if desired. If you want to reduce fat, remove the skin before cooking.

From Ellie's Kitchen to Yours

Maple Dijon–Glazed Chicken

This recipe is typical of the haute cuisine, low-cholesterol dining at Canyon Ranch: it aims to make guests feel pampered, to please the tastebuds, and to skimp on the calories. Each serving contains approximately 180 calories and only 6 grams of fat.

MAPLE DIJON GLAZE:
½ cup Dijon mustard
2½ teaspoons white wine
¼ teaspoon Worcestershire
  sauce
Pinch of black pepper

1 teaspoon finely diced
  shallot
2½ teaspoons pure maple
  syrup

Prepare coals for grilling, or preheat the broiler. Combine the ingredients in a small bowl and blend well.

4 chicken breast halves,
  boned, skinned, and defatted

Grill the chicken until done, brushing from time to time with glaze. Serves 4.

A recipe from Canyon Ranch, Lenox, MA.

Best Recipes of Berkshire Chefs

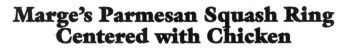

Marge's Parmesan Squash Ring Centered with Chicken

This is delicious served hot or cold with either chicken or turkey and is an excellent way to use leftover turkey.

SQUASH RING:

½ cup chopped green onion
2 tablespoons butter or
    margarine
4 eggs
2 (12-ounce) packages frozen
    squash, defrosted, or 4 cups
    fresh squash, cooked, mashed

¼ teaspoon salt
¼ teaspoon red pepper
1 cup Parmesan cheese

In skillet, cook onion in butter until tender. Set aside. Beat eggs in mixer until blended and add the squash, salt, pepper, Parmesan cheese, and onion mixture. Pour into oiled baking ring. Bake at 350° for 30-40 minutes or until set. Let stand 8 minutes. Loosen edges and turn onto serving dish.

CHICKEN MIXTURE:

2 cups cooked chicken
2 cups celery, finely sliced
½ cup toasted almonds,
    chopped
½ teaspoon salt

1 cup mayonnaise
2 tablespoons lemon juice
2 teaspoons onion, grated
½ cup Parmesan cheese,
    grated

While squash is baking, combine chicken, celery, almonds, salt, mayonnaise, and lemon juice. Grate the onion on top. If chicken is served cold, place in center of ring and top with cheese. If served hot, heat the mixture in a casserole about 10 minutes in a 450° oven. Add to ring and add the cheese.

Memories from Brownie's Kitchen

Ski Day Chicken Casserole

Actually, good for any day.

8 tablespoons butter or
  margarine
¼ cup flour
1½ cups chicken broth
1 cup sour cream
⅛ teaspoon nutmeg
⅛ teaspoon pepper
Salt to taste
¼ cup dry sherry

½ pound flat egg noodles,
  cooked and drained
4½ cups cut-up cooked
  chicken
½ pound mushrooms, sliced
  and sautéed
1 cup soft bread crumbs
½ cup freshly grated
  Parmesan cheese

Melt 4 tablespoons butter; stir in flour, and add broth and sour cream, stirring until thick. Add nutmeg, pepper and salt. Remove from heat and stir in sherry. Arrange noodles in 9x13-inch baking dish. Cover with chicken, mushrooms, and sauce. Melt remaining 4 tablespoons butter and mix with crumbs. Top casserole with crumbs and cheese. Bake in preheated 350° oven for 30 minutes or until hot and bubbly. May be made day in advance, refrigerated, and baked when needed. Serves 8.

Merrymeeting Merry Eating

Oven Fried Chicken

1 (2½-3-pound) fryer, cut
  into eighths
Salt and pepper
¼ cup Dijon-style mustard

¼ cup sour cream
1 cup cornflake crumbs or
  bread crumbs

Wash chicken and pat dry. Salt and pepper to taste. Spread with mustard, then sour cream. Coat with crumbs. Spread out on baking sheet. Bake in a 350° oven for 1 hour.

Dining on Deck

Phyllo Chicken Pie

Your luncheon guests will exclaim at the puffy, fluffy crust; they will exclaim again when they taste the pie–and they will come back for more.

1 cup chopped onions
½ pound mushrooms, coarsely chopped
½ cup cubed celery
¾ cup plus 2 tablespoons (1¾ sticks) margarine
3 cups chopped cooked chicken

¾ (10¾-ounce) can cream of mushroom soup
1½ cups sour cream
2 tablespoons sherry
1 tablespoon soy sauce
1 tablespoon catsup
1 teaspoon prepared mustard
8 leaves phyllo, thawed

Sauté onions, mushrooms, and celery in 2 tablespoons margarine. Mix in chicken, mushroom soup, sour cream, sherry, soy sauce, catsup, and mustard. Combine well. (Can be prepared 1 day in advance and refrigerated.)

The remaining preparation can be done several hours before cooking. Remove chicken mixture from refrigerator. Slowly melt ¾ cup (1½ sticks) margarine. Grease a 9x13-inch baking dish. Handle phyllo according to package directions. Place 4 full phyllo leaves, 1 at a time, on bottom of dish. This is done in the following way: The leaves measure approximately 18x13-inches. Hold first leaf at right angles to dish and smooth half of it in bottom of dish. Brush all over with melted margarine—not too much. Fold other half of phyllo leaf into dish and brush with margarine. Repeat process with 3 more leaves, thus making 8 layers of phyllo. Spread phyllo with chicken mixture. Cover with 8 more layers (4 full leaves) of phyllo, each brushed with melted margarine. Spread top with any remaining margarine. Finally, with a sharp knife, cut the pie into 12 pieces. Store in refrigerator until ready to cook. Bake in a preheated 350° oven for 45 minutes and serve at once. Serves 12.

The Lymes' Heritage Cookbook

Once nearly extinct from excessive hunting, the Atlantic Puffin lays only one egg each year and doesn't usually breed until it is five years old. Project Puffin, begun in 1973 and funded by private contributions, has been slowly successful. The beautiful puffin can be watched in June and July on several breeding islands in the Gulf of Maine with binoculars from the water, or by a guided National Audubon Society tour.

Chicken, Broccoli with Pasta

3 tablespoons vegetable oil
1½ inches fresh ginger, grated
3 cloves garlic, mashed
1 pound chicken breast (boned, cut up into 1-inch cubes)
1 tablespoon sesame oil
1 pound fettucini, linguini, or other flat pasta

1 bunch broccoli florets
⅓ cup low-sodium soy sauce
⅓ cup red wine or sherry
2 tablespoons butter or margarine
½–1 cup freshly grated Parmesan cheese

Using a large pot or wok, heat vegetable oil on medium high heat, then stir in ginger and garlic for 30 seconds. Then add chicken and stir well until chicken is no longer pink. Add sesame oil, toss well, and remove with slotted spoon. Set aside and keep warm.

Cook pasta in plenty of boiling, salted water until just al dente. While pasta is cooking, dump broccoli into remaining hot oil and stir for 1 minute. Add the soy and the wine and stir once, then cover for 1½ minutes. Drain pasta, add butter, and toss well.

Turn heat to low, add pasta to broccoli, add in reserved chicken, and toss well. Add cheese and mix well. Serve immediately. Makes 4 servings.

Hasbro Children's Hospital Cookbook

Crab and Chicken Casserole

4 chicken breasts
¼ cup chopped onion
1-2 tablespoons butter
1 (3-ounce) can chopped,
  drained mushrooms
½ pound crab meat
2 tablespoons snipped
  parsley
½ cup crumbled saltine
  crackers

Pepper to taste
4 tablespoons butter
¼ cup flour
¾ cup milk
¾ cup chicken broth
⅓ cup dry white wine
½ pound grated Swiss cheese
Paprika

Cut deboned chicken breasts in half and pound between Saran Wrap until flat. Place in buttered rectangular Pyrex dish. Sauté the onion in skillet in 1-2 tablespoons butter until soft. Add mushrooms, crab meat, parsley, saltine crackers, and pepper to taste. Toss to blend and spoon mixture generously atop each piece of chicken. Melt 4 tablespoons of butter in a saucepan. Add flour and stir. Gradually stir in milk, chicken broth, and wine, whisking to keep a smooth sauce. Pour the sauce over the chicken-crab. Cover with aluminum foil and bake at 350° for 1 hour. Uncover, sprinkle with Swiss cheese and paprika, returning to oven to melt. Serves 6-8.

A Hancock Community Collection

Baked Chicken Reuben

4 boneless chicken breasts
¼ teaspoon salt
⅛ teaspoon pepper
1 (16-ounce) can sauerkraut,
  drained (press out liquid)

4 slices (each 4x6 inches)
  Swiss cheese
1¼ cups Thousand Island
  dressing
1 tablespoon chopped parsley

Place chicken in a greased baking pan. Sprinkle with salt and pepper. Place sauerkraut over chicken; top with Swiss cheese. Pour dressing evenly over cheese. Cover with foil; bake at 325° for 1½ hours or until fork can be inserted with ease. Sprinkle with chopped parsley and serve. Makes 4 servings. Can be cooked in electric fry pan, 325°, covered.

Great Island Cook Book

Quick Stir-Fried Chicken

3 tablespoons peanut oil
4 tablespoons soy sauce
¾ teaspoon garlic salt
2 teaspoons cornstarch
3 tablespoons cold water
2 cups raw chicken, sliced
  julienne
1 (6-ounce) package frozen
  Chinese pea pods
1 (8-ounce) can water
  chestnuts, drained and
  sliced

¾ cup chopped fresh
  broccoli
2 oranges, sectioned
1 bunch green onions,
  trimmed and quartered
½ cup sliced mushrooms
2 cups cooked rice or chow
  mein noodles

Heat oil in wok or skillet over medium heat. When hot, add soy sauce and garlic salt, and stir. Combine cornstarch and water, and set aside. Add chicken to pan and stir-fry, about 3 minutes. Add pea pods, water chestnuts, and broccoli, and stir-fry 2 minutes. Reduce heat then add orange sections, green onions, mushrooms, and cornstarch. Stir until thickened and serve over rice or noodles.

What's Cooking at Moody's Diner

Chicken Breasts Stuffed with Boursin Cheese and Sun-Dried Tomatoes

4 boneless chicken breasts,
  pounded flat
1 package boursin cheese
Sun-dried tomatoes (can be
  purchased in a jar with
  olive oil or dried)

Olive oil and dried basil
  for basting

On flat chicken breasts spread boursin cheese to cover. Chop finely 6 sun-dried tomatoes and sprinkle over cheese. Roll this in jelly-roll fashion. Secure with wooden toothpick. Place in oiled baking dish. Baste with a mixture of olive oil which has dried basil added to it. Bake at 350° for about 30 minutes. Serves 4.

More Than Sandwiches

Hunter's Chicken with Wild Rice

¾ cup wild rice mix
1½ cups water
1 tablespoon butter
4 slices bacon, or about
　¼ pound
4 (8-ounce) chicken breasts,
　skinned and boned
¼ cup butter

2 cups mushrooms, sliced
1 cup onions, diced large
½ teaspoon thyme
1 clove garlic, minced
2 tablespoons sherry
2 tablespoons chives, sliced
4 slices raw bacon
Sprinkles of thyme

Combine rice mix, water, and butter in a small saucepan, bring to a boil and simmer over low heat for 20–25 minutes. Cook 4 slices bacon until crisp and set aside. Pound chicken breasts with a meat mallet to an even thickness, and set aside.

In a large skillet melt butter; add mushrooms, onions, thyme, and garlic and sauté 5 minutes, over high heat, until golden. Stir in quickly 2 tablespoons sherry until evaporated. Stir in and mix well the cooked rice, cooked bacon, chopped coarsely, and 2 tablespoons chives, sliced.

Stuff chicken breasts with filling, dividing evenly. Place chicken breasts in a baking dish with seam sides down so that they do not touch and brush with melted butter or oil. Cut 4 slices raw bacon in half and place criss-cross over chicken breasts. Sprinkle with thyme and bake at 375° for 25 minutes or until chicken is cooked through. Serves 4.

Peter Christian's Favorites

Turkey Meatloaf

1½ pounds ground turkey (grind twice if possible)
½ cup chopped green bell pepper
½ cup chopped yellow onion
⅓ cup seasoned bread crumbs
¼ cup thinly sliced scallions

2 teaspoons minced garlic
6 tablespoons egg substitute
¼ cup chili sauce
¼ cup skim milk
½ teaspoon ground cumin
¼ teaspoon ground nutmeg
¼ teaspoon freshly ground pepper
⅛ teaspoon cayenne pepper

TOMATO SALSA:
2 cups chopped plum tomatoes
¼ cup chopped fresh cilantro

1 cup sliced scallions
1 tablespoon olive oil

In a bowl, combine the turkey and the next 5 ingredients. In another bowl, combine the egg substitute, chili sauce, milk, cumin, nutmeg, and peppers. Add to the turkey mixture and combine thoroughly. Form a round loaf 7 inches across. Bake for 50 minutes in a 375° oven. While the loaf bakes, combine the Tomato Salsa ingredients. Set aside. Let the cooked loaf stand for 10 minutes before slicing. Serve topped with salsa. Serves 8.

Note: Commercial salsa may be used, though homemade is better!

As You Like It

Why Be Normal Burger

This original recipe was entered in the Stowe, Vermont, Annual Best Burger Contest—it took First Place!

1 pound ground turkey
2 cups cooked wild rice
¼ cup cooking wine
¾ cup whole cranberry sauce

1½ cups bread crumbs
Chopped onions (½-1 cup)

Combine all ingredients. Shape into patties and grill. Serves 6-7.

Note: Cooking time for these burgers is longer than for regular hamburgers—about 7 minutes a side.

The Marlborough Meetinghouse Cookbook

Barbequed Chicken

Down behind Uncle Billy's Barbeque, Nephew Jonny works every day in a converted steel sugar shack where he has a 9-foot tall metal double-barrel cooker with about 75 hooks in it. Jonny hangs halved chickens on these hooks and cooks them over red oak. Awful hot work in August, damned chilly about mid-February, but Jonny claims to enjoy it, or at least he pretends to. Here's a recipe that doesn't take quite as much dedication to the out-of-doors, but still gives you a chicken "like you ain't ever had nowhere before."

2 (3½-4-pound) split broiler chickens

1 heaping tablespoon Segabo Pig & Poultry Rub (page 233)

1 small handful of soaked chips

Purchase whole chickens and ask the butcher to split them with his bandsaw. When picking out chicken, try to avoid the ones with bright yellow skins. They may look better, but chickens don't come by yellow skin naturally so you're better off spending a little less for a paler bird.

Rub the inside of the chicken halves with the Sebago Pig & Poultry Rub, salt and pepper. If there's any rub left on your hands when you're done, rub it on the chicken's skin. Wrap the chicken halves in plastic wrap, put in the refrigerator, and let them sit overnight. Soak some fruitwood or corn cob chips overnight as well.

The next day, build a medium-hot to hot grill, remove the wrap, and place the chickens, skin-side-down, on the grill directly over the coals. Sear the chickens for 2 minutes and then jerk them over to an indirect heat, skin-side-up, and cover, with the damper vents half-open. Cook for 2 hours, at which time you'll be able to twist the drumstick at the joint and it will separate easily, without a crack. The meat will appear pink, but that's normal for barbeque cooking. To double-check, jab a fork into the thickest part of a thigh. The juice that flows should be clear. The internal temperature of the cooked chicken should be 185° on your cooking thermometer.

While some recipes call for slathering all manner of syrups, sauces, and gyppos on the birds while they cook, Jonny prefers to serve them at the table. In real life, barbeque sauce doesn't adhere to chicken the way it does on TV commercials, but it does adhere to the grill. Rather than scrape the mess off the grill, serve the chicken with barbeque sauce on the side, coleslaw, and baked beans.

Uncle Billy's Downeast Barbeque Book

Turkey Curry Crêpes

Perfect for using up the leftover bird.

12 basic crêpes
½ cup chutney, cut up
2 cups cubed cooked turkey
   (or chicken)
2 slices bacon
¼ cup thinly sliced celery
¼ cup chopped onion
1 clove garlic, minced

2 tablespoons flour
1½ cups milk
½ cup applesauce
3 tablespoons tomato paste
1 tablespoon curry powder
2 teaspoons instant chicken
   bouillon granules

GARNISH:
Toasted coconut and chopped peanuts

Preheat oven to 375°; grease a 13x9x2-inch baking dish. On each crêpe, spread chutney and sprinkle with a handful of cubed turkey. Roll up crêpe and place, seam-side-down, in baking dish.

To prepare sauce: Cook bacon; drain and crumble. Reserve drippings. In bacon drippings, sauté celery, onion, and garlic. Blend in flour; add milk, applesauce, tomato paste, curry, and bouillon granules. Cook and stir until bubbly. Pour sauce over turkey-filled crêpes in dish. Top with bacon. Bake 15-20 minutes. Sprinkle with coconut and peanuts. Yield: 6 servings.

Christmas Memories Cookbook

Because of cold nights, Vermont turkeys have an extra layer of fat, which is good for natural basting. No Vermont turkey can be sold out of the state because there is no federal turkey inspection.

Chestnut Stuffing

1 pound chestnuts
2 cups chopped celery
½ cup minced onion
½ cup butter
1 egg

6 cups bread crumbs
1 cup hot stock or water
2 teaspoons celery salt
¾ teaspoon pepper

Boil chestnuts 30 minutes; remove shells and skins while hot, and press through potato ricer. Sauté celery and onion in butter several minutes; add egg, bread crumbs, chestnuts, stock, and seasonings. This recipe will fill a 10-pound turkey.

Good Maine Food

Duck L'Orange–Pauplis' Style

Prepare a 5-pound duck by salting cavity and rinsing thoroughly with cold water.

Place duck on oven rotisserie skewer, securing wings and legs with cooking string so that duck parts stay in place while duck is in rotation. Place a large roasting pan under duck to catch grease as it is cooking.

Prick duck often with a long pronged fork to allow grease to drip out. If there seems to be too much grease in the roasting pan, take roasting pan out of oven, drain grease out of pan, and return pan back in the oven. This will eliminate the smoking of the grease. (Use extreme caution when handling pan of grease.) Cooking time for duck is 2½-3 hours.

FRESH ORANGE SAUCE:

I recommend preparing the orange sauce a couple of hours ahead of time to let the ingredients blend and meld together.

½ jar orange marmalade
1 tablespoon fresh grated orange peel
1 cup orange juice (fresh, preferred)
¼ fresh lemon, squeezed
½ bottle honey
¼ teaspoon allspice (ground)
⅛ teaspoon cloves (ground)

Place ingredients in a small saucepan and simmer, stirring often, for 15-20 minutes. If mixture appears too thick add more orange juice; if too thin, add additional honey and marmalade. Remove pan from burner and pour orange sauce into a gravy boat.

Presentation and serving of duck: Heat serving platter for duck. Place sliced duck on platter and decorate with fresh orange slices and curls of orange peel around the duck. Add parsley sprigs between orange slices.

Serve with white rice, fresh garden salad, and homemade bread or biscuits. Serves: 3-4 people.

Hint: To keep the duck crispy, it is recommended that the orange sauce not be poured over the duck on the general serving platter. Sauce should be passed to guests for individual serving.

Heritage Cooking

Roast Duck with Cornbread Stuffing

Sausage, nuts, and cornbread make an unusual and tasty stuffing for this hearty autumn dish.

½ pound pork sausage
1 medium onion, diced
2 cloves garlic, minced
Duck livers and peeled
   gizzards, chopped (optional)
2 teaspoons fresh thyme or 1
   teaspoon dried thyme
4 cups cubed cornbread
3 or 4 scallions, sliced
2 tablespoons parsley,
   chopped

1 tablespoon fresh sage,
   chopped, or 1½ teaspoons
   dried sage
½ cup lightly toasted pecans,
   chopped
Salt
Freshly ground black pepper
¼ cup Marsala or sherry
   wine
2 (4-5 pound) ducks

Preheat oven and roasting pan to 350°. To prepare stuffing: In a heavy skillet over medium heat, cook crumbled sausage until lightly browned. Remove to a mixing bowl. Add onions to skillet, and cook until soft, and add garlic. Cook for 1 minute and then cook the livers, gizzards, and fresh thyme. Cook briefly and add to mixing bowl with cornbread, scallions, parsley, sage, and pecans. Toss well. Season with salt and pepper and moisten with Marsala or sherry.

To prepare ducks: Trim extra fat from neck and inside of ducks. Rinse and pat dry. Season inside and out with salt and pepper. Stuff and sew up or truss the birds with wings folded underneath the back. Pierce the skin with a fork to allow fat to drain while roasting.

Place on a lightly oiled wire rack in the roast pan. Cook for about 2 hours or until juices run clear when the thigh is pierced with a skewer. To brown the ducks further, turn the oven to 500° and roast for 5-10 minutes. Remove to a heated platter, cover loosely with foil for 10-15 minutes. Remove thread or string and serve with turnips, carrots, parsnips, or sweet potatoes. Serves 4.

Fresh from Vermont

Meats

The view is great from easily accessible Owl's Head Lighthouse.
Owl's Head, Maine.

Stuffed Leg of Lamb

1 (6-pound) leg of lamb
  (most skin and fat removed)
1 clove garlic (finely
  chopped)
4 sprigs parsley (finely
  chopped)
Salt and pepper
Provolone cheese
4 slices bacon (each slice
  cut in 4 pieces)
Melted shortening
Fine bread crumbs
1½ cups of water

Cut slits in leg of lamb as deeply as possible. With fingertips, place in every slit a mixture of garlic, parsley, salt and pepper, 1 bite-size piece of provolone cheese, and 1 piece of bacon. Repeat this procedure in each slit. Baste leg of lamb with melted shortening and roll in bread crumbs. Place lamb on rack in roasting pan in preheated oven of 425°. Pour 1½ cups of water in pan and cook for about 3½-4 hours. Add water to lamb while cooking, if needed.

Cuisine à la Mode

Roast Leg of Lamb with Herb Crust

2 tablespoons olive oil
3 cloves garlic, minced
1 teaspoon crushed rosemary
1 teaspoon thyme
Salt and pepper to taste
1 boned and rolled leg of
  lamb, 3½-4 pounds
2 ounces bread crumbs
4 tablespoons finely chopped
  parsley

Mix together olive oil, garlic, rosemary, and thyme. Season generously with salt and pepper. Spread the mixture over the lamb and let it marinate 3 hours.

Preheat oven to 300° and roast the lamb for 1½ hours. Mix bread crumbs and parsley. Add sufficient meat juices to make a paste. You may need to add a little butter. Spread the paste over the lamb and bake another 30 minutes to finish cooking and to brown the crust. Yield: 6-8 portions.

Hospitality

 Vermont government is distinctive for its local tradition of Town Meeting Day, held the first Tuesday in March. In many towns and villages, municipal and school budgets are voted from the floor as they have been for nearly 200 years.

Seldom Seen Farm Lamb Chops in Foil

So easy, anyone will become the "Chef of the Day."

For each serving allow:

2 lamb chops
1 sliced zucchini, unpeeled
1 small onion, sliced
**1 small green pepper, cored
and sliced**

1 small tomato, quartered
Dash of basil
Salt and pepper
Garlic powder

Make a packet with the above in each, wrapped tightly. Grill on low about 25-30 minutes. Be sure to turn several times. Another great way to use this recipe is to bake at 350° for 1¼-1½ hours.

A recipe from Seldom Seen Farm, Harmony, RI.

The Island Cookbook

Apple-Stuffed Pork Chops
(Microwave)

4 pork chops, 1 inch thick
¼ cup butter or margarine,
  melted
½ cup chopped apple
½ cup herb seasoned
  stuffing mix
¼ cup (1 ounce) shredded
  Cheddar cheese

2 tablespoons chopped celery
1 tablespoon chopped onion
1 tablespoon chopped raisins
2 tablespoons orange juice
¼ teaspoon salt
1 tablespoon Worcestershire
  sauce
1 tablespoon water

Cut horizontal slit in each pork chop to form a pocket. Combine butter, apple, stuffing mix, cheese, celery, onion, raisins, orange juice, and salt in small bowl. Mix well.

Fill each pocket with stuffing mix; secure opening with wooden toothpicks. Arrange pork chops in 12x8-inch dish. Mix Worcestershire sauce with water and brush on chops.

Cover with wax paper and cook in microwave at MEDIUM for 17-20 minutes. Let stand, covered, 5 minutes. Serves 4.

Come Savor Swansea

Pork Piccata

2½ pounds center pork
  loin, boned and trimmed
Salt
White pepper
Flour

4 eggs, beaten
½ cup grated Parmesan
  cheese
¼ cup parsley, chopped
Butter and oil for sautéing

Preheat oven to 350°. Remove all fat and membrane from pork, slice ¼-inch thick, and flatten slightly with a meat tenderizer or cleaver. Season cutlets and dredge in flour, shaking off all excess. In a medium-sized bowl, combine eggs, cheese, and parsley. Mix well and allow to stand several minutes. Dip cutlets into batter, which should coat and cling to pork easily. If batter is too thin, add more cheese, if too thick, add a little cream. Sauté cutlets until golden brown on both sides in 3 parts of very hot butter and 1 part very hot oil. Transfer to a baking pan and cook in the oven 5 minutes. Serves 6.

A recipe from Edson Hill Manor, Stowe, VT.

Country Inns and Back Roads Cookbook

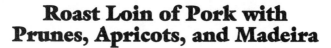

Roast Loin of Pork with Prunes, Apricots, and Madeira

I served this roast at dinner parties well before we became innkeepers. It is simple to prepare, and looks beautiful when carved.

1 pound large pitted prunes	½ teaspoon salt
Dry Madeira wine	¼ teaspoon fresh-ground
15 large dried apricot	pepper
halves	½ cup dry white wine
1 (4-5-pound) center loin	1 cup heavy cream
pork roast, boned, rolled,	Salt and fresh-ground pepper
and tied	to taste
½ teaspoon ground ginger	

In a medium bowl, combine the prunes with enough Madeira to cover. Let stand at room temperature for 3 hours. Preheat the oven to 325°.

With a long, sharp knife, cut a lengthwise slit in the center of the roast. Using a wooden spoon handle, push a prune and apricot half until the cavity is completely filled, using all of the apricot halves; some prunes should be left over.

In a small bowl, combine the ginger, salt, and pepper. Rub the mixture all over the pork roast. Place the meat, fat-side-up, in a narrow, deep baking dish that holds the pork snugly (a bread pan works well). Place the pan in the oven and roast for 30 minutes.

Drain the remaining prunes, reserving the Madeira. Mix the Madeira and white wine, and pour the wine mixture over the roast. Continue roasting the pork for 1 hour, basting it frequently with the pan juices. Add the cream and continue roasting, basting frequently, for 45 minutes.

Remove the roast from the pan, and keep it warm. Skim off the fat from the pan. Over high heat, reduce the juices in the pan until they are thickened. Add the remaining prunes and heat, stirring. Add salt and pepper. Keep the sauce warm.

Carve the pork roast into 1-inch slices, so that each slice shows a prune or an apricot in the center, and spoon some of the sauce over the slices. Serve immediately with the remaining sauce on the side. Serves 6-8.

Chris Sprague's Newcastle Inn Cookbook

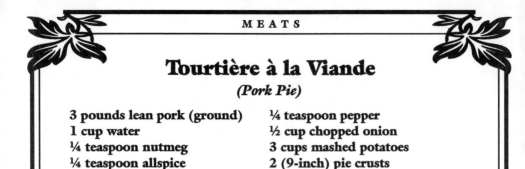

Tourtière à la Viande
(Pork Pie)

3 pounds lean pork (ground)
1 cup water
¼ teaspoon nutmeg
¼ teaspoon allspice
1 tablespoon salt

¼ teaspoon pepper
½ cup chopped onion
3 cups mashed potatoes
2 (9-inch) pie crusts

Put meat in saucepan and add water, nutmeg, allspice, salt, pepper, and onion. Cook for 30 minutes over moderate heat, stirring often to prevent sticking. Remove from heat and add 3 cups mashed potatoes. Mix well and cool. Line a pie plate with pie crust, add filling, and top with second crust. Make incision in top of crust for vent. Bake in hot 450° oven about 30 minutes or until well browned. Serve hot or cold as preferred. Makes enough for 2 (9-inch) pies.

Maine's Jubilee Cookbook

Pork Tenderloin in Currant Sauce

1½ teaspoons salt
½ teaspoon pepper
2 pounds pork tenderloin
2 tablespoons butter
½ teaspoon rosemary

4 tablespoons butter or
   margarine
½ cup currant jelly
½-1 cup light cream
3 tablespoons flour

Salt and pepper the whole tenderloin and brown in butter. Place in casserole and sprinkle with rosemary. Spread with butter and top with currant jelly. Cover and bake at 325°, for about 35 minutes per pound. Blend flour and cream and stir into the liquid. Bake an additional 10 minutes. On a platter slice into pieces about ⅜-inch thick and overlap on individual plates. Spoon about 2-3 tablespoons of sauce on each serving and serve the remainder in a small pitcher. Serves 6.

A Taste of New England

Tortière is a traditional French Canadian dish on Christmas Eve, usually served to family and friends after midnight mass. It has become a tradition in many Vermont families as well, and says "Christmas Eve" to many of us.

—*Vermont Kitchens Revisited*

Tourtière

2 pounds ground pork	Bread crumbs
1 pound ground beef	Cinnamon
1 chopped onion	Ground cloves
Salt and pepper	Pie crust for 2 pies

Cover meat, onion, salt and pepper with 3 or 4 cups water. Stir well. Bring to a boil. Continue simmering for 5 minutes. Thicken with bread crumbs. Add cinnamon and ground cloves to taste. Put between 2 pie crusts and bake (about 30 minutes at 450°). Makes 2 big pies.

Cuisine à la Mode

Baked Vermont Ham

1 (10-pound) ham, cooked and skinned	1 teaspoon dry mustard
1 cup sugar	¼ teaspoon allspice
2 tablespoons dark molasses	¼ teaspoon ginger
¼ teaspoon cinnamon	Whole cloves
	Bread crumbs

The only skin that needs to be removed from my favorite ham is a piece around the shank. Yours may need more removed. Score the fat in diagonal lines about ¾-inch apart, making diamonds. Mix sugar, molasses, and spices together and rub mixture into the surface of the ham. Press whole cloves into the intersections of scored lines. Sprinkle fine bread crumbs over the whole surface.

BASTING SAUCE:

| ½ cup ginger ale | ½ teaspoon ginger |
| ½ cup fizzy cider | |

Mix ginger ale, cider, and extra ginger and pour mixture into a roasting pan. Place the ham on a rack in the roaster. Insert meat thermometer so that it touches neither fat nor bone. Set the pan into a preheated 200° oven. Baste ham twice during the first hour, then cover with aluminum foil and forget it until morning.

The next day the thermometer should register 165° and the ham should be a golden brown. If necessary, let it go on cooking until it reaches this stage. Set in a cool place but do not refrigerate it. Serve at room temperature.

Mrs. Appleyard's Family Kitchen

Ham Uncatena

This reliable meat sauce, like the ferry that runs between Woods Hole and Martha's Vineyard, is packed full. It can be used on tongue and Canadian bacon slices as well as on ham.

½ cup pitted beach plums
¼ cup raisins
¼ cup dark brown sugar
1 teaspoon dry mustard
¼ teaspoon ground ginger
⅛ teaspoon ground cloves
4 drops red pepper sauce
  (such as Tabasco)
Juice of ½ orange (about
  ¼ cup)

⅓ cup dry red wine
⅓ cup fruit brandy or
  liqueur (such as beach plum,
  plum, orange, or cherry)
¼ cup pecan pieces
2 tablespoons peanut oil
6 thick slices boneless,
  cooked ham (about 2 pounds)

Place the beach plums, raisins, sugar, mustard, ginger, cloves, red pepper sauce, orange juice, wine, and brandy or liqueur in a saucepan. Simmer, stirring occasionally, for 20 minutes or until the sauce is clear and slightly thickened.

Meanwhile, brown the pecan pieces in the oil, taking care not to burn them. Remove the pieces with a slotted spoon, drain them on paper towels, and add them to the sauce.

Sauté the ham slices in the oil in which the pecans were browned, turning once. Arrange the slices on a warm serving platter. Serve the sauce separately. Makes 6 servings.

Plum Crazy

Beach plums grow wild on low bushes in the sand. Cherry-like in size and color, plums have high pectin content, therefore jelly can be made by simply boiling the fruit or juice with sugar and water.

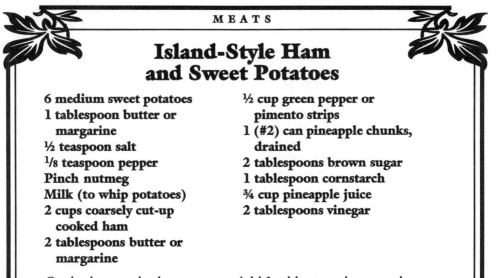

Island-Style Ham and Sweet Potatoes

6 medium sweet potatoes	½ cup green pepper or
1 tablespoon butter or	pimento strips
margarine	1 (#2) can pineapple chunks,
½ teaspoon salt	drained
⅛ teaspoon pepper	2 tablespoons brown sugar
Pinch nutmeg	1 tablespoon cornstarch
Milk (to whip potatoes)	¾ cup pineapple juice
2 cups coarsely cut-up	2 tablespoons vinegar
cooked ham	
2 tablespoons butter or	
margarine	

Cook, then mash the potatoes. Add 1 tablespoon butter, salt, pepper, nutmeg, and enough milk to whip. Heat oven to 375°. In a skillet sauté the ham in 2 tablespoons butter stirring until golden. Add green pepper (or pimento) and pineapple chunks. Cook 2 or 3 minutes. Stir in combined brown sugar, cornstarch, juice, and vinegar. Cook, stirring until thickened and clear. Pour mixture into 9-inch pie plate or casserole dish. Drop spoonfuls of potato on top. Bake until hot in 375° oven about 20–25 minutes. Serves 4–6.

All-Maine Cooking

Polynesian Kielbasa

1 pound kielbasa, cut into	1 (12-ounce) can pineapple
½-inch pieces	chunks, drained (save juice)
1 cup sliced onions	1 cup beef broth
2 cloves of minced garlic	1 tablespoon brown sugar
(or more)	¼ teaspoon pepper (or
1 cup green peppers, sliced	more)
1 (16-ounce) can whole	2 tablespoons cornstarch
tomatoes, drained and	
quartered	

Cook kielbasa, onions, garlic, and peppers in 3 tablespoons of oil until onion is transparent, about 5 minutes. Add tomatoes, pineapple, broth, sugar, and pepper. Cover and simmer for 5 minutes. Mix cornstarch with pineapple juice. Add to kielbasa mixture and stir until thickened. Let season a few minutes. Serve with rice.

A Taste of Salt Air & Island Kitchens

Pork Shoulder Sandwich

For the purist, barbeque is pork shoulder—period. It's an understand-able attitude, especially after you've tasted one.

1 (3½–4-pound) pork butt
2 tablespoons Sebago Pig &
  Poultry Rub (recipe follows)
8 large hamburger-type rolls
Killer Gene's Tar Heel
  Vinegar Sauce (recipe
  page 234)

Barbeque sauce
2 handfuls soaked wood or
  corn cob chips

Get your chips soaking at least 2 hours before starting out. Then build a medium-hot fire in your grill. Rub all sides of the shoulder with Sebago Pig & Poultry Rub, and set it, fat-side-up, over an indirect heat on which you've just sprinkled a small handful of chips. Cover and cook for 4½-5 hours. Check the fire every couple of hours and add more chips and charcoal to keep the temperature medium-hot.

When the pork shoulder's internal temperature reaches 190°, remove it from the grill and cool awhile. The meat will make a hollow hissing sound as you handle it. Put on a pair of heavy rubber gloves, the kind your oil deliveryman wears, locate and pull out the only bone remaining in the shoulder—a small piece of shoulder blade—and put it aside to use for stock in next week's jambalaya. If the meat has been properly cooked, the bone will pull out without a struggle.

Continue to pull apart the cooked shoulder with a fork and your gloved hands, then roughly chop the meat with a cleaver. This is what we mean by pulled and chopped.

Pile the pork onto rolls, or Wonder bread, squirt on some Killer Gene's Tar Heel Vinegar Sauce and a little barbeque sauce (or serve them on the side if you'd rather).

Pulled and chopped and made into sandwiches, a cut this size will feed 8 hungry people.

Uncle Billy's Downeast Barbeque Book

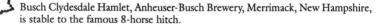

Busch Clydesdale Hamlet, Anheuser-Busch Brewery, Merrimack, New Hampshire, is stable to the famous 8-horse hitch.

Sebago Pig & Poultry Rub

Nephew Jonny, Uncle Billy and some of their friends were up to camp on Sebago Lake visiting relatives when, as usually happens, Jonny was designated that evening's cook. He was in the kitchen, pondering possible dinner entrées, when a bunch of chickens burst through the screen door, chased by an assortment of children, angry adults, and one wet dog. The chickens headed for the pantry and ran straight into the spice shelf. An open jar of Oriental Five Spice Powder fell down, covering the chickens, pantry, dog, and one of the kids with a pretty liberal dose of the spice powder.

A good-sized mess was the result. Jonny lost his characteristic laissez-faire attitude, and since the kid belonged to a relative and everyone was partial to the dog, dinner that night was arrived at by deductive reasoning—it would be chicken.

To this day Jonny swears the story is true, and what's more, he said those chickens, all tossed with Oriental Five Spice Powder, were the best he'd ever eaten. Which is exactly why he puts it in his Sebago Pig & Poultry Rub.

3½ ounces granulated garlic
3 ounces Hungarian paprika
2½ ounces granulated sugar
2½ ounces Oriental Five Spice Powder

1½ ounces salt
1½ ounces black pepper
½ ounce ground marjoram
½ ounce ground anise
¼ ounce ground sage
⅛ ounce ground allspice
⅛ ounce ground ginger

Combine all ingredients. There's enough here for a pound of rub. Store it on a shelf (minding the kids and dogs); it'll come in handy time and time again.

Uncle Billy's Downeast Barbeque Book

Killer Gene's Tar Heel Vinegar Sauce

A word about Killer Gene. Hailing from the Tar Heel state of North Carolina, Gene boxed in the basement ring under Jonny's kitchen when the restaurant first opened. The ceiling was a little low and the ring wasn't regulation, but Gene had a jab-and-hook combo that cracked ribs and loosened teeth with frightening regularity. He liked to come upstairs, chat with Jonny, eat pork shoulder sandwiches, and mix up batches of this sauce to put on them. To those who knew him outside the ring, a sweeter, kinder man never lived.

2½ cups cider vinegar   1 tablespoon granulated garlic
1 cup sugar   2 teaspoons salt
¼ cup Tabasco sauce   2 teaspoons ground black pepper
¼ cup pickle brine

Combine the ingredients in a clean jar with a tight-fitting lid and shake well before each use.

This recipe makes a pint, which is enough for an entire Tar Heel pig roast. It will keep for months refrigerated.

Uncle Billy's Downeast Barbeque Book

Hallowell Hash House Harriers
Sweet and Sour Barbecued Spareribs

4 quarts thick tomato sauce
2 quarts pineapple juice
2 cups cider vinegar
2 cups honey
1 cup molasses

½ cup Lea & Perrins
  Worcestershire Sauce
4 cases beer of choice
20 pounds spareribs

Mix the sauce ingredients in a big canning pot. Include 2 cans of beer and leave the rest aside. Cook over low heat until honey and molasses are fully mixed in. Layer sauce and spareribs in a 5 gallon glazed ceramic crock and let marinate for 6-24 hours.

Cook the spareribs on a large grill (the Hash uses a 50-gallon drum cut in half lengthwise). Turn and baste the ribs approximately every 5 minutes until they are evenly browned and the meat begins to pull away from the bone. Eat the ribs with the remaining beer. Serves 40.

A Taste of Hallowell

Veal Birds

2 pounds veal cutlet (or
  round, cut ¼-inch thick)
Salt and pepper
4 ounces ham, finely chopped
  (1 cup)
2 tablespoons finely chopped
  shallots
1 clove garlic, minced

½ teaspoon dried rosemary,
  crushed
2 tablespoons clarified butter
1 cup white wine
2 cups chicken broth
1 tablespoon cornstarch
2 tablespoons cold water
Minced parsley

Cut veal into 16 even-sized pieces. Pound each piece to ⅛-inch thickness. Sprinkle with salt and pepper. Combine ham, shallots, garlic, and rosemary; top each veal slice with about 1 tablespoon of mixture. Roll veal around filling and fasten with toothpick. Melt butter in large fry pan over medium heat; add veal rolls and brown quickly. Add wine and simmer a few minutes. Add chicken broth; cover and simmer 20 minutes. Remove veal birds to a warm platter. Rapidly boil broth to reduce to 1½ cups. Combine cornstarch and cold water; stir into broth. Cook and stir until slightly thickened. Spoon sauce over veal birds; sprinkle with parsley. Makes 4-6 servings.

Home Cookin' is a Family Affair

Vealburgers in Mustard Cream

These are as quick and easy as anything you can prepare, yet delicate and still unusual. Since the veal is tender, the interior should be rare and juicy, the exterior crusty brown. The meat needs only a little onion juice for seasoning. The sauce is smooth and very sharp.

2 tablespoons onion juice
2 pounds good-quality ground
  veal, with little fat
6 tablespoons sweet butter
  or margarine
½ cup Dijon-style mustard

½ cup heavy cream or
  yogurt
1 tablespoon lemon juice
6 rolled anchovies
Watercress or parsley sprigs

Mix onion juice with veal and shape into 6 cylindrical patties about 1½ inches thick, flat on tops and bottoms and straight on sides.

Melt butter in skillet and sauté patties over brisk heat, turning until nice crust forms on all sides and patties have reached desired state of doneness. Remove meat to warm platter while preparing sauce. Stir mustard, cream, and lemon juice into pan juices. Blend well.

Pour sauce onto hot platter and arrange patties on it. Top each patty with rolled anchovy, garnish with watercress or parsley, and serve. Yield: 4 or 5 servings.

Favorite New England Recipes

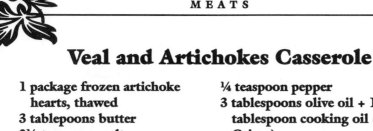

Veal and Artichokes Casserole

1 package frozen artichoke
  hearts, thawed
3 tablepoons butter
2½ teaspoons salt
12 veal scallops (chicken
  can be substituted)
1 egg, beaten
½ cup flour

¼ teaspoon pepper
3 tablespoons olive oil + 1
  tablespoon cooking oil (like
  Crisco)
¼ cup beef broth
⅓ cup grated Parmesan
  cheese

Sauté the artichokes in butter 5 minutes. Season with 1 teaspoon salt. Dip veal scallops in eggs, then in a mixture of flour, pepper, and remaining salt.

Heat the oil in a skillet; brown veal on both sides. Arrange in greased shallow casserole.* Add broth; cover veal with artichokes and sprinkle with cheese. Bake for 10 minutes (or until browned) at 375°. Serves 6-8.

*Can be done up to this point day before and add broth and cheese just before baking and serving.

Hasbro Children's Hospital Cookbook

Beef Burgundy

2 large onions
4 pounds beef sirloin tip,
  cut in cubes
Flour
Salt
Pepper
Celery salt

Garlic
A little nutmeg
1 box fresh mushrooms
Butter
1 cup beef stock
1 cup red wine

Chop onions and brown in a little fat in skillet. Remove to deep casserole or Dutch oven. Dust meat with flour and brown well in skillet with salt, pepper, celery salt, garlic, and a little nutmeg. Add to casserole.

Brown a box of fresh mushrooms in butter and add. Pour beef stock and red wine over all. Cover tightly and cook in a slow oven (325°) for at least 2½ hours. Serve with rice or wild rice.

Note: I find 2 cans of sliced water chestnuts add much to this dish as well. Serves 6-10.

Berkshire Seasonings

Viennese Beef Tenderloin

This is, without doubt, one of our favorite entrées. Wunderbar!

SAUCE:

1 cup orange juice	2 cups beef stock
1 cup marsala wine	1 cup heavy cream
½ cup burgundy wine	Pan drippings
¼ cup brandy	

In a small saucepan, combine orange juice, wines, and brandy. Simmer to reduce by half. Add the beef stock and reduce by half again. Add the cream, and again reduce by half. Later, add the meat juices from the roasting pan.

FILLING:

3 strips bacon	1 teaspoon fresh minced
2 shallots or ½ red onion,	parsley
finely chopped	¼ teaspoon fresh minced
2 cloves garlic, mashed	marjoram
5 ounces mushrooms, chopped	¼ teaspoon fresh minced
¼ teaspoon fresh minced	thyme
rosemary	3 tablespoons bread crumbs

Fry, drain, and dice the bacon; set aside. In the same pan, sauté onion for 10 minutes, add garlic, mushrooms, and herbs and sauté briefly. Mushrooms should be soft but not wilted. Remove to a bowl and mix with bacon and crumbs. Let cool. Preheat oven to 425°.

TENDERLOIN:

1 whole (5-5½-pound) beef	2 teaspoons Dijon mustard
tenderloin, trimmed and	¼ cup butter, softened
peeled	6 bay leaves
Fresh ground pepper	

Butterfly the tenderloin and lightly pound evenly flat between 2 sheets of waxed paper. Sprinkle with pepper and brush with mustard. Spread the filling, stopping ½ inch from edges. Close the tenderloin and tie with kitchen string in about 6 intervals. Sprinkle with pepper, smear with butter, place bay leaves across top. Place the meat in a well-greased roasting pan and roast for 30 minutes (meat will be medium-rare). Remove and let rest for 5 minutes before carving. Spoon sauce across center of slices and serve. Serves 10-12.

Recipes from a New England Inn

Braciole

2½ pounds round steak, ¼-½-inch thick
½ pound bulk Italian sausage
1 tablespoon parsley
1 teaspoon leaf oregano
2 small cloves garlic, minced
1 large onion, finely chopped
1 teaspoon salt
1 (16-ounce) can Italian-style tomatoes
1 (6-ounce) can tomato paste

Trim all excess fat from steak. Cut into 8 evenly shaped pieces. Pound steak pieces between waxed paper until very thin and easy to roll.

In skillet, lightly brown sausage. Drain well and combine with parsley, ½ teaspoon oregano, garlic, onion, and ½ teaspoon salt; mix well. Spread each steak with 2-3 tablespoons sausage mixture. Roll up jelly-roll fashion and tie.

Stack steak rolls in crockpot. Combine tomatoes, tomato paste, ½ teaspoon salt, and ½ teaspoon oregano; pour over rolls. Cover and cook on low setting for 7-10 hours. Serve steak rolls with sauce.

Cuisine à la Mode

Yankee Pot Roast

Really good. This recipe is for the pot roast famous at Clay Hill Farm.

4-6 pounds round roast or
   rump roast
2 cups red wine
2 cups tomato juice
1 large onion, minced
2 carrots, finely minced

1 clove garlic, minced
½ cup brown sugar
2 bay leaves
¼ teaspoon nutmeg
Salt and pepper to taste

Do not brown the pot roast. Place the meat in a heavy roasting pan that has a tight-fitting lid. Mix all the other ingredients together and pour over the meat. Cover and cook at 300° for about ¾ hour per pound. Turn roast over about halfway through cooking time. Let roast rest; thicken gravy and serve.

Visions of Home Cook Book

Corned Beef Hash

1 large corned beef (raw)
4-6 potatoes (peeled)
1 large onion (diced)
4-5 stalks celery (diced)
4 tablespoons butter

¼ cup flour
¼ cup Worcestershire sauce
Salt and pepper
1-1½ cups cooking liquid

Cook corned beef in a large pot, covered with water, for 6 hours or until tender. In the last hour of cooking, add the potatoes to pot and cook till soft. Drain, reserving 1½ cups cooking liquid. When cooled enough to handle, shread the corned beef into a large bowl. Mash the potatoes and add to the beef. Sauté the onion and celery in the butter till tender. Add to the beef with flour and Worcestershire. Season with salt and pepper to taste. Add the liquid as needed to hold the mixture together. Form into patties (approximately 5-ounce patties). Lightly brown in skillet in hot oil. Serves 16-20.

Note: Use leftover corned beef or smaller cuts of meat for fewer portions. You may substitute roast beef, turkey, or pork for a nice variation. These freeze well!

Washington Street Eatery Cook Book

New England Boiled Dinner

6 pounds brisket or rump of
  corned beef
½ clove garlic
6 peppercorns
6 carrots
3 large yellow turnips, cut
  in quarters

4 small parsnips
8 small peeled onions
6 medium-sized potatoes,
  pared and cut in quarters
1 head cabbage, quartered

Place corned beef in cold water with garlic and peppercorns and cook slowly until tender, skimming now and then. If you use very salty corned beef, drain when it comes to a boil and use fresh water for the rest of the cooking time. Allow from 4-5 hours for simmering, testing tenderness with a fork. When done, remove the meat, and cook the vegetables in the stock. When the vegetables are done, return the meat to the pot and reheat.

Serve with grated fresh horseradish beaten with sour cream, or use prepared horseradish with sour cream, adding a little lemon juice. Serves 4-8, depending on the size of the beef.

We like the beef sliced thin, not in chunks. We arrange the slices overlapping on an ironstone platter, arrange the vegetables around them with a slotted spoon, and serve the stock in an ironstone tureen (never thicken it).

We like to corn our own beef. We put it down in a crock for 36 hours, weighted down with a plate and a clean stone. The brine is 8 cups of water, 1 cup of salt, 3 tablespoons of sugar, 6 peppercorns, 1 clove of garlic, 2 bay leaves, and 2 teaspoons of mixed spices. Add ¼ teaspoon of saltpeter and ½ cup of warm water. All I can say is, Oh, my....

My Own Cookbook

New England Boiled Dinner
(Microwave)

This traditional New England meal can be microwaved in about an hour and a half instead of the usual three hours of conventional cooking time.

3 pounds boneless corned beef brisket	3 medium potatoes, about 6 ounces each
1 tablespoon whole cloves	1 medium turnip (optional)*
6 peppercorns	2 medium onions
2 bay leaves	4 medium carrots
1 clove garlic, halved	1 head of cabbage, about
2 cups water	1½ pound

Discard any spice packages packed with the beef. Rinse beef; put in a deep 4-quart casserole or bowl. Put the cloves, peppercorns, bay leaves, and garlic on top of the beef. Add the water. Cover with vented plastic wrap. Heat at HIGH (100%) power for 10 minutes. Rotate casserole a half turn. Heat at MEDIUM (50%) power for 30 minutes.

While the meat cooks, prepare the vegetables. Peel potatoes; cut each one in 8 pieces. Peel onions; cut each one in 8 wedges. Peel carrots; cut into 2-inch-long pieces. Core and rinse the cabbage; cut into 6 wedges.

At the end of the 30-minute cooking period, carefully turn the meat over. Put the potatoes in the liquid around the meat. Add carrots, then onions. Push vegetables down into liquid as much as possible. Cover with vented plastic wrap. Heat at MEDIUM for 30 minutes.

Put the cabbage wedges on top of the meat, arranging them around the edge of the casserole. Cover with vented plastic wrap. Heat at MEDIUM for 10–15 minutes, or until the cabbage is tender. Let stand for 10 minutes before serving.

To serve, slice corned beef thin and arrange on a platter. Arrange the vegetables around the meat. If you want to reheat the food before serving, be sure to use a microwaveable platter. Cover with waxed paper and heat at MEDIUM for 3–4 minutes, until heated through. Makes 6 servings.

*If you want to use the turnip, peel it and cut in 1-inch chunks. Add with the potaotes. Cook an additional 10 minutes before adding the cabbage.

Classic New England Dishes from Your Microwave

Red Flannel Hash
(Microwave)

2 tablespoons minced onion

3 cups finely diced cooked
corned beef

2 cups finely diced boiled
potatoes

1 cup finely diced cooked
beets

1 teaspoon Worcestershire
sauce

Ground black pepper to taste

3 tablespoons bacon
drippings (or butter or
margarine)

2 tablespoons chopped
parsley

Put the minced onion in a custard cup. Cover with vented plastic wrap. Heat at HIGH (100%) power for 1 minute. Let stand, covered, for 2 minutes.

Mix the diced corned beef, potatoes, and beets together. Add the onion and its liquid, Worcestershire sauce, and pepper to taste. The mixture should not need any added salt, as the beef is usually very salty.

Preheat a 10-inch browning dish at HIGH for 5 minutes, or as directed in manufacturer's instructions. Put the bacon drippings in the preheated dish, tilting to spread evenly. Spoon the corned beef mixture into the dish. Press down to cover bottom completely. Heat at HIGH for 4 minutes. Carefully turn hash over with a spatula. Heat at HIGH for another 2 minutes. Serve sprinkled with the chopped parsley. Makes 4-6 servings.

Classic New England Dishes from Your Microwave

Meatloaf

1-2 tablespoons olive oil
1 cup diced onion
½ cup diced celery
2 minced garlic cloves
1 teaspoon basil
1 teaspoon oregano
2 teaspoons thyme
1½ pounds ground beef
¾ pound sweet Italian
  sausage, casings removed

½ cup chopped sun-dried
  tomatoes
½ cup minced Italian
  parsley
2 beaten eggs
½ cup fine dry bread
  crumbs
1 teaspoon salt
1 teaspoon pepper

Preheat oven to 350°. Put olive oil in skillet and sauté onion, celery, garlic, basil, oregano, and thyme until tender, about 15 minutes. In large bowl, combine ground beef, sausage, and sautéed vegetables. Stir in the tomatoes, parsley, eggs, crumbs, salt and pepper. Mix thoroughly with hands. Form into 2 loaves and place in large shallow baking dish. Bake 1 hour or a little more, occasionally pouring off the juices. Serves 4-6.

The Maine Collection

Dynamites

3 pounds green peppers
4 large onions
½ bunch celery
2 pounds lean ground beef
1 (11-ounce) can tomato
  paste

2 teaspoons salt
Crushed red pepper seeds,
  to taste
½ teaspoon black pepper
Small, hard-crusted rolls

Chop green peppers, onions, and celery into half-inch pieces and cook over medium heat until done but not overcooked. Brown hamburg in a separate skillet and add to vegetables while they are cooking. You will note that a liquid will form. When vegetables and meat are cooked, add tomato paste and mix well. This will thicken the mixture. Add salt, crushed red pepper seeds, and black pepper to taste, being careful not to do it in excess.

Serve in a small, hard-crust roll. Especially delicious with a cold bottle of beer.

Cuisine à la Mode

Beef and Pepper Roll

1 pound ground beef (lean)
1 cup bread crumbs
1 lightly beaten egg
1 (16-ounce) jar spaghetti
  sauce (meatless)
1 cup shredded Swiss cheese

4 tablespoons grated
  Parmesan cheese
¼ teaspoon garlic powder
1 red and 1 green sliced
  pepper
6 large fresh mushrooms

Preheat oven to 350°. Combine ground beef, bread crumbs, egg, and ¼ cup spaghetti sauce. Combine in separate bowl, cheeses, and garlic; set aside. Place beef mixture between 2 pieces plastic wrap. With rolling pin, roll beef flat to approximately 12x12 inches, remove top plastic wrap, and spread cheese mixture over beef. Top with sliced pepper and mushrooms. Roll beef into long roll and tuck ends lightly; place seam-side-down. Sprinkle 2 tablespoons Swiss cheese over top and bake for 30 minutes on a cookie sheet. Remove and serve with remaining 1¾ cups sauce. Makes 8 servings.

Note: Beef rolls may be made ahead and chilled, or frozen to be cooked later. Joann O'Flaherty says you may substitute mozzarella for Swiss and Marinara sauce for spaghetti sauce.

A *Culinary Tour of the Gingerbread Cottages*

Mock Stuffed Cabbage

1 small head cabbage,
  shredded
1½-2 pounds ground
  beef, turkey, or chicken
1 egg
¾ cup bread crumbs
½ teaspoon garlic powder

1 (15-ounce) can tomato
  sauce
8-12 ounces whole or
  "crushed berry" cranberry
  sauce
2 tablespoons brown sugar

Place shredded cabbage in a Dutch oven. Combine ground beef, egg, bread crumbs, and garlic. Shape into meatballs and place on top of cabbage. Combine tomato sauce, cranberry sauce, and brown sugar and pour over meatballs. Cover and cook on top of stove or in a 350° oven for 1 hour. Serve with noodles or rice.

Hint: This tastes almost like stuffed cabbage, but without all the work! To keep this recipe as low in cholesterol as possible, substitute ground chicken or turkey for the beef and use an egg substitute or 2 egg whites instead of the whole egg. This freezes well.

From Ellie's Kitchen to Yours

Bildner's Chili

Good chili, like chowder, gets better after a couple of days. We sell so much of this chili in our Boston stores it's a wonder Boston isn't famous for chili instead of baked beans. If you prefer, you can make this classic chili with strips of lean beef rather than ground beef.

3 medium onions
10 medium cloves garlic
2 tablespoons vegetable oil
4 pounds lean ground beef
1 tablespoon sugar
6 tablespoons chili powder
1 teaspoon cayenne pepper
1 tablespoon ground
  cumin
1 teaspoon dried oregano
Salt and freshly ground
  pepper to taste
2 tablespoons corn flour
  (masa harina—in the
  imported foods section)

3 (3-ounce) cans chopped
  mild green chilies, drained
  (or hot if you prefer your
  chili very spicy)
2 (16-ounce) cans red kidney
  beans, drained
1 (1-pound, 13-ounce) can
  whole tomatoes, undrained
1 (6-ounce) can tomato paste
1 cup beef broth
Grated Cheddar or Monterey
  Jack cheese, diced red
  onion, sour cream, and
  chopped green chilies for
  topping

Chop the onions into ½-inch dice. Mince the garlic. Heat the oil in a large, heavy non-aluminum pot over medium-high heat until hot but not smoking. Sauté the chopped onions and garlic for about 3 minutes, stirring, until the onions are translucent. Add the ground beef and sear, breaking up any large chunks of beef with a spoon.

In a small bowl, mix together the sugar, chili powder, cayenne, cumin, oregano, salt, pepper, and corn flour. Sprinkle the mixture over the meat, reduce the heat to medium, and stir. Add the chopped chilies, kidney beans, canned tomatoes with their liquid, tomato paste, and beef broth. Stir well, breaking up the tomatoes with the spoon. Bring the chili to a boil, raising the heat if necessary.

Reduce the heat to low and simmer the chili for 2-3 hours. Serve with grated cheese, diced red onion, sour cream, and chopped green chilies to top. Yield: 8-10 servings.

J. Bildner & Sons Cookbook

Peter's Red Hot Chili

3 tablespoons oil
2 pounds stew beef
5 cups water
1 diced green pepper
1 diced onion
1 diced tomato
1½ tablespoons salt
2 teaspoons cayenne pepper

1 tablespoon granulated
 garlic
¼ cup chili powder
2 tablespoons cumin
1½ cups water
⅓ cup cornmeal
1 (6-ounce) can tomato paste

Brown beef in oil. Add next 9 ingredients and simmer for 2 hours. In a small bowl mix the water, cornmeal, and tomato paste. Stir cornmeal mixture into chili to thicken. Simmer another 20 minutes. Garnish with sliced raw onions and grated Monterey Jack cheese. Serves 4.

Peter Christian's Recipes

The Salem Witch Museum recounts true events which took place in 1692 during the famed witch trials, whereafter 19 accused "witches" were hanged on Gallows Hill, one was crushed to death, and more than 100 were imprisoned. Salem, Massachusetts.

Cakes

A village nestled in an eastern Vermont valley. East Topsham, Vermont.

Vermont Pumpkin Cheesecake

This dessert was made for a company member's birthday by our stage manager. At my request, she passed along the receipt—I had never tasted anything so delicious.

1½ cups zwieback crumbs
¼ cup sugar
6 tablespoons butter, melted
24 ounces cream cheese, softened
¾ cup sugar
¾ cup firmly packed light brown sugar

5 eggs
1 (16-ounce) can pumpkin purée
1¾ teaspoons pumpkin pie spice
¼ cup heavy cream

WALNUT TOPPING:
6 tablespoons butter, softened
1 cup firmly packed light brown sugar

1 cup coarsely chopped walnuts

Combine the zwieback crumbs, the ¼ cup sugar, and the melted butter in a small bowl. Butter a springform pan and firmly press the crumb mixture onto the bottom and side of the pan. Beat the cream cheese in a large bowl at medium speed until it is smooth. Gradually add the ¾ cup sugar and the brown sugar, mixing well after each addition. Beat in the eggs, 1 at a time, until the mixture is light and fluffy. With the mixer at low speed, beat in the pumpkin purée, pumpkin pie spice, and heavy cream. Pour the mixture into the prepared pan and bake at 350° for 1 hour and 35 minutes.

While the cake is baking, prepare the Walnut Topping. Combine the softened butter and the brown sugar and stir in the walnuts. Remove the cake from the oven and spread the topping over the surface. Bake for an additional 10 minutes. Cool the cheesecake on a wire rack and chill overnight before serving. Serves 15.

As You Like It

Cheesecake Supreme

¼ pound melted butter
1 pound cream cheese
1 pint ricotta cheese
4 eggs
1½ cups sugar
3 tablespoons flour

3 tablespoons cornstarch
1½ teaspoon lemon juice
1 pint sour cream
1 teaspoon vanilla
1 (20-ounce) can crushed
    pineapple, well drained

Melt and cool butter. Mix all ingredients in order given, except pineapple. Lightly grease a 9-inch springform pan. Spread can of pineapple on bottom of pan. Pour in the cheese mixture and bake for 1 hour at 350°. Turn oven off and let cake stand for 2 hours before removing.

Do not open oven door during baking or cooling of cheesecake. Remove from pan and invert so pineapple is on top.

This cheesecake is not too sweet. It stores well and maintains its texture. Easy to make and everyone loves it. Serves 16.

Great Island Cook Book

Apple Cheese Cake

4 ounces cream cheese,
    softened
½ cup butter, softened
1 egg
¾ cup sugar

1 cup flour
1 teaspoon baking powder
3 apples, sliced
½ cup brown sugar
1 teaspoon cinnamon

Beat cream cheese and butter together until creamy. Add egg and sugar and beat until very fluffy. Sift together flour and baking powder, and gently fold into cheese mixture. Spoon into a deep 9-inch pie plate which has been well buttered and dusted with flour. Cover the top with apple slices, pinwheel fashion.

Sprinkle with mixture of brown sugar and cinnamon. Bake at 350° for 40-45 minutes. Serve warm with sweetened whipped cream. Yield: One 9-inch cake.

Note: Maple sugar makes an elegant substitute for the brown sugar.

Apple Orchard Cookbook

Lime Cheesecake

"The most luscious, creamy cheesecake you've ever had! Yes, it's totally fattening. But some things you've just got to do," says chef Stephen Daoust.

1 (9-ounce) package
   chocolate wafers, finely
   crushed
4 tablespoons butter, melted
3 extra-large eggs
1 cup sugar

½ cup fresh lime juice
1 tablespoon vanilla
24 ounces cream cheese
16 ounces sour cream
¼ cup sugar

Preheat the oven to 300°.

Mix the crushed chocolate wafers with the melted butter and press the mixture into the bottom and 1 inch up the sides of a 9-inch springform pan. Chill.

Mix the eggs and the 1 cup sugar with a blender for several minutes until pale yellow. Add the lime juice and vanilla and combine.

In a bowl, cream the cream cheese until soft, and slowly add the egg-and-sugar mixture. Fill the prepared pan and bake at 300° for 50 minutes or until the top is set. Allow to cool.

In a separate bowl, mix the sour cream with the ¼ cup sugar and spoon over the top of the cooled cake. Bake for 10 minutes more. Chill overnight.

Run a sharp knife between the crust and the pan before you unmold the cake. Serves 8.

A recipe from The Williamsville Inn, West Stockbridge, MA.

Best Recipes of Berkshire Chefs

The song "Yankee Doodle" had its origins in Norwalk, Connecticut. In 1756, a brigade of volunteers assembled at the home of Colonel Thomas Fitch where the young recruits set out to assist the British during the French and Indian War. Fitch's young sister stuck a feather into the hatband of each soldier as he pulled out on his plow horse. The British, amused by the appearance of the troops, wrote and sang the jingle in mockery. The rest is history. Yankee Doodle became the rallying song for the colonial troops during the Revolution and in 1979 became the official song of Connecticut.

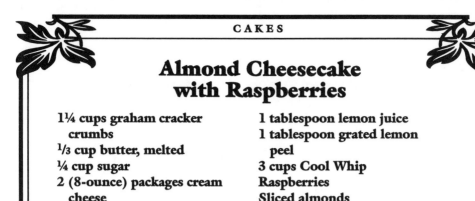

Almond Cheesecake with Raspberries

1¼ cups graham cracker
  crumbs
⅓ cup butter, melted
¼ cup sugar
2 (8-ounce) packages cream
  cheese
1 (16-ounce) can ready-to-
  spread vanilla frosting

1 tablespoon lemon juice
1 tablespoon grated lemon
  peel
3 cups Cool Whip
Raspberries
Sliced almonds

Stir together crumbs, butter, and sugar in a small bowl; press onto bottom and ½ inch up sides of a 9-inch springform pan or pie plate. Chill. Beat cream cheese, frosting, juice, and peel in a large mixing bowl at medium speed with electric mixer until well blended. Fold in whipped topping; pour over crust. Chill until firm. Arrange raspberries and almonds on top.

Sandy Hook Volunteer Fire Co. Ladies Aux. Cookbook

Chocolate Amaretto Cheesecake

CRUST:
25 chocolate wafers, crushed
¼ cup margarine, melted

½ teaspoon cinnamon

FILLING:
24 ounces cream cheese,
  softened
1 cup sugar
3 eggs
1 (16-ounce) package
  semi-sweet chocolate, melted

1 tablespoon cocoa
1 teaspoon vanilla
1 tablespoon amaretto
2 cups sour cream

Mix ingredients for crust and press into lightly buttered 10-inch springform pan. Chill. Preheat oven to 350°. In a large bowl, beat cream cheese until fluffy and smooth. Add sugar and beat in eggs. Stir in chocolate, cocoa, vanilla, and amaretto. Add sour cream and continue beating until very smooth and well blended. Pour into crust. Bake for 1 hour and 10 minutes. Cake may appear to be liquid, but it will become firm when chilled. Cool to room temperature, then chill for at least 5 hours. Garnish with whipped cream.

A Taste of New England

Cherry Walnut Delight

1¼ cups flour
¾ cup brown sugar
½ cup margarine
¾ cup coconut
¾ cup chopped walnuts
1 (8-ounce) package cream
   cheese
½ cup sugar
1 egg
1 teaspoon vanilla
1 (1 pound 5-ounce) can
   cherry pie filling
½ cup chopped walnuts
   (for topping)

Combine flour, brown sugar, and butter; blend to fine crumbs. Add coconut and walnuts; mix. Reserve ⅓ cup crumb mixture and press the rest into bottom of a greased 9x13-inch pan. Bake at 350° for 12-15 minutes or until lightly browned. Beat cream cheese until fluffy. Add sugar, egg, and vanilla. Spread over baked layer and bake 10 minutes. Put cherry filling over cream cheese. Sprinkle with walnuts and crumb mixture. Bake for 15 minutes.

The Parkview Way to Vegetarian Cooking

Strawberry Crunch Cake

2 cups flour
2 tablespoons whole wheat
   flour
4 teaspoons baking powder
½ cup sugar
¾ teaspoon salt
¾ cup milk
2 eggs
½ teaspoon lemon extract
1 teaspoon vanilla
2 cups fresh sliced
   strawberries
½ cup sugar
⅓ cup sugar
⅓ cup flour
2 tablespoons whole wheat
   flour
⅓ cup soft butter
¼ teaspoon nutmeg
Whipped cream

Combine first 9 ingredients and mix well (it is quite thick). Spread in a greased 10-inch springform pan. Sprinkle sliced strawberries and ½ cup sugar over top of batter. In another bowl, combine ⅓ cup sugar, flours, butter, and nutmeg. Mix with a fork until crumbly and sprinkle over strawberries. Bake at 425° 30-40 minutes. Serve warm with whipped cream. Serves 10-12.

Peter Christian's Recipes

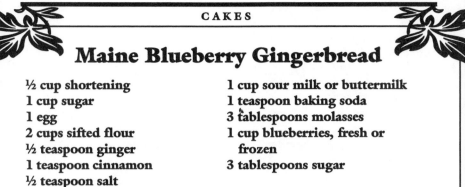

Maine Blueberry Gingerbread

½ cup shortening
1 cup sugar
1 egg
2 cups sifted flour
½ teaspoon ginger
1 teaspoon cinnamon
½ teaspoon salt

1 cup sour milk or buttermilk
1 teaspoon baking soda
3 tablespoons molasses
1 cup blueberries, fresh or
    frozen
3 tablespoons sugar

Cream shortening and sugar. Add egg and mix well. Mix and sift together flour, ginger, cinnamon, and salt. Add to creamed mixture alternately with sour milk, in which soda has been dissolved. Add molasses. Carefully fold in blueberries and pour batter into greased and floured 9x9-inch pan. Sprinkle 3 tablespoons of sugar over batter. Bake in preheated 350° oven for 50 minutes to 1 hour. Sugar makes sweet, crusty topping when cake is baked. Makes 9-12 servings.

Merrymeeting Merry Eating

Melt-In-Your-Mouth Blueberry Cake

A wonderful light summer dessert and especially good for picnics. A family favorite!

2 eggs, separated
1 cup sugar
½ cup margarine, softened
¼ teaspoon salt
1 teaspoon vanilla
1½ cups flour, sifted, and
    1 tablespoon for coating
    blueberries

1 teaspoon baking powder
⅓ cup milk
1½ cups fresh blueberries
Cinnamon sugar for topping

Preheat oven to 350°. Beat egg whites until stiff. Beat in ¼ cup of sugar. Cream margarine; add salt, vanilla, and remaining sugar gradually. Add egg yolks and beat until creamy. Sift flour with baking powder. Add alternately to creamed mixture with milk. Fold in beaten egg whites. Add 1 tablespoon of flour to coat blueberries. Fold in berries. Turn into 8x8-inch pan. Sprinkle cinnamon sugar on top. Bake in 350° oven 50 minutes. Cool on rack. Wrap any leftovers and store in refrigerator. May be frozen. Serves 8.

The Maine Collection

Blueberry Pudding Cake

2 cups blueberries	½ cup milk
2 tablespoons lemon juice	1 egg
1 cup flour	¼ cup melted butter
2 teaspoons baking powder	1 teaspoon vanilla
¼ teaspoon salt	1 cup sugar
½ teaspoon nutmeg	1 tablespoon cornstarch
¾ cup sugar	1 cup boiling water

Place blueberries and lemon juice in an 8x8-inch pan. Mix flour, baking powder, salt, nutmeg, and ¾ cup sugar. Beat in milk, egg, melted butter, and vanilla. Spread over berries. Mix 1 cup sugar with cornstarch and sprinkle over batter. Pour boiling water over all. Bake at 350° for 40-45 minutes.

Note: Other fruits may be used in place of the blueberries.

Windjammer Cooking

White Raspberry Truffle Cake

1 package white cake mix	1 (16-ounce) container dairy
1 large container fresh	whip
raspberries or large package	1 large bar white chocolate,
frozen raspberries, thawed	shaved

Prepare white cake mix according to directions in a 9x13-inch pan. Cool thoroughly. Cut cake into 4-inch squares. (Use a truffle dish or attractive, deep crystal bowl for the container of this dessert.)

For the first layer, place enough cake squares to cover bottom of dish. Next, sprinkle shaves of white chocolate. Place a layer of raspberries on the white chocolate. Place a light layer of dairy whip on top of raspberries. Repeat until all the ingredients have been used, ending with the dairy topping.

Just before serving, place a layer of raspberries on top of the dairy whip and it is ready for the presentation and enjoyment of your guests. Serves 12 people.

Heritage Cooking

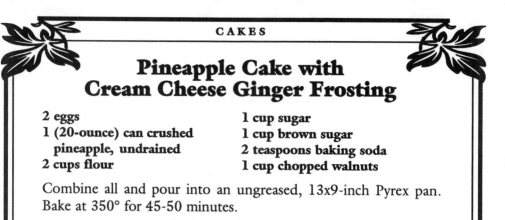

Pineapple Cake with Cream Cheese Ginger Frosting

2 eggs
1 (20-ounce) can crushed
  pineapple, undrained
2 cups flour

1 cup sugar
1 cup brown sugar
2 teaspoons baking soda
1 cup chopped walnuts

Combine all and pour into an ungreased, 13x9-inch Pyrex pan. Bake at 350° for 45-50 minutes.

CREAM CHEESE GINGER FROSTING:

1 (3-ounce) package cream
  cheese
¼ cup butter

1 teaspoon vanilla
2 cups powdered sugar
½ teaspoon ginger

Combine and spread on cooled pineapple cake.

Berkshire Seasonings

Raw Apple Cake

1 cup vegetable oil
2 cups sugar
2 eggs
2 teaspoons vanilla extract
2½ cups flour
1 teaspoon baking soda
½ teaspoon salt

1 teaspoon cinnamon
¾ cup apple juice
3 cups diced tart apples
  (Granny Smith or Northern
  Spy work well)
½ cup walnuts (optional)
½ cup raisins (optional)

Combine oil and sugar in bowl, mix well. Add eggs 1 at a time, then vanilla. Sift together dry ingredients. Add to oil and egg mixture alternately with the apple juice. Blend well. Fold in remaining ingredients. Grease well a 10-inch Bundt pan. Spread batter evenly in pan; bake at 325° for approximately 1½ hours. Test with a toothpick. Cool well before turning out of pan.

GLAZE:

1 stick butter
1 cup brown sugar

¼ cup evaporated milk
1 teaspoon vanilla extract

Melt butter and sugar over low heat. Stir in milk and bring to a boil. Remove from heat and stir in vanilla. Cool. Spread on cooled cake. Yields 1 Bundt cake.

Washington Street Eatery Cook Book

Apple Pie Cake

Mrs. Hunter cooked for my grandfather for years, and everything she cooked was good and made from scratch. Surely nothing this tasty comes from a mix. It's easy, bright with cinnamon, and delicious hot or cold.

½ cup (1 stick) margarine
¾ cup sugar
1 egg, slightly beaten
1 cup flour
1 teaspoon baking powder
1 teaspoon ground cinnamon
½ teaspoon salt

½ teaspoon ground nutmeg
¼ teaspoon ground cloves
⅛ teaspoon vanilla
2 cups chopped and peeled
   apples
½ cup chopped pecans

Thoroughly grease a 9-inch pie pan. Melt margarine, remove from heat, and blend with sugar and egg. Mix in flour, baking powder, cinnamon, salt, nutmeg, cloves, vanilla, apples, and pecans. Spread into pan. Bake in a preheated 350° oven for 40-45 minutes. Serve warm with ice cream. Serves 6-8.

The Lymes' Heritage Cookbook

Yankee Apple Cake

2 cups sugar
2 cups flour
4 eggs
3 teaspoons baking powder

½ cup oil
3 teaspoons vanilla
⅓ cup orange juice
¼ teaspoon salt

APPLE MIXTURE:
4 large apples, cored,
   peeled and sliced

4 teaspoons sugar
1 teaspoon cinnamon

Beat everything but Apple Mixture with mixer for 10 minutes. Grease 2 loaf pans or 1 tube pan and make several layers of batter and apples, beginning with batter and ending with apples. Bake at 350° for 1 hour or until tester is dry when inserted in center. A tube pan will take 10-15 minutes longer. (If glass pans are used, turn oven to 325° after first 10 minutes.) Serves 10-12.

Come Savor Swansea

The *U.S.S. Constitution*, more commonly know as "Old Ironsides," is the oldest commissioned warship afloat in the world. Boston Massachusetts.

Carrot Cake

This is the best carrot cake I have ever tasted.

1½ cups vegetable oil
2 cups granulated sugar
3 whole eggs and 1 egg
  white, well beaten
2 cups flour
1 teaspoon salt

2 teaspoons ground cinnamon
2 tablespoons baking powder
1 cup chopped pecans
½ cup golden raisins
3 cups grated carrots

Preheat oven to 325°. Coat 2 (9-inch) square Teflon cake pans with vegetable spray. In a large bowl, mix vegetable oil and sugar and beat well. Add the eggs and blend. Sift together the dry ingredients and add to egg mixture. Add the nuts, raisins, and grated carrots, a small amount at a time, and blend thoroughly.

Pour the batter into prepared cake pans and bake 1 hour, or until toothpick inserted into center comes out clean. Turn onto wire rack to cool. When cool, spread Cream-Cheese Frosting between layers and on the top (but not on the sides) of the cake. Finish off with some fancy swirls. Yield: 16 or more servings.

CREAM-CHEESE FROSTING:

4 ounces (1 stick) butter or
  margarine
1 (8-ounce) package cream
  cheese

2 cups confectioners' sugar
2 teaspoons vanilla extract
  (or substitute brandy if
  desired)

Allow the butter and cream cheese to reach room temperature. Then cream butter and cream cheese and gradually beat in confectioners' sugar and vanilla (or brandy). Spread between layers and on top of Carrot Cake. Yield: Enough frosting for top and filling for 2-layer cake.

Favorite New England Recipes

Chocolate Sin Cake

In all my days, I have never had a chocolate cake as good as this!

2 sticks butter
1½ cups sugar
4 eggs
1 (6-ounce) package semi-
  sweet chocolate morsels
1½ cups chocolate syrup
1½ cups applesauce
1 teaspoon vanilla extract

1 teaspoon almond extract
  (pure)
½ teaspoon baking soda
½ teaspoon salt
2½ cups flour
1 cup chopped nuts
  (optional)

Preheat oven to 325°. Cream butter and sugar well. Add eggs 1 at a time. Beat until light and fluffy. Melt the chocolate morsels with the syrup in a double boiler. Add to the butter and egg mixture. Add remaining ingredients, and blend well. Pour batter into a well-greased 10-inch Bundt pan or 10-inch round pan. Bake for 1 hour or until a toothpick inserted comes out clean. Cool well before turning out of pan. This cake is very moist and requires no frosting, but is delicious with whipped cream. Yields 1 Bundt cake.

Washington Street Eatery Cook Book

Chocolate Mousse Cake

SPONGE:

1 cup sifted all-purpose
  flour
1 teaspoon baking powder
3 large eggs

1 cup sugar
⅓ cup water
1 teaspoon vanilla

Heat oven to 375°. Grease a jelly roll pan (15½x10½x1-inch) and line with greased wax paper. Blend flour and baking powder; set aside. Beat eggs until thick and lemon colored. Gradually add sugar and continue beating. Blend water and vanilla and add dry ingredients on very low speed just until mixed and batter is smooth. Pour into pan and spread. Bake 12-15 minutes. Turn upside down on a towel that has been sprinkled with confectioners' sugar, and remove wax paper carefully as cake cools. When cool, cut off edges and cut into pieces to line the loaf pan to prepare for the mousse.

MOUSSE:

12 ounces semi-sweet
  chocolate morsels
3 tablespoons water
3 tablespoons confectioners'
  sugar

7 eggs, separated
1 teaspoon vanilla

Melt chocolate morsels with water in the top of a double boiler. Add sugar and mix well; cool slightly. Add egg yolks and mix well. Cool slightly and add vanilla. In a separate bowl beat egg whites until stiff and fold into chocolate mixture. Line 9x5x2¾-inch loaf pan with transparent wrap. Cut sponge into pieces to line the bottom and all sides and top. Pour in mousse and put top piece of sponge in place, cover with plastic wrap, chill, and then freeze. Next day remove from refrigerator ½ hour before using. Turn upside down on serving plate and remove plastic wrap. You can cover with meringue as for Baked Alaska, or top with whipped cream and chocolate sprinkles or curls.

The Fine Art of Holiday Cooking

 Shakers made an important contribution to New Hampshire through their culture and religion. Canterbury and Enfield are home to Shaker villages where you can learn about the history and lifestyle of the Shakers.

Rocky Roadhouse Cake

8 eggs
¼ cup oil
1¾ cups sour cream
1 (8-ounce) box butterscotch
   instant pudding mix
1 package of devil's food
   chocolate cake mix

1 cup chopped walnuts
½ bag mini-marshmallows
8 ounces chocolate mini-
   chips
8 ounces butterscotch
   mini-chips

Break eggs into a large bowl and mix in the oil, sour cream, and butterscotch pudding mix. Add cake mix. Stir, but do not overmix. Stir just long enough for the mix to be absorbed but not completely smooth. This will be a heavy mix. Add the rest of the ingredients. Spoon into a greased and floured cake pan. Bake at 350° for about ¾ hour.

A recipe from The Roadhouse Café, Hyannis, MA.

Cape Cod's Night at the Chef's Table

Famous Rum Cake

1 cup chopped pecans or
   walnuts
1 (18½-ounce) package
   yellow cake mix
1 (3¾-ounce) package
   instant vanilla pudding mix

4 eggs
½ cup cold water
½ cup cooking oil
½ cup dark rum

Preheat oven to 325°. Grease and flour a 10-inch tube or 12-cup Bundt pan. Sprinkle nuts over bottom of pan. Mix all cake ingredients together. Pour batter over nuts in pan. Bake at 325° for 1 hour.

Set on rack to cool. Invert on serving plate. Prick top; drizzle and brush glaze evenly over top and sides.

GLAZE:

¼ pound butter
¼ cup water

1 cup granulated sugar
½ cup dark rum

Melt butter in saucepan. Stir in water and sugar. Boil 5 minutes, stirring constantly. Stir in rum.

Perennials

Gillie Whoopers

¾ cup sifted flour
¼ teaspoon baking powder
¼ teaspoon salt
2 tablespoons cocoa
¾ cup sugar
½ cup shortening

2 eggs
1 teaspoon vanilla
½ cup walnuts
1 package miniature
   marshmallows

Combine flour, baking powder, salt, cocoa, and sugar. Blend in shortening, eggs, and teaspoon vanilla. Add walnuts. Spread in greased baking pan and bake at 350° for 20 minutes. Take from oven; sprinkle miniature marshmallows over the top, keeping away from sides. Put back into oven for 3 minutes.

FROSTING:
½ cup brown sugar
¼ cup water
2 squares baking chocolate

3 tablespoons butter
2 tablespoons vanilla
1½ cups powdered sugar

Combine brown sugar, water, chocolate. Boil for 3 minutes; take from burner and add butter, vanilla, and powdered sugar (enough to make smooth icing). Spread over marshmallows and let cool. Cut in squares.

All-Maine Cooking

Apricot Pound Cake

1 cup unsalted butter,
  softened
3 cups granulated sugar
6 large eggs
1 cup sour cream
½ cup apricot brandy

1 teaspoon vanilla extract
2 teaspoons dark rum
3 cups all-purpose flour
½ teaspoon salt
½ teaspoon baking soda

In a large bowl, cream butter and sugar. Beat until mixture is light and fluffy. Add eggs 1 at a time, beating well after each addition. Beat in sour cream, brandy, vanilla, and rum.

In another bowl, sift together the flour, salt, and baking soda. Stir the flour mixture into the butter and egg mixture.

Pour batter into a buttered Bundt pan and bake for 1 hour at 325°, or until a cake tester inserted in the center comes out clean.

Cool the cake in the pan on a rack for 1 hour. Then, turn it out of the pan on a rack to cool completely.

Dining on Deck

Worster House Hot Fudge Sunday Cake

Here's one for you gals who need a quick dessert for a last-minute party.

First—Preheat oven to 350°. Use a 9x9-inch pan and do NOT grease the pan. Stir with a fork in the baking pan:

1 cup flour
¾ cup sugar
2 tablespoons cocoa

2 teaspoons baking powder
¼ teaspoon salt

Second—Mix in separate bowl; then spread evenly on top of your flour and sugar mixture:

½ cup milk
2 tablespoons oil

1 teaspoon vanilla
1 cup nuts

Third—Sprinkle over everything evenly:

1 cup brown sugar

¼ cup cocoa

Fourth—Pour over the entire cake:

1⅓ cups very hot water

Bake for 35-40 minutes. Serve hot from the oven on top of your best vanilla ice cream.

A Taste of Hallowell

Cookies and Candies

A barrel of Maine pumpkins sits on the dock of the bay amidst crates of goods from near and far.

Country Raisin Gingersnaps

1½ cups seedless raisins
¾ cup shortening
1 cup sugar
1 egg
¼ cup molasses
2¼ cups sifted flour

2 teaspoons soda
½ teaspoon salt
1 teaspoon ginger
½ teaspoon cinnamon
½ teaspoon cloves

Chop raisins, as this makes the cookie chewy as well as crunchy. Beat together shortening, sugar, and egg. Blend in molasses. Blend in flour sifted with soda, salt, and spices. Mix in raisins. Chill dough. Shape dough into small balls and roll in additional sugar, if desired. Place on lightly greased baking sheet. Bake in moderately hot oven 375°, 8–10 minutes. Remove to cooling rack. Makes about 3 dozen cookies.

Maine's Jubilee Cookbook

Gingerbread Men

My father was an architect, among other things, but I don't recall seeing his designing any gingerbread houses. I hope that the real houses he designed were sturdier than my gingerbread house. But then, just about anything would be—my house was eaten by a dog.

½ cup butter
¾ cup molasses
¼ cup sugar
1 egg, lightly beaten
3 cups sifted flour
1 tablespoon ginger

¼ teaspoon nutmeg
½ teaspoon cinnamon
¼ teaspoon salt
3 teaspoons baking powder
Seedless raisins—for eyes
    and buttons

Melt the butter. Stir in molasses, sugar, and beaten egg. Stir in the flour, sifted with spices, salt and baking powder. Chill the mixture in refrigerator at least 2 hours. Roll out dough, not too thin, using a pastry cloth and covered rolling pin. Use as little flour as possible. Cut dough with gingerbread man cutter. Lift with 2 nylon spatulas and place on a Teflon cookie sheet. Roll up small bits of raisins for eyes and buttons and push them into the dough. Use the edge of a spoon to make marks for the nose, mouth, chin, and collar. Bake at 375° for about 10 minutes. Be sure they do not scorch. Cool.

Notes: With loops of gold cord, hang the finished men on your Christmas tree, or make a fence of them in front of it. This amount of dough will bake about 16 men. The same mixture, rolled rather thicker, may be used for a gingerbread house if you are in the architectural mood.

Mrs. Appleyard's Family Kitchen

The internationally known phenomenon "Old Man of the Mountain" is a natural, granite profile jutting from a sheer cliff 1,200 feet above Profile Lake in Franconia Notch State Park, New Hampshire. Carved by nature thousands of years ago, the profile is formed by five separate ledges. It measures 40 feet from chin to forehead.

Joe Froggers

Legend says that Uncle Joe, an old man who lived on the edge of a frog pond in Marblehead, made the very best molasses cookies in town. They were called "Joe Froggers" because they were as large as lily pads and as dark as the frogs in the pond. Fishermen found the cookies would keep well on long sea voyages and began trading them for rum. Today the big molasses cookies will keep as well in the cookie jar as they did in the fishermen's sea chests—if they last that long!

1 cup butter or margarine	1 teaspoon allspice
2 cups sugar	1 teaspoon nutmeg
2 cups dark molasses	1 tablespoon ginger
7 cups flour	2 teaspoons baking soda
1 tablespoon salt	¾ cup water
1 teaspoon ground cloves	¼ cup rum

Cream butter and sugar together. Add molasses. Sift dry ingredients together. Mix water with the rum. Add flour mixture alternately with the liquid mixture to the creamed mixture. Stir well between additions. Dough should be sticky. Chill dough overnight in the refrigerator.

Preheat oven to 375°. On a well-floured surface, roll dough to ¼-½-inch thick. Cut with a 4-inch round cutter, or use the bottom of a 1-pound coffee can. Bake 10-12 minutes on greased cookie sheets. Yield: 5 dozen.

Hospitality

Meltaway Nut Squares

These are not very sweet and are good for a coffee or tea.

1 stick butter, softened	2 cups flour
1 stick margarine, softened	1 cup chopped nuts
1 cup sugar	½ cup seedless jam
2 egg yolks	

Preheat oven to 325°. Cream butter, margarine, and sugar. Add egg yolks and flour; blend well. Fold in nuts. Spoon ½ of the mixture in the bottom of a lightly buttered 8-inch square pan; top with jam and cover with the remaining dough. Bake 1 hour. Cool before cutting.

Home Cookin' is a Family Affair

Brownie Crisps

½ cup butter
1 ounce unsweetened
  chocolate
1 teaspoon instant coffee
½ cup sugar

1 egg
¼ teaspoon vanilla
¼ teaspoon salt
¼ cup flour
½ cup finely chopped
  nuts

Melt butter and chocolate over low heat in a heavy saucepan. Stir until smooth. Add instant coffee and stir to dissolve. Remove from heat and stir in sugar, then egg and vanilla. Mix thoroughly. Add salt and flour; mix until smooth. Pour into a greased 15x10-inch jelly roll pan and spread evenly. Sprinkle with nuts. Bake in a 375° oven on center rack exactly 15 minutes, reversing position of pan once during baking to insure even browning. Remove from oven and without waiting, cut carefully with a sharp knife. Immediately, before cookies cool and harden, remove them with a wide spatula. Cool on rack. Store in airtight container. Yield: 5 dozen.

Boston Tea Parties

Turtles

Keep copies of this recipe handy—everyone will ask for one.

CRUST:

2 cups flour

1 cup brown sugar

½ cup (1 stick) butter, at
  room temperature

Preheat oven to 350°. Mix crust ingredients in mixer bowl at medium speed until well mixed and dough forms fine particles. With hands pat dough into a 13x9x2-inch pan.

CARAMEL:

1 cup (2 sticks) butter

1½ cups brown sugar

3 tablespoons corn syrup

2 cups chopped pecans

12 ounces chocolate chips

In a saucepan over medium heat, mix butter, syrup, and brown sugar for caramel. Bring to a boil; boil for 1 minute, stirring constantly. Sprinkle nuts over crust; pour caramel over all. Bake 18-22 minutes, until surface bubbles. Immediately after removing pan from oven, pour chocolate chips evenly over all. Let stand briefly to melt, then spread chocolate. Cool; cut into squares. Yield: 48 squares.

Christmas Memories Cookbook

Oatmeal Carmelitas

8 ounces (about 32) light
  candy caramels

5 tablespoons light cream

1 cup all-purpose flour

1 cup quick-cooking rolled
  oats

½ cup chopped pecans

½ teaspoon baking soda
  sugar

¾ cup margarine, melted

¼ teaspoon salt

1 (6-ounce) package
  semi-sweet chocolate chips

Melt caramels in cream in top of double boiler. Cool slightly. Set aside. Heat oven to 350°. Lightly spoon flour into measuring cup; level off. Combine flour with remaining ingredients except chocolate chips and pecans. Press ½ of crumbs in bottom of ungreased 11x7-inch or 9-inch-square pan. Bake for 10 minutes. Remove from oven. Sprinkle with chocolate chips and pecans. Spread carefully with caramel mixture. Bake for 15-20 minutes longer until golden brown. Chill 1-2 hours. Cut into bars. Makes about 2 dozen.

More Than Sandwiches

Tollhouse Brownies

2 (16-ounce) packages
   chocolate chip cookie
   dough, softened (found
   in dairy section)
1 (8-ounce) package cream
   cheese, at room temperature

2 eggs
½ cup sugar
1 teaspoon vanilla

Grease well a 9x13-inch pan; spread 1 softened package cookie dough in bottom of pan. Mix cream cheese, eggs, sugar, and vanilla well and pour over dough. Drop pieces of dough from second package over filling. Bake at 350° for 35 minutes. If top is not brown enough, place under broiler for desired browning. Watch carefully. Refrigerate when cooled. Can also be frozen and eaten as an ice cream-type sandwich. Yield: 2 dozen.

RSVP

Cheesecake Fudge Nut Brownies

1 pound cream cheese
¼ pound butter
1 cup sugar

2 teaspoons vanilla
2 teaspoons lemon juice
1 egg

Grease and lightly flour the 10x12-inch cookie sheet.

Cream the cream cheese and butter together, then add the sugar, vanilla, and lemon juice. When they are well mixed, beat in 1 egg until the mixture is smooth.

2 cups all-purpose flour
2 teaspoons baking powder
1 teaspoon salt
1 pound unsweetened
   chocolate

¼ pound butter
8 eggs
4 cups sugar
1 tablespoon vanilla
1 cup chopped walnuts

Make the fudge part separately by combining the flour, baking powder, and salt. Melt the chocolate and butter together over a low flame. Beat the eggs, sugar, and vanilla together, add the flour mixture, and finally fold in the melted chocolate.

Spread a thin layer of the brownie mix over the bottom of the cookie sheet. Pour the cheesecake mix in, then "plop" the rest of the brownie on top. To get a marbled effect, trail a rubber spatula through the two top layers, but don't overdo, or the finished product will be muddy.

Sprinkle the top with walnuts, then bake for half an hour at 350°.

The Loaf and Ladle Cook Book

Chocolate Sin
Raspberry Truffle Brownies

BROWNIES:

1½ cups semi-sweet real
  chocolate morsels
½ cup margarine
¾ cup brown sugar
2 large eggs

1 teaspoon instant coffee
  crystals
2 tablespoons water
½ teaspoon baking powder
¾ cup all-purpose flour

In saucepan over low heat, melt morsels and margarine; cool slightly. In large mixing bowl, beat sugar and eggs. Add chocolate mixture and coffee dissolved in water. Mix well.

Stir in baking powder and flour; blend well. Spread in greased 9x9-inch pan. Bake at 350° for 30-35 minutes or until toothpick tests clean.

RASPBERRY TRUFFLE FILLING:

1 cup semi-sweet real
  chocolate morsels
¼ teaspoon instant coffee
  crystals
1 (8-ounce) package cream
  cheese, softened

¼ cup powdered sugar
⅓ cup seedless red
  raspberry preserves

Melt chocolate with coffee in pan over low heat. Set aside. In small mixing bowl, beat softened cream cheese until fluffy; add powdered sugar and preserves. Beat until fluffy. Beat in melted chocolate mixture until well blended. Spread over cooled browned layer.

GLAZE:

¼ cup semi-sweet real
  chocolate morsels

1 teaspoon solid vegetable
  shortening

In small saucepan over low heat, melt chocolate and shortening. Drizzle over truffle layer. Chill 1-2 hours. Cut into bars.

The Marlborough Meetinghouse Cookbook

It was at Old North Church in Boston that lanterns were hung to signal Paul Revere to begin his ride to Lexington and Concord. Actually two riders, Revere and his North Street neighbor William Dawes, both set off to sound the alarm to be sure the message got through if one was captured. Revere was in fact captured, and Dawes got through, but it was Revere that Longfellow immortalized in his famous poem, "Paul Revere's Ride."

Brickle Bars

½ cup margarine or butter
2 squares (2 ounces)
   unsweetened chocolate
1 cup sugar
2 eggs
1 teaspoon vanilla

¾ cup all-purpose flour
¾ cup almond brickle
   pieces
½ cup miniature semi-sweet
   chocolate pieces

In a 2-quart saucepan, cook and stir margarine or butter and un-sweetened chocolate over low heat until melted. Remove from heat; stir in sugar. Add eggs and vanilla; beat lightly with a wooden spoon just until combined (don't overbeat or brownies will rise too high, then fall). Stir in flour.

Spread batter in a greased 8x8x2-inch baking pan. Sprinkle al-mond brickle pieces and chocolate pieces evenly over batter.

Bake in a 350° oven for 30 minutes. Remove pan from oven and cool brownies in pan on a wire rack. Cut into bars. Makes 16 bars.

Home Cookin' is a Family Affair

Oh Henry Bars

²/₃ cup oleo
1 cup brown sugar
½ cup Karo syrup
3 teaspoons vanilla

4 cups oatmeal
Chocolate bits
²/₃ cup crunchy peanut
   butter

Mix first 4 ingredients, then add oatmeal. Put in greased 9x13-inch pan and bake at 350° for no more than 15 minutes (will not look done). Melt chocolate bits and peanut butter. After 10 min-utes, spread on oatmeal for topping.

Cooking with H.E.L.P.

273

Frosted Carrot Bars

4 eggs	1 teaspoon salt
2 cups sugar	1½ cups oil
2 cups flour, sifted	3 cups grated carrots
2 teaspoons baking powder	1½ cups grated coconut
2 teaspoons cinnamon	1½ cups walnuts, chopped

Beat eggs until light. Gradually add sugar. Sift flour, baking powder, cinnamon, and salt. Add flour mixture alternately with oil. Fold in carrots, coconut, and walnuts. Spread in two 13x9x2-inch pans. Bake at 350° for 25-30 minutes. Cool and frost.

CREAM CHEESE FROSTING:

1 (3-ounce) package cream cheese	1 teaspoon vanilla
1 tablespoon light cream	⅛ teaspoon salt
2½ cups confectioners' sugar	

Blend together cream cheese and cream. Add the sugar and more cream, if necessary, to make frosting spreadable. Add vanilla and salt and beat well.

A Hancock Community Collection

Brownie Meringues

1 (6-ounce) package semi-sweet chocolate pieces, melted and slightly cooled	Dash of salt
	½ teaspoon vinegar
	½ teaspoon vanilla
	½ cup sugar
2 egg whites	¾ cup broken walnuts

Preheat oven to 350°. Beat egg whites with salt, vinegar, and vanilla until soft peaks form. Gradually add sugar, beating to stiff peaks. Fold in chocolate and nuts. Drop from teaspoon onto greased cookie sheet. Bake for 8-10 minutes. Makes 3 dozen.

Connecticut Cooks

Connecticut's jagged coastline dotted with coves and inlets was well-suited to the exploits of pirates, including the notorious Captain Kidd. Although locals have their favorite tales of buried treasure, no one has ever really substantiated the stories.

Half-Way-to-Heaven Bars

A brown-sugar meringue crowns these chocolate chip bars, transforming them from the mundane to the ethereal. Perfect for holiday gift-giving.

½ cup (1 stick) butter	2 cups flour
½ cup sugar	¼ teaspoon salt
½ cup brown sugar	¼ teaspoon baking soda
2 egg yolks	1 teaspoon baking powder
1 tablespoon water	1 (12-ounce) package
1 teaspoon vanilla extract	chocolate chips

In large bowl, cream together butter and sugars; add egg yolks, water, and vanilla. Mix well. Mix together flour, salt, baking soda, and baking powder. Add to butter mixture. Preheat oven to 350°. Lightly grease 15-inch jelly roll pan. Pat dough into pan. Sprinkle evenly with chocolate chips.

TOPPING:

2 egg whites	1 cup brown sugar

In small bowl of mixer, beat egg whites until stiff. Gradually beat in brown sugar. Spread mixture over top of chocolate chips. Bake 20-25 minutes. Cool, then cut into bars. Yield: 4½ dozen bars.

All Seasons Cookbook

Ali's Cookies
(Cholesterol Free)

1 cup dates, cut up, or ½ cup each dates and apricots	1 cup confectioners' sugar
1 cup chopped pecans	1 egg white (as is)

Combine all ingredients. Do not beat egg white. Line cookie sheet with parchment. Drop by teaspoonfuls. Bake at 350° for 10 minutes.

Perennials

Spritz Butter Cookies

1 cup butter, softened
1 cup sugar
2 teaspoons vanilla extract, or more

2 eggs, unbeaten
3 cups sifted flour
¼ teaspoon salt

Cream together the butter, sugar, and vanilla. Add the eggs and beat well. Add the flour and salt and mix until well blended. Using a cookie press, press the dough into long strips onto an ungreased baking sheet. Cut the strips into pieces about 1½ inches long. Bake at 375° until golden brown, 10-12 minutes. About one-half minute after removing the baking sheet from the oven, loosen the cookies with a spatula to keep them from sticking to the pan. Cool on wire racks. Makes 4-6 dozen.

As You Like It

Oatmeal Butterscotch Cookies

This recipe is sometimes varied at The Red Lion Inn by using currants in place of the butterscotch bits.

1 cup butter, softened
1½ cups light brown sugar, firmly packed
2 eggs
4 teaspoons water
2 cups flour

2 teaspoons baking powder
1 teaspoon baking soda
1 teaspoon salt
1½ cups rolled oats
2 cups butterscotch bits

Preheat the oven to 350°. Line a baking sheet with lightly oiled parchment paper. Cream the butter and brown sugar together in a bowl, until fluffy. Add the eggs and water, and blend them in well. Beat in the flour, baking powder, baking soda, and salt. Finally, stir in the oats and butterscotch bits.

Drop 1½-inch balls of the dough onto the prepared cookie sheet. Bake at 350° for 8-12 minutes, until golden. Allow the cookies to cool slightly (about 3 minutes) on the baking sheet, then transfer them to a wire rack to cool. Yields 3-4 dozen cookies.

The Red Lion Inn Cookbook

Chocolate Chip Cookies

¾ pound butter
1 cup packed brown sugar
1 egg
1 cup chocolate chips (or carob, butterscotch, or vanilla chips)
½ cup sunflower seeds
½ cup sesame seeds
½ cup walnut pieces

2 teaspoons molasses
¼ cup juice (orange, pineapple) or milk (optional)
2½ cups flour
1 teaspoon baking powder
An ice cream or cookie scoop with a 3-tablespoon capacity

Cool ingredients make a good cookie. Cream the butter with the brown sugar. Add the egg immediately followed by the chips, seeds, nuts, molasses, and juice until well mixed. Stir in the flour with the baking powder and a pinch of salt. Scoop the dough with a 3-table-spoon ice cream scoop and place on a lined or lightly greased pan 4-5 inches apart. Dip your 3 fingers in a glass of cool water and squash the batter flat on the sheet pan to make a flattened ball about 2½ inches in diameter.

Bake for about 20 minutes in an oven at 350°. The finished cookie will be 3½-4 inches in diameter.

If cooked on the lighter side, until the very edges get light brown, the cookies will be very chewy for the remainder of that day. These cookies, however, are more of a short cookie and keep for a month in a tin under cool and dry conditions. If you make this batch of cookies without the egg, you will have a rich, crunchy cookie.

Baba À Louis Bakery Bread Book

The Richest Lunch Box Cookies Ever

Gourmet cookies have become a staple of the eighties. Start making these for friends and neighbors, and you may find yourself becoming the new Mrs. Fields or David. These lunch box gems make wonderful gifts, too—just fill a tin for birthdays, Christmas gifts, or last-day-on-the-job parties.

2 (3½-ounce) bars
  caramel-filled Swiss
  chocolate, such as Lindt
2 ounces bittersweet or
  semi-sweet chocolate
2 ounces white chocolate
1 cup pecan halves
1½ cups regular oatmeal
  (not quick-cooking)

1 cup butter, softened
1½ cups brown sugar,
  lightly packed
½ teaspoon salt
2 teaspoons vanilla
2 eggs
1½ cups flour
½ teaspoon baking powder
½ teaspoon baking soda

Preheat the oven to 350°. Break the caramel bars into natural sections. Cut the sections into small chunks with a sharp knife. (You may chill the bars first if you like—it helps to keep the caramel from oozing out too much as you cut them.) Set the chunks aside. Grate the bittersweet or semi-sweet chocolate and the white chocolate.

Chop the pecans. Place ½ cup of the oatmeal in a blender and blend at high speed until the oatmeal turns to powder. In a large bowl, beat the butter with the sugar, salt, and vanilla until creamy. Add the eggs and beat well. Stir in the flour, powdered oatmeal, remaining oatmeal, baking powder, and baking soda. Add the caramel chunks, both grated chocolates, and the pecans and mix just to combine.

Using 2 spoons or your hands, form balls the size of large walnuts. Place them in rows about 3 inches apart on ungreased cookie sheets. Bake for 10-15 minutes until golden brown. Remove the cookies from the sheet and cool on a rack. When cool, store the cookies in an airtight container. Yield: about 4 dozen cookies.

J. Bildner & Sons Cookbook

Cream Cheese Cut-Out Cookies

1 cup sugar
1 cup (2 sticks) butter,
  softened
1 (3-ounce) package cream
  cheese, softened
¼ teaspoon salt

1 teaspoon vanilla (or half
  almond or lemon) extract
1 egg yolk
2¼ cups flour
Confectioners' Sugar Glaze
Colored sugars (optional)

CONFECTIONERS' SUGAR GLAZE:
1 cup confectioners' sugar
2-3 tablespoons milk

¼ teaspoon extract of
  choice

Cream sugar, butter, cream cheese, salt, extract, and egg yolk until light. Add flour, blending well. Chill dough several hours or overnight. When ready to bake, preheat oven to 375°.

Using a section at a time, roll dough to ⅛ inch on a floured cloth. Cut into desired shapes and bake on ungreased cookie sheets for 7-10 minutes or until light golden. Cool on a rack. Brush with Confectioners' Sugar Glaze and sprinkle with colored sugars if desired. Yield: 3-4 dozen.

Note: Cut-out cookie batter can also be rolled into logs, wrapped, and refrigerated to be sliced when needed. Saves time and fuss when you are not concerned about decorative shapes.

Christmas Memories Cookbook

Chocolate-Glazed Shortbread Cookies

1 cup (2 sticks) butter
1 cup confectioners' sugar
2 cups flour
2 cups almonds or pecans,
  finely chopped

6 ounces semi-sweet
  chocolate

Cream butter and sugar; gradually add flour; stir in half the nuts. Chill dough 1 hour. Preheat oven to 325°.

Form 1 tablespoon dough into a 2-inch-long finger. Cut in half lengthwise and place cut-side-down on ungreased cookie sheet. Bake 15 minutes or until pale golden brown. Cool. Melt chocolate. Dip 1 end of cookie into chocolate then into chopped nuts. Cool on waxed paper until set. Yield: about 5-6 dozen.

Christmas Memories Cookbook

Peanut Butter Squares
(Microwave)

No baking required. Good "Kid" recipe.

1 cup peanut butter	2 sticks (1 cup) margarine
1 cup confectioners' sugar	3 cups graham cracker crumbs

Mix above ingredients in a bowl. Pat into a 9x13-inch pan. Top with the following ingredients, melted together:

1 can condensed milk (not evaporated milk)	1 (12-ounce) package chocolate chips

The milk and chips can be put into microwave oven for 1½ minutes at FULL POWER. Whip quickly and spread over squares quickly. The milk and chips can also be put into a saucepan, on the stove, to melt. Refrigerate for about 1 hour; then cut into squares.

Berkshire Seasonings

Alice's Almond Apricot Cookies

6 tablespoons butter, (not margarine), softened	1¼ cups flour
1 "log" almond paste	½ teaspoon soda
½ cup brown sugar	A capful of vanilla
1 large egg	Dried apricots (about 3 dozen)

Combine all ingredients, except dried apricots, in mixer. Mix well. Place dough on wax paper and refrigerate overnight.

When ready to make cookies, take a tablespoonful of dough and, with fingers, flatten dough and wrap around 1 apricot, sealing the edges. Try to get the best-quality dried apricots possible—during the holidays there are usually good ones available. Continue with the rest of the dough. Place on greased cookie sheet and bake at 350° for 8-10 minutes. Makes approximately 3 dozen cookies.

Hints: Work with the tips of your fingers only. If the dough gets sticky, put a bit of flour on your fingers and only work with a portion of the dough while keeping the rest in the refrigerator.

A Taste of Hallowell

Apricot Nut Snowballs

No-bake and oh, so easy.

6 ounces dried apricots	1 cup chopped nuts
¼ cup apricot jam	1 cup sweetened coconut
1 tablespoon sugar	Confectioners' sugar

Put all ingredients in food processor, except confectioners' sugar, and pulse until a mass is formed. Form balls using a rounded teaspoon and roll in confectioners' sugar. Chill, covered loosely, in refrigerator.

Note: Wet hands with water when rounding cookies.

The Island Cookbook

Illumination Night Apricot Bars

When I first asked Doris MacGillvray for some recipes, she had just made these for Illumination Night and insisted I have one. I admit that after one bite, I gave her no peace until I had the recipe for this collection!

¾ cup butter (at room temperature)	2 cups flour
	1½ cups shredded coconut
1 cup sugar	1 (8-ounce) jar apricot
1 egg	preserves
1½ teaspoons vanilla	1 cup walnuts, chopped
½ teaspoon salt	

Cream butter, sugar, egg, and vanilla until fluffy. Mix in salt, flour, and coconut; stir well. Reserve ¾ cup for topping; spread the rest in a greased 9x11-inch pan. Spread apricot preserves over mixture. Sprinkle nuts over preserves. Dot reserved ¾ cup batter over top. Bake for 30 minutes in preheated 350° oven. Cool slightly and cut into bars. Makes 24.

A Culinary Tour of the Gingerbread Cottages

Amaretto Cheesecake Cookies

1 cup all-purpose flour
1/3 cup brown sugar, packed
6 tablespoons butter, softened
1 (8-ounce) package cream cheese, softened

1/4 cup granulated sugar
1 egg
4 tablespoons amaretto
1/2 teaspoon vanilla
4 tablespoons chopped almonds

In a large mixing bowl, combine flour and brown sugar. Cut in butter until mixture forms fine crumbs. Reserve 1 cup crumb mixture for topping. Press remainder over bottom of ungreased 8-inch-square baking pan. Bake for 12-15 minutes at 350° or until lightly browned.

In mixer bowl, thoroughly cream together cream cheese and granulated sugar. Add egg, amaretto, and vanilla; beat well. Spread batter over partially baked crust. Combine almonds with reserved crumb mixture; sprinkle over batter. Bake for 20-25 minutes. Cool and cut into squares. Yield: 16 cookies.

Dining on Deck

Toffee Crunch

1 package (about 42) saltines
2 sticks (½ pound) butter
1 cup light brown sugar

1 (12-ounce) package chocolate chips, butterscotch chips, or peanut butter chips

Arrange saltines in single layer in bottom of foil-lined 17x14-inch baking sheet or use whatever pan you have that will accommodate the saltines in a single layer. Turn up edges of foil to form a rim.

In large saucepan, combine butter and brown sugar. Bring to a boil and boil gently for 3 minutes. Immediately pour over saltines, making sure all are covered. Bake at 400° for 7 minutes, watching carefully to be sure that mixture doesn't burn. Sprinkle chips evenly over surface as soon as pan is removed from oven. Allow to stand for a few minutes until the chips soften; then spread with a spatula. If desired, finely chopped nuts may be sprinkled over chocolate. Set aside to harden. Break into pieces and store in covered container. Makes 2 quarts of candy pieces.

Visions of Home Cook Book

Truffles

Great for Christmas.

1 (12-ounce) package
  semi-sweet chocolate chips
¾ cup sweetened condensed
  milk

1 teaspoon vanilla
⅛ teaspoon salt
½ cup cocoa or 1 cup
  chopped, flaked coconut

In double boiler over hot, not boiling water, melt chocolate chips. Stir in condensed milk, vanilla, and salt until well mixed. Refrigerate mixture about 45 minutes or until easy to shape. With buttered hands, shape mixture into 1-inch balls. Roll balls in cocoa or coconut. Yields 36 truffles.

Connecticut Cooks III

Almond Butter Crunch

Before starting to make this candy, have all ingredients ready. This candy cooks and cools rapidly.

1 cup chopped, toasted
  almonds
½ cup butter (1 stick) *no*
  substitute

1 cup sugar
2 cups (12-ounce package)
  chocolate bits, melted
Chopped almonds for topping

Lightly toast almonds, blanched or unblanched, in a slow oven, 250°. Cool. Put through medium blade of food chopper. Measure ½ cup of almonds; set aside.

In saucepan, mix butter and sugar. Stir and cook over high heat until mixture melts and becomes a brown liquid; do not burn. Stir constantly. When mixture is liquid and "smokes," it is nearly ready to remove from heat. Add ½ cup chopped almonds. Stir quickly and pour onto buttered marble or cookie sheet; spread to ⅛-inch thickness. Mark in squares. Have ready in double boiler the chocolate which has been melted over warm, not hot, water. Spread chocolate over candy and sprinkle with chopped almonds. Cool until chocolate hardens; with a spatula, flop candy over and repeat with chocolate and nuts. Break candy into pieces when cold. Makes about 1¼ pounds.

Memories from Brownie's Kitchen

Creamy Nutcracker Fudge

Perfect for holidays.

4½ cups sugar
1½ cups half-and-half
¼ cup butter
Dash salt
1 (12-ounce) package
   semi-sweet chocolate pieces

4 (1-ounce) squares
   unsweetened chocolate,
   chopped
1 (7-ounce) jar marshmallow
   cream
1 cup chopped nuts

Combine first 4 ingredients in heavy 3-quart saucepan. Bring to full rolling boil for 6 minutes, stirring frequently. Add chocolate and marshmallow cream. Beat until melted. Add nuts. Pour into buttered 13x9-inch pan. Let stand several hours before cutting. Store in cool place. Makes 4 dozen.

Connecticut Cooks

Peanut Butter Bon Bons

½ cup butter
½ cup peanut butter
2 cups powdered sugar
1 cup graham crackers
¾ cup chopped nuts

½ cup flaked coconut
1½ cups semi-sweet
   chocolate
3 tablespoons Crisco

Melt butter and peanut butter together. Add to dry ingredients. Make 1-inch balls. Melt chocolate and shortening. Dip the balls into melted chocolate and put on waxed paper until hardened.

The Fine Art of Holiday Cooking

Cyclone Candy

1 cup sugar
1 cup molasses
3 tablespoons vinegar

2 tablespoons butter
1 teaspoon vanilla
1¼ teaspoons baking soda

Cook sugar, molasses, vinegar, and butter in a heavy saucepan until it forms a hard ball when tried in cold water. Then add vanilla and soda, and stir well. Pour into a shallow, lightly buttered pan and do not touch or move until cool.

Good Maine Food

Pies and Desserts

Everything's dee-licious at the "Taste of Rhode Island" food festival which takes place every fall in Newport.

Apple Baked Alaska

5 apples, thinly sliced
3 tablespoons sugar
2 teaspoons cornstarch
½ teaspoon each, nutmeg
  and cinnamon

¼ teaspoon salt
1 quart vanilla ice cream,
  softened slightly

Arrange sliced apples in a 9-inch pie plate. Combine sugar, cornstarch, spices, and salt; sprinkle evenly over apples. Cover with aluminum foil; bake at 425° for 30 minutes or until apples are just tender. Remove from oven, cool, and refrigerate.

At serving time, cover with an even layer of ice cream; place in the freezer.

MERINGUE:
3 egg whites   ¼ cup confectioners' sugar
⅛ teaspoon cream of tartar

While ice cream is hardening in the freezer, beat egg whites with cream of tartar until frothy. Gradually add confectioners' sugar, a tablespoon at a time, and continue beating until the mixture stands in peaks.

Spread meringue over the ice cream, making sure to spread it to the rim of the pie plate so that the edges are sealed. Place the pie plate in a roasting pan, and surround the pie plate with ice cubes. Bake at 500° for 3 minutes or until lightly browned. Yield: 8-10 servings.

Note: If time permits, keep the apples covered with ice cream in the freezer until the ice cream is really hardened and the apples are well chilled.

Apple Orchard Cookbook

Bogberry Apple Tart

Great warm with ice cream! (and cold, every time you pass through the kitchen!)

6 apples, peeled and sliced	**½ cup brown sugar**
1½ cups whole cranberries	**½ cup white sugar**
½ cup chopped nuts	**2 eggs**
1 teaspoon cinnamon	**½ teaspoon vanilla**
⅛ teaspoon salt	**½ cup melted butter**
¼ cup sugar	**1 cup flour**

Grease a 9-inch pie pan or 8-inch square pan. Layer apples in pan; alternate cranberries with apples. Sprinkle nuts, cinnamon, salt and ¼ cup sugar over fruit. Mix together sugars, eggs, vanilla, butter, and flour. Pour this mixture over apples and berries, spreading evenly to cover (mixture will run down through the fruit.) Bake in 325° oven for 45 minutes or until knife inserted into the center comes out clean. Serves 4-8.

Savory Cape Cod Recipes & Sketches

Apple-Crumb Pie

Make 1-crust pie shell. Fill with following mixture:

12 apples, peeled and cored;	**¾ cup sugar**
slice with slicer or into 15	**2 tablespoons flour**
pieces	**½ teaspoon cinnamon**
¼ cup lemon juice	

Mix all ingredients, put in pie shell with decorative edge; cover with crumb topping.

CRUMB-ALMOND TOPPING:

½ cup sugar	**6 tablespoons butter**
¾ cup flour	**¾ cup slivered almonds**
½ teaspoon salt	

Blend sugar, flour and salt together, then cut into butter till crumbly. Mix in almonds. Use crumb mixture on apple-filled pie. Bake at 425° for 15 minutes, then at 350° for 30 minutes.

A Taste of Hallowell

Red Inn Apple Pie

This unusual recipe appears to have no crust. However, the custard forms a kind of crust under the apples. It is delicious and so easy to make!

**7 Granny Smith apples, pared
  and thinly sliced**

**Pinch of cinnamon
Pinch of nutmeg**

CUSTARD:
2 eggs
1 cup sugar

½ cup Bisquick
¾ cup milk

CRUMBLE:
1 cup Bisquick
⅓ cup brown sugar
½ cup walnuts

3 tablespoons butter (hard)
Heavy cream

Butter a 10-inch pie plate. Sprinkle the sliced apples with cinnamon and nutmeg and mix together. Place the apples in the pie plate.

Beat together the ingredients for the custard and pour it over the apples. Mix together the ingredients for the crumble and cut in the butter. Sprinkle this over the apples and press down lightly. Bake in a preheated oven at 325° for 1 hour. Serve with whipped cream. Serves 6-8.

A recipe from The Red Inn, Provincetown, MA.

A Taste of Provincetown

Lemon-Rosemary Apple Cobbler

You won't believe how good this is until you try it.

FILLING:

½ teaspoon dried rosemary
  leaves
⅓ cup granulated sugar
2 tablespoons freshly
  squeezed lemon juice

Grated rind of ½ a lemon
1½ pounds apples, peeled,
  cored, and thinly sliced
  (5 cups)

Heat oven to 450°. Have ready a heavy dish, a 9-inch pie plate, or a single-layer cake pan.

Crush the rosemary as fine as possible. Place in a large bowl. Add sugar, lemon juice, and rind. Stir to mix. Add apples, stirring to coat. Arrange in baking dish.

TOPPING:

1 cup all-purpose flour
1 tablespoon granulated
  sugar
1 teaspoon baking powder
⅛ teaspoon salt
½ teaspoon dried rosemary
  leaves, crushed as fine as
  possible

3 tablespoons cold, unsalted
  butter, cut up
⅓ cup light cream or milk

Mix dry ingredients into medium-sized bowl. Add butter and cut in with pastry blender or knives until mixture is the consistency of coarse cornmeal. Add cream or milk and stir until a soft dough forms. Knead on lightly floured surface 10-12 times. Roll to fit baking dish, place over apples, seal edges, and cut slits. Bake 25-30 minutes, until golden. Serve warm with cream. Serves 6.

Vermont Kitchens Revisited

 Vermont sugar maple trees yield their harvest in late winter when the days are warmer, but the nights are still cold. Four maple trees will yield 30-40 gallons of sweet, waterlike sap that boils down to make one gallon of maple syrup.

Brown Betty

Once, overcome with enthusiasm and immodesty, Grandmother labeled this in her notebook "Perfect Brown Betty." Realizing that she was just beginning to be considered a Vermonter (after only 40 years) and not wishing to jeopardize her position, she promptly apologized for her mistake. There are as many rules for Brown Betty in Vermont as there are catamounts (imagined or real) in the Green Mountains. I happen to believe that this one is pretty good, and blush for having again bragged about a family recipe.

2 cups cubed homemade
   bread (no crusts)
2 tablespoons melted butter
3 cups pared and thinly
   sliced apples (4 large
   Macs or 6 medium)
1 cup white sugar

½ teaspoon nutmeg
⅛ teaspoon cloves
¼ teaspoon cinnamon
2 tablespoons butter, in
   small dots
Grated rind and juice of
   1 lemon

Put a layer of cubed bread into a straight-sided, buttered baking dish, either a French soufflé dish or a Swedish enameled iron dish, that will hold 1½-quarts. Mix the apples, sugar, and spices. Cover the bread with a layer of the mixture. Dot with butter, add a little lemon juice and rind. Put in more layers, alternating bread cubes and the apple mixture until the dish is well heaped. Finish with cubed bread. Cover.

Bake at 375° for half an hour. Uncover. Bake until the apples are tender and the crumbs golden brown—about half an hour longer. Serve at once with thick cream or vanilla ice cream. Like a soufflé, it will collapse if allowed to stand. Serves 6.

Mrs. Appleyard's Family Kitchen

 Every year since 1776, on July 4th, the Declaration of Independence is read from the same balcony it was first read from, the Old State House. Built in 1713, it is the oldest public building in Boston. The oldest wooden building in Boston is Paul Revere's House. It was nearly 100 years old when the patriot took his famous midnight ride to warn "every Middlesex village and farm" that the British were coming.

Microwave Fresh Fruit Betty

This is especially delicious in late summer and early fall when these fruits are in season. A combination of apples and peaches is marvelous!

6-7 large apples,
   nectarines, peaches, or
   pears (or combination)
¼ cup raisins
1 tablespoon lemon juice
1½ cups flour
¾ cup light brown sugar,
   firmly packed

1 teaspoon cinnamon
½ teaspoon ginger
   (optional)
⅛ teaspoon mace (optional)
½ cup butter or margarine,
   softened

Peel fruit and remove seeds or pits. Cut into thin slices. Place fruit in a 9-inch pie plate. Sprinkle with raisins and lemon juice. Combine flour, brown sugar, and spices. Add butter or margarine. Blend until well mixed and crumbly. Spread over fruit, patting firmly into place. Cook on HIGH for 10-12 minutes or until fruit is tender, rotating plate a half turn after 5 minutes. Cool for 10 minutes. Serve warm. Top with vanilla ice cream, frozen yogurt, or whipped cream.

Hint: If you don't have a microwave, just bake in a conventional oven at 350° for about 30-40 minutes, or until fruit is tender and top is golden.

From Ellie's Kitchen to Yours

Rhubarb Cheesecake Pie

A nice combination of tastes.

3 cups rhubarb, cut into
  ½-inch pieces
½ cup sugar

1 tablespoon flour
1 (9-inch) unbaked pie shell

CHEESE TOPPING:
2 eggs
1 cup sugar

1 (8-ounce) package cream
  cheese, softened

Toss rhubarb with ½ cup sugar and flour. Add to pie shell. Bake in preheated 425° oven for 15-20 minutes.

Beat eggs with 1 cup sugar and cream cheese until smooth. Pour over rhubarb. Reduce heat to 350° and continue baking for 30 minutes. Cool before serving. Makes 6-8 servings.

Merrymeeting Merry Eating

Rhubarb Pie

A Vermont cookbook would be incomplete without a rule for rhubarb pie. The showing of rhubarb is one of the first true signs of spring. While dirt roads are still making automobiles wallow in mud, and neither daffodils nor apple blossoms have yet shown their beauty, the rhubarb may be spotted in the garden patch. For pie or any other rhubarb concoction, pick the rhubarb when the first stalks come up. By the time its ivory plumes of flowers appear, it will be tough and stringy. Young "strawberry rhubarb" makes the best pie.

For a 9-inch pie, use:

3 cups rhubarb
Pastry for a double crust
2 tablespoons flour
1½ cups sugar
⅛ teaspoon each of
  cinnamon and nutmeg

1 egg, well beaten
2 tablespoons butter cut
  into 12 bits

Use the youngest, tenderest "strawberry rhubarb"—the kind that needs no peeling. Discard leaves and lower ends of stalks and cut into ½-inch pieces.

Line a 9-inch pie tin with pastry. Leave a good margin of pastry to be turned up over the top crust and crimped with a fork so that no juice will run out. I dislike any drippings in the oven, because I resent spending time cleaning it, so I always place a cookie sheet under fruit pies just in case they drip. In my experience, they have never failed to do so.

Sift flour, sugar, and spice together. Scatter ¼ cup of this mixture over the lower crust. Add half of the rhubarb, half of the remaining sugar mixture, then the rest of the rhubarb and the last of the sugar and spice. Heap the rhubarb slightly toward the center of the pie; it will sink while baking.

Pour the beaten egg over the pie and dot it with bits of butter. Set the top crust in place and gash it well so that steam can escape. Bake at 450° for 15 minutes. Reduce the heat to 350° and continue baking until the fruit is tender and the crust is brown and puffed—about 40 minutes longer. If it browns too quickly, cover it with a tent of aluminum foil, but remove the tent during the last 10 minutes of baking. Enjoy the coming of spring!

Mrs. Appleyard's Family Kitchen

Beehives

If peaches happen to be out of season at the time you read this recipe, save it in a very special place for use the next year. We think you will declare it well worth the wait! Prepare this recipe in the cool of the morning, as we do in the inn, and then pop dessert into the oven while you enjoy your dinner.

Make a double recipe of pie crust. Roll into an oblong and cut strips 1-inch wide. Wash and dry 8 extra-large, perfect peaches. They must be *perfect*. Wrap the strips of pie crust around starting from the bottom until the peach is entirely covered. Pat and patch the crust as you go along so there are no holes. Seal the edges. Place "beehives" on a cookie sheet and bake for 40 minutes at 400°. Serve hot with hard sauce.

To eat: Break the "beehive" in half, remove the stone, and spoon a heaping tablespoon of hard sauce into the cavity. The peach skin has disappeared! What an absolutely divine dessert!

8 extra large perfect peaches
HARD SAUCE:
4 tablespoons sweet butter   **1 teaspoon vanilla**
1 unbeaten egg   **Nutmeg**
2 cups powdered sugar

Cream butter. Add egg and mix well. Gradually work in 2 cups or more powdered sugar. The definite amount of sugar you add will depend upon whether you like tight or not-so-tight hard sauce. Flavor with 1 tablespoon brandy. Pile sauce into peach cavity and sprinkle with nutmeg. Serves 8 lucky people.

From the Inn's Kitchen

294

Peacheesy Pie

PEACHES 'N' CHEESECAKE FILLING:

1 (1-pound 13-ounce) can
  peach slices
½ cup sugar
2 tablespoons cornstarch

2 tablespoons corn syrup
2 teaspoons pumpkin pie spice
2 teaspoons vanilla

Drain peaches; save syrup. Mix peaches, sugar, cornstarch, corn syrup, pumpkin pie spice, and vanilla.

CHEESECAKE TOPPING:

2 eggs, slightly beaten
⅓ cup sugar
1 tablespoon lemon juice

1 (3-ounce) package cream
  cheese
½ cup yogurt or sour cream

Combine eggs, ⅓ cup sugar, lemon juice, and 2 tablespoons peach syrup in small saucepan. Cook, stirring constantly until thick. Soften cream cheese; blend in yogurt. Add hot mixture and beat smooth.

CRUST:

⅔ cup shortening
2 cups flour, sifted
1 teaspoon salt

6-7 tablespoons peach syrup
2 tablespoons margarine

Cut shortening into flour and salt until size of peas. Sprinkle peach syrup over mixture, stirring until dough holds together. Roll out and fit into 9-inch pie pan. Fill with peach mixture. Dot with butter. Cover with Cheesecake Topping. Roll out remaining dough. Cut into circles. Brush with peach syrup and arrange on topping. Bake at 425° for 10 minutes, then cover edge with foil. Bake at 350° for 30-35 minutes.

The Parkview Way to Vegetarian Cooking

You can still throw a bale of tea overboard just for the fun of it from the *Beaver II*, an authentic replica of one of the three British brigs moored that historic night, when 342 chests (equalling 90,000 pounds of tea) were dumped into Boston Harbor.

Pumpkin Cheese Pie

1 (1-crust) pastry
1 (8-ounce) package cream
  cheese, softened
¾ cup sugar
2 tablespoons flour
1 teaspoon ground cinnamon
¼ teaspoon ground nutmeg

¼ teaspoon ground ginger
1 teaspoon grated lemon peel
1 teaspoon lemon juice
¼ teaspoon vanilla
3 eggs
1 (16-ounce) can pumpkin

SOUR CREAM TOPPING:
¾ cup sour cream
1 tablespoon sugar

¼ teaspoon vanilla

Heat oven to 350°. Prepare a 1-crust pastry in a pie plate. Beat cream cheese, sugar, and flour in large mixing bowl until blended. Add remaining ingredients, except topping; beat on medium speed until smooth. Pour into pastry-lined pie plate. Bake in oven for about 60 minutes. Remove from oven and immediately spread with the Sour Cream Topping you have mixed together. Cool; refrigerate for about 4 hours.

A Taste of Salt Air & Island Kitchens

Pumpkin Gingersnap Pie

1½ cups milk or
  half-and-half
1 package instant vanilla
  pudding
3½ cups Cool Whip
½ cup canned pumpkin

1 cup chopped pecans
1 cup crushed gingersnaps
1½ tablespoons pumpkin
  pie spice
1 (9-inch) graham cracker
  pie crust

Beat chilled half-and-half and instant pudding in a large bowl for 1 minute. Let stand 5 minutes. Fold in topping and remaining ingredients. Spoon into pie crust. Freeze until firm. Let stand at room temperature for 10 minutes before serving. Stores well in freezer.

Recipes from Smith-Appleby House

The American country inn is one of the oldest continuing institutions in our country. Town records from the mid-17th century indicate that many communities were required by law to provide some type of accommodations and provender for travelers.

Old-Fashioned Blueberry Pie

This is really superb. The recipe can be used for many other fruits as well.

1 baked (9-inch) pie shell
1 generous quart fresh
   blueberries
1 cup sugar
3 tablespoons cornstarch

¼ teaspoon salt
¼ cup water
1 tablespoon margarine
Whipped cream

Wash and sort berries. Measure 1½ cups of the softer berries into a saucepan and crush slightly. Add sugar, cornstarch, salt, and water and cool until thickened—about 3 minutes. Add margarine. Cool slightly. Pour the uncooked berries into the pie shell, then spread the cooked berries on top. Refrigerate 3-4 hours. Serve with whipped cream. Serves 6-8.

Variation: If using other berries, crush them well. Do not add water. Use less sugar for strawberries and raspberries, more for blackberries.

The Lymes' Heritage Cookbook

New England Blueberry Pie

3½ cups blueberries
¾ cup sugar
⅛ teaspoon salt
¼ teaspoon cinnamon

3 tablespoons flour
Butter
Pastry crust for a 2-crust
   (9-inch) pie

Mix blueberries and all other ingredients (except butter) in a large bowl. Line a shallow pie plate with crust. Pour in berry mixture. Dot with 5-6 small pieces of butter. Moisten edge of crust with water.

Roll top crust to fit plate. Spread lightly with shortening and sprinkle with flour. Fold over and cut 3 or 4 small slits on the fold. Place over berries. Unfold and press down around the edge. Trim crust close to the edge of the plate and press again around the edge with floured tines of a fork. Hold pie over sink and pour about ¼ cup milk over crust, letting surplus drain off. Bake at 475° for 15 minutes. Reduce heat to 350° for 15 minutes longer. If frozen berries are used, increase last baking time to 30 minutes.

Homespun Cookery

Blackberry Pie

Pastry (for single crust
pie)
1 (4-ounce) container
whipped cream cheese
1/8 cup sugar
1/8 cup sour cream
5 cups fresh blackberries

1 cup sugar (more or less,
depending on sweetness of
berries)
3 tablespoons cornstarch
1 tablespoons lemon juice
Whipped cream

Cook pie shell and cool. Combine next 3 ingredients and spread in
bottom of cooked pie shell. Arrange 1 cup of blackberries on the
cream cheese mixture. Combine remaining berries and sugar in
saucepan and mash and cook. Add the cornstarch and lemon juice.
Cook until very thick. Pour into pie shell. Chill to set. Top with
whipped cream.

A Taste of Salt Air & Island Kitchens

Chocolate Roulade with Raspberries

6 ounces unsweetened
chocolate
5 eggs
6 ounces fine sugar

3 tablespoons hot water
Powdered sugar
1 cup heavy cream
½ pint fresh raspberries

Preheat oven to 350°. Break chocolate into a small bowl and place
over hot water to melt. Stir occasionally until melted. Separate
eggs, placing yolks into a large bowl, and the whites into a smaller
bowl. Add sugar to yolks and beat until pale in color. Add the hot
water to the melted chocolate. Stir thoroughly and add to egg yolk
mixture. Whisk egg whites until stiff and fold gently through the
chocolate mixture. Pour into a greased and lined jelly roll pan.
Bake for 15 minutes.

Cover with a sheet of parchment paper and a damp cloth. Leave
overnight. Turn roulade onto a sheet of paper dusted well with
powdered sugar. Peel away parchment paper. Spread with whipped
cream and raspberries. Roll up like a jelly roll using sugared paper
to help. Chill for several hours. To serve, dust with more powdered sugar and slice on the diagonal with a sharp knife. Yield: 8
portions.

Hospitality

Cranberry-Glazed Cheese Pie

CRUST:

1½ cups graham cracker or
   cookie crumbs

3 tablespoons sugar
⅓ cup butter, melted

Combine crumbs, sugar, and butter; mix well. Press into a 9-inch pie plate. Bake at 350° for 10 minutes. Cool.

FILLING:

1 (3-ounce) package lemon
   gelatin
1¼ cups boiling water
1 (8-ounce) package cream
   cheese, softened

1½ cups grated apple
1 tablespoon sugar

Dissolve gelatin in boiling water; add cream cheese and blend until well mixed. Refrigerate until slightly jelled. Beat again. Mix grated apple with sugar; add to gelatin mixture, blend, and pour into prepared crust. Chill.

TOPPING:

2 teaspoons cornstarch
1 tablespoon sugar
½ cup cranberry or
   cranapple juice

1 apple, thinly sliced

Mix cornstarch and sugar; add juice and heat, stirring until thickened. Add apple slices and cook until soft. Arrange slices on top of pie, pouring any remaining juice mixture over. Chill. Yield: 1 (9-inch) pie.

Apple Orchard Cookbook

Strawberries Brulée

1 (8-ounce) package cream
  cheese, softened
1½ cups dairy sour cream
6 tablespoons granulated
  sugar

2 pints fresh strawberries,
  hulled, sliced, and
  sweetened to taste
1 cup packed brown sugar

Beat cream cheese until fluffy. Add sour cream and granulated sugar, blending thoroughly. Arrange berries in a 9x12-inch glass baking dish. Spoon cream cheese mixture over berries. Bake in a 300° oven for 10 minutes—remove and sprinkle with brown sugar. Place on lowest broiler rack, broiling until sugar bubbles and browns lightly (about 5 minutes). Serve at once. Makes 6-8 servings.

Great Island Cook Book

Acorn Squash Holiday Pie

2 cups steamed acorn squash
  (approximately 1¾ pounds)
¼ cup sugar, honey, or
  maple syrup
2 eggs, slightly beaten
½ teaspoon salt
¾ cup heavy cream

¾ cup light cream
2 tablespoons butter, melted
¼ teaspoon ginger
1 teaspoon cinnamon
½ teaspoon nutmeg
1 jigger brandy
1 (10-inch) unbaked pie crust

Cut the acorn squash into quarters. Scoop out the seeds and retain. *Steam the squash until soft (20 minutes). Cool the squash in a cold water bath, then scoop the meat off the skin. Combine all of the ingredients in a food processor and whip until frothy. Pour into the pie crust. Place in a 400° oven, reducing the heat to 350°. Bake until a knife inserted in the center comes out clean (45 minutes.) Cool and serve with whipped cream.

The Chef's Treat: Place the squash seeds on a metal pan (clean off large pieces of pulp but leave some on the seeds). Place several pats (⅓ tablespoon) of butter or margarine on the seeds. Roast in a 350° oven, turning frequently. Remove from oven when golden brown and spread on a paper towel to drain. Salt lightly.

The Fine Art of Holiday Cooking

Mocha Macaroon Pie

5 egg whites
1 cup minus 2 tablespoons
  sugar
1 teaspoon vanilla
2 teaspoons instant coffee
½ teaspoon almond extract

6 ounces grated unsweetened
  chocolate
1 cup graham cracker crumbs
¼ cup coconut
1 teaspoon baking powder

Whip egg whites at high speed until it forms soft peaks. Add sugar, vanilla, coffee, and almond extract and whip to stiff peaks. Fold in gently by hand the chocolate, cracker crumbs, coconut, and baking powder. Pour into a greased and floured 9-inch springform pan and bake at 350° 30-35 minutes.

TOPPING:
1½ cups heavy cream
¼ cup confectioners' sugar
1 tablespoon instant coffee

1 teaspoon vanilla
½ teaspoon almond extract

Combine ingredients and whip until stiff. Spread topping over chilled pie.

2 tablespoons grated
  chocolate

2 tablespoons toasted coconut

Sprinkle grated chocolate and coconut over topping. Serves 8-10.

Peter Christian's Recipes

Lemon Lush

Great anytime, but especially in summer. Pistachio or chocolate pudding may be substituted.

FIRST LAYER:

¾ cup butter or margarine
1½ cups all-purpose flour

1½ cups chopped nuts

Blend butter and flour well and add nuts. Spread in bottom of a 13x9x2-inch pan. Bake at 350° for 20 minutes; cool and set aside.

SECOND LAYER:

1 cup confectioners' sugar
1 (8-ounce) package cream
  cheese, softened

1 cup whipped topping (use
  only 1 cup from 12-ounce
  container, reserve rest)

Mix all well; spread over cooled first layer.

THIRD LAYER:

2 (3¾-ounce) packages
  lemon-flavor instant
  pudding mix

3 cups milk
Chopped nuts

Beat pudding with milk for 2 minutes or until thickened. Pour over second layer and top with remaining whipped topping. Garnish with nuts and refrigerate. May be made a day ahead. Serves 10-12.

Connecticut Cooks III

Quick Eggnog Pie

1 envelope unflavored
  gelatin
3 tablespoons cold water
2 cups commercially prepared
  eggnog
1 cup heavy cream, whipped
¼ cup sugar

¼ teaspoon salt
2 teaspoons vanilla or rum
  flavoring
1 (9-inch) graham cracker
  pie shell

Soften gelatin in cold water. Warm eggnog over direct low heat. Stir in softened gelatin and continue heating until completely dissolved. Chill until partially set, then beat until smooth. Into stiffly whipped cream, beat sugar, salt, and flavoring. Fold into eggnog mixture. Pour into pie shell. Chill 2-4 hours. Garnish with nutmeg.

A Hancock Community Collection

Lime Pie in Meringue Crust

A light, airy, and tart dessert. The meringue crust and lime custard are a heavenly combination. Allow for seconds, or at least be prepared to allow your guests to lick the pie plate.

5 egg whites, at room
   temperature
¼ teaspoon cream of tartar
¾ cup sugar
5 egg yolks
⅛ teaspoon salt
⅓ cup sugar

⅓ cup freshly squeezed
   lime juice
2 tablespoons grated lime
   peel
2 cups whipping cream,
   divided in half
Lime slices for garnish

Preheat the oven to 275°. Grease a 10-inch pie plate and set it aside. In a large bowl, beat the egg whites with the cream of tartar until soft peaks form. Slowly add ¾ cup sugar, a little at a time, beating until stiff and glossy.

Spoon the meringue into the prepared pie plate, mounding it up the sides and over the edge. Bake 1 hour and cool at room temperature.

To prepare the filling: beat the egg yolks and salt in a medium-size bowl until fluffy. Whisk in ⅓ cup sugar, lime juice, and peel, and place the mixture in the top of a double boiler over boiling water. Whisk constantly until thick and smooth, about 10 minutes. Remove from the heat and let cool.

Beat 1 cup of the cream until stiff. Fold this into the cooled lime custard and pour into the cooled meringue shell. Refrigerate the pie at least 4 hours. Serve garnished with the additional cup of cream, whipped, and lime slices. Serves 8.

Tony Clark's New Blueberry Hill Cookbook

French Silk Pie

This is our favorite Saturday night dessert. So you jog that extra mile; it's worth it!

3 egg whites, room temperature	1 cup butter, room temperature
Pinch of salt	4 eggs
¼ teaspoon cream of tartar	1½ cups sugar
½ teaspoon vanilla	2 teaspoons vanilla
¾ cup sugar	1 cup heavy cream
⅓ cup finely chopped walnuts	1 tablespoon crème de cacao
2 ounces unsweetened chocolate	Semi-sweet chocolate shavings for garnish

Preheat oven to 275°.

Beat egg whites with salt, cream of tartar, and vanilla until just fluffy, then gradually add the sugar. Beat until meringue is light and firm. Spread into an ungreased 9-inch pie pan. Using a small rubber spatula, build a free-form rim of meringue at least ½-inch higher than rim of pie pan; it should resemble a mountain panorama, with some peaks here and there. Sprinkle rim and bottom with walnuts. Bake meringue for 1 hour, then turn off heat but leave meringue in the oven to cool and dry.

Make the filling. Melt 2 ounces chocolate in a small double boiler. Briefly beat the softened butter in the food processor. Add the eggs, sugar, vanilla, and melted chocolate and process for 15 minutes (color will change from a light to a dark brown). Empty filling into a bowl, cover, and chill for at least 4 hours to set.

An hour before serving, fill the meringue shell with the now firm chocolate cream. Whip the heavy cream with the crème de cacao and spread over the pie. Sprinkle with chocolate shavings and serve. Serves 8.

Recipes from a New England Inn

Chocolate Marquise

This is a light creamy chocolate terrine served on a white chocolate custard sauce.

TERRINE:

½ cup dried apricots, chopped
⅔ cup Armagnac, Cognac, or Cointreau liqueur
24 ounces bittersweet chocolate, chopped
1 cup butter, room temperature
1½ cups powdered sugar
10 eggs, separated
½ teaspoon cream of tartar

Combine apricots and liqueur. Set aside to steep for 30 minutes. Melt chocolate over a double boiler, then cool until it is lukewarm. In a mixing bowl, beat butter and sugar until light and fluffy. Mix melted chocolate into the butter/sugar mixture by hand. Blend egg yolks into the chocolate mixture, 1 at a time, by hand. In a separate bowl beat egg whites with cream of tartar until they form soft peaks. Fold ⅓ of the egg whites into the chocolate mixture to lighten it, then fold in the rest of the egg whites. Pour this mixture into 2 small loaf pans lined with Saran Wrap and refrigerate overnight.

SAUCE:

¼ cup butter, at room temperature
1 cup sugar
3 eggs
1 cup milk
1 teaspoon vanilla extract
8 ounces white chocolate, chopped fine

Beat butter and sugar in a mixing bowl until light and fluffy. Beat in eggs 1 at a time. In a small saucepan, bring milk and vanilla extract to a boil. Whisk hot milk into butter-egg mixture. Immediately whisk in chopped chocolate while sauce is hot. Continue to whisk until sauce is smooth. Let sauce cool and then refrigerate.

Serve 2 thin slices of chocolate terrine per person on a puddle of white chocolate custard sauce.

A recipe from Audrey's, Seekonk, MA.

A Taste of Providence

Rhode Island's nickname is the Ocean State. The smallest state in the U.S., it is only 48 miles north to south and 37 miles east to west. However, because of its numerous bays, inlets, and islands, it has over 400 miles of coastline.

Carob Cream Pie

½ cup raw cashews
2 cups boiling water
20 pitted dates
2 tablespoons carob powder
1 teaspoon vanilla

½ teaspoon salt
¼ cup cold water
¼ cup cornstarch
1 or 2 bananas
1 baked pie shell

Grind cashews until powdered into a fine meal. Blend cashew meal and boiling water until smooth, then add dates, vanilla, carob powder, and salt. Pour into saucepan; bring to a boil, stirring constantly to prevent scorching. Combine cold water and cornstarch in small cup or bowl. Pour slowly into hot mixture, stirring vigorously to distribute quickly and evenly. As mixture begins to thicken, stir gently to prevent scorching. Cook 1 minute until thick.

Slice bananas lengthwise into baked pie shell. Cover bottom of crust with banana slices. Pour filling into pie shell. Cool 15-20 minutes. Garnish with sliced bananas. Cool 1 hour at room temperature, then refrigerate at least 3 hours before serving.

Variation: This could be used as a custard or chocolate-like pudding served in a parfait glass.

The Parkview Way to Vegetarian Cooking

Boston Cream Pie

Boston Cream Pie isn't a pastry at all, and is here purely because of its name.

1/3 cup butter	2 teaspoons baking powder
1 cup sugar	1½ cups King Arthur Un-
2 eggs, separated	bleached All-Purpose Flour
½ teaspoon salt	½ cup milk
½ teaspoon vanilla	1 recipe chocolate frosting

Preheat your oven to 375°. Cream the butter; add the sugar and cream until light. Add the egg yolks and beat until fluffy. Stir in the salt and the vanilla.

Combine the baking powder with the flour and add this to the batter alternately with the milk. Stir only as much as is necessary to blend the ingredients. Beat the egg whites until they are stiff and fold them into the batter.

Pour the batter into 2 greased, 8-inch cake pans. Bake for 30 minutes. While the batter bakes, prepare the filling.

CREAM FILLING:

1/3-½ cup King Arthur Un-	2 cups milk
bleached All-Purpose Flour	2 eggs
2/3 cup sugar	1 teaspoon vanilla
1/8 teaspoon salt	

Combine the flour, sugar and salt. Scald the milk and pour it over the dry ingredients gradually. Cook until it has thickened.

Beat the eggs slightly and add them to the hot, thickened custard. Allow the custard to remain heating for 1 minute. Cool and add the vanilla flavoring.

When the cake layers are cool, put the cooled cream filling between them and top with your choice of chocolate frosting.

The King Arthur Flour 200th Anniversary Cookbook

Paul Revere supplied the copper for the dome of the "new" State House, built in 1775 in Boston, Massachusetts, on land owned and used as a cow pasture by John Hancock. The Sacred Cod, a reminder of the importance of the fishing industry, still hangs in the House Gallery. (It was "codnapped" briefly in 1933, but quickly returned.)

Chocolate Pecan Pie

2 squares chocolate
2 tablespoons butter
3 eggs, beaten
½ cup sugar

¾ cup dark corn syrup
¾ cup pecan halves
1 (9-inch) unbaked pie shell

Melt chocolate and butter together. Add beaten eggs, sugar, and syrup. Mix in pecan halves. Pour into pie shell. Bake at 375° for 40-50 minutes until set. Serve warm or cold with whipped cream or ice cream.

Great Island Cook Book

Moody's Walnut Pie

¾ cup melted oleo
1½ cups sugar
9 eggs
3 heaping tablespoons flour
¾ teaspoon salt

1½ teaspoons vanilla
2½ cups dark corn syrup
2 cups milk
2 cups chopped walnuts
2 (9-inch) pie shells, uncooked

In large bowl, beat together melted oleo, sugar, eggs, flour, salt, vanilla, and corn syrup. Beat well and stir in milk. Spread nuts in each uncooked, 9-inch pie shell. Pour batter over nuts. Bake 30-40 minutes at 350°.

What's Cooking at Moody's Diner

Charlotte au Chocolat

*This is our house dessert which we have been serving since we opened.
It continues to rank among our most popular desserts.*

1 (8-ounce) package
   semi-sweet chocolate
	½ pound sweet butter,
	   softened

1 cup sugar	2 tablespoons liqueur of
½ cup brewed coffee, hot	your choice, if desired
4 eggs, beaten	

Grate chocolate. Add sugar and ½ cup brewed coffee. Add the
butter and eggs and mix together well. Add 2 tablespoons of liqueur if desired, and mix again.

    Place double-folded heavy-duty aluminum foil in an 8-10 cup
charlotte mold or soufflé pan. Pour in batter. Cook at 350° for 45
minutes to 1 hour. Chill. Portion out into approximately 8 equal
servings and cover with piped whipped cream or crème Chantilly.
Add candied violets as a garnish.

A recipe from Upstairs At The Pudding, Cambridge, MA.

A Taste of Boston

Angel Food Delight

1 tablespoon plain gelatin	Juice of 1 lemon
3 tablespoons cold water	1 cup sugar
1 cup boiling water	½ pint cream, whipped
1 cup orange juice	1 large angel cake

Dissolve the gelatin in the cold water, add to the cup of boiling
water, and dissolve thoroughly. Mix together the orange and lemon
juice with the sugar and add to the gelatin mixture. Let cool. Fold
in the whipped cream. Break the angel cake in pieces. Put a layer
of cake in bottom of pan and cover with gelatin mixture, another
layer of cake etc., using last a layer of gelatin mixture. Do not press
down. Let stand at least 48 hours in refrigerator. Serve with whipped
cream and a cherry. A good dish to use for this is a square Pyrex
dish. Will serve 9.

Maine's Jubilee Cookbook

On July 11, 1992, the world's glorious Tall Ships sailed into Boston Harbor,
launching a six-day celebration. Viewed by seven million people, "Sail Boston"
was the largest single event in Boston history.

Baked Indian Pudding

The fame of the Durgin-Park Indian pudding is worldwide. Long before Durgin, Park, and Chandler took over the restaurant, the pudding made according to this recipe was taken to sea by clippership captains who were restaurant patrons. It was made by chefs in ships' galleys from Valparaiso to Hong Kong. The secret of its excellence lies in its slow and careful cooking.

1 cup yellow granulated corn meal	¼ teaspoon each salt and baking soda
½ cup black molasses	2 eggs
¼ cup granulated sugar	1½ quarts hot milk
¼ cup of lard or butter	

Mix all the ingredients thoroughly with ½ of the hot milk and pour into a stone crock, well greased inside. Bake in a very hot oven until the milk boils. Then stir in the remaining ½ of hot milk, and return to a slow oven to bake for 5-7 hours. Serve hot with whipped cream or ice cream.

A recipe from Durgin-Park, Boston, MA.

A Taste of Boston

Indian Pudding II

This is an old-fashioned dessert which does not resemble what passes for Indian Pudding in some restaurants. It is moist and light and calls for second helpings.

4 cups milk	½ cup sugar
3 tablespoons yellow cornmeal	1 whole beaten egg
1/3 cup molasses	Butter (size of a walnut)
2 teaspoons salt	½ teaspoon powdered ginger
	½ teaspoon cinnamon

Scald 3 cups milk and stir the cornmeal in slowly. Add molasses and salt and stir until thickened. Remove from the heat and add sugar, egg, butter, ginger, and cinnamon. Pour into a buttered baking dish and place in a 300° oven. After 30 minutes pour 1 cup of milk over pudding and bake for 2½ hours. Serve with rich cream or vanilla ice cream.

Stillmeadow Cook Book

Indian Pudding

This rule was weaseled out of a cook from a small Vermont inn not far from the Connecticut River. It was the best Indian pudding Mr. and Mrs. Appleyard had ever tasted. The difference from other rules is that the cornmeal has already been cooked in the form of johnny cake.

**Square of cold johnny cake
(6-8 inches) (Spider Corn
Cake can be used)
1 quart milk
½ cup molasses**

**½ teaspoon salt
½ teaspoon nutmeg
½ teaspoon cinnamon
2 eggs**

Crumble johnny cake very fine. Pour milk over it and soak it well. Add molasses and seasonings, mix well, and let stand on back of stove for a while. Beat 2 eggs and add them. Taste it and add more molasses if you like. Put mixture into a buttered baking dish and bake it for 1½ hours at 350°. Stir it 3 times the first hour, slipping the spoon in at the side and taking care not to break the skin.

Serve the pudding with thick cream and powdered maple sugar or vanilla ice cream. As a variation you might like to add ½ cup raisins before you bake the pudding.

Mrs. Appleyard's Family Kitchen

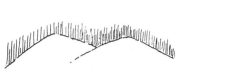

Native Americans probably taught the Pilgrims at Plymouth how to make a type of griddle cake from stone-ground cornmeal which the Indians called "jonakin." New Englanders still make this regional specialty 350 years later—johnnycakes! And the unequivocal ingredient in any variation is still stone-ground cornmeal.
—*All Seasons Cookbook* from the Mystic Seaport

Paradise Pudding

1 (8-ounce) graham cracker crust	1 (20-ounce) can crushed pineapple, well drained
1 cup heavy or whipping cream	¼ cup currant jelly

About 3 hours before serving, have crust ready. In a bowl, with electric mixer at high speed, whip cream. Fold in pineapple.

Spoon half the mixture into the crust. Top with jelly. Repeat, covering last layer with a sprinkling of crushed graham crackers. Freeze until firm.

Berkshire Seasonings

Cranberry Pudding

This is a family favorite. A wonderful combination of sweet and tart.

1½ tablespoons butter	1½ teaspoons baking powder
1 cup sugar	
½ cup milk	2 cups raw cranberries
1 cup flour	

Preheat oven to 375°.

Cream the butter and sugar. Add the milk, flour, and baking powder. Add the cranberries. Pour into buttered and floured dish. Bake at 375° for 30 minutes. Serve with vanilla sauce.

VANILLA SAUCE:

1 stick butter	A little vanilla
1 cup sugar	½ cup cream

Combine all ingredients except cream in the top of a double boiler until sugar is melted. Add cream and stir. Serve warm over cranberry pudding. Serves 6.

The Maine Collection

Blueberry Pudding

2 cups blueberries
Juice of ½ lemon
½ teaspoon cinnamon
1 cup flour
¾ cup sugar
1 tablespoon baking powder

½ teaspoon salt
½ cup milk
3 tablespoons margarine
1 cup sugar
1 tablespoon cornstarch

Grease a 9x9-inch pan. Pour blueberries in pan. Sprinkle with lemon juice and cinnamon. Mix flour, ¾ cup sugar, powder, salt, milk, and margarine; pour over berries. Mix 1 cup sugar, cornstarch, and dash of salt; pour over dough. Pour 1 cup boiling water over all and bake at 375° for 45 minutes.

The Parkview Way to Vegetarian Cooking

Vanilla Bread Pudding with Butter Rum Sauce

6 eggs
2 cups milk
½ pound sugar
2 teaspoons ground cinnamon
½ cup raisins

2 teaspoons vanilla extract
1 loaf French bread,
 approximately
½ cup walnuts
½ cup brown sugar

In a large bowl, mix together the eggs, milk, sugar, cinnamon, raisins, and vanilla. Cut up enough French bread in small cubes to absorb the mixture. Pour mixture into a greased deep baking pan and top with ½ cup walnuts and ½ cup brown sugar. Bake in oven for 45 minutes at 350°.

BUTTER RUM SAUCE:
½ cup melted butter
¾ cup powdered sugar

¼ cup Meyer's rum

Combine all ingredients and cook over medium heat for 15 minutes.

To serve: Cut bread pudding into squares and serve warm topped with heated rum sauce.

A recipe from Muriel's Restaurant, Newport, R.I.

A Taste of Newport

Ginger Poached Pears

6 ripe firm pears
1 cup water
1 cup sugar
2½ teaspoons lemon juice
Pinch of salt

1 teaspoon vanilla
4 or 5 pieces preserved or
candied ginger, cut in
slivers

Peel the pears but leave the stems on. In a saucepan, combine remaining ingredients except ginger and bring to a boil. Add the pears and simmer, covered, for about 25 minutes, or until tender. If the pears are large, cook 3 at a time in the syrup. Put the pears in a shallow serving dish, pour the syrup over, and lay the ginger in a star-shaped design in the center so there will be a sliver or two for each serving. Chill and serve cold. Serves 6.

Stillmeadow Cook Book

Brandied Peach Ice

This masterpiece was created by the Executive Chef of a very famous hotel, who refused to give the recipe to even his best friends. We enjoyed it so many times that we were finally able to reconstruct it well enough that nobody (including the Executive Chef) could tell the difference between ours and the original.

2 cups ripe, peeled, and
chopped peaches
1 cup sugar
2 tablespoons brandy,
divided

2 cups light cream
2 teaspoons unflavored
gelatin
¼ cup cold water
1 cup heavy cream, whipped

Mix the peaches and sugar and let stand for 30 minutes. Force the mixture through a sieve, add 1 tablespoon brandy, and stir in the 2 cups light cream.

Sprinkle the 2 teaspoons gelatin over the ¼ cup cold water. Dissolve over hot water. Stir into the peaches and cream mixture. Pour into covered molds or refrigerator trays covered with foil and place in the freezer. While still soft, beat twice in half-hour intervals to reduce the size of the crystals. Whip the heavy cream, add the remaining tablespoon brandy, and fold the whipped cream into the ice after the last beating. Return to the freezer.

Remove from the freezer about 20 minutes before serving. Beat once more and pile into 8 champagne glasses. Serves 8.

The Country Innkeepers' Cookbook

Lemon Snow with Grand Marnier Sauce

LEMON SNOW:

^{2}/$_3$ cup sugar
1 envelope gelatin
1½ cups boiling water
^{1}/$_3$ cup fresh lemon juice

½ tablespoon finely grated
    lemon peel
3 egg whites

Combine sugar and gelatin in a large bowl. Add boiling water, stirring until gelatin dissolves. Stir in lemon juice and lemon peel. Chill mixture until syrupy. (Set bowl in a larger bowl partly filled with ice.) Beat egg whites until stiff. Add the syrup mixture, beating until it thickens slightly, approximately 5 minutes. Pour into a serving dish and chill at least 2 hours.

SAUCE:

3 egg yolks
¼ cup sugar
^{1}/$_3$ cup butter, melted
3 tablespoons fresh lemon
    juice

3 tablespoons Grand Marnier
½ cup heavy cream
½-1 teaspoon finely grated
    lemon zest

Beat egg yolks until thick and light colored. Gradually beat in sugar, butter, lemon juice, and Grand Marnier. Beat cream until thick and glossy, but not stiff. Fold into egg mixture along with lemon peel. Chill 3 hours.

To serve, decorate lemon snow with mint leaves and pass Grand Marnier sauce in a separate bowl. Yield: 6 portions.

Hospitality

Warm Bananas Kahlua

1 ounce light brown sugar
1 ounce table sugar
6 large bananas

4 ounces Kahlua liqueur
2 ounces butter

Caramelize sugars in a hot, dry sauté pan, being careful not to burn the sugar. Add sliced bananas, Kahlua, and butter. Remove pan from burner (butter and Kahlua should not cook). This is excellent served directly, or over ice cream.

A recipe from The Chatham Squire, Chatham, MA.

Cape Cod's Night at the Chef's Table

Sizzle

This was a favorite dessert served in my grandmother's house when I was a girl. This is just as the recipe was given to me.

1 large teacup thick, dark
  molasses (West Indies,
  unsulphured)
A piece of butter, size of
  an egg

12 slices very thin bread,
  crust cut off
Pitcher of cold heavy cream

Melt butter in spider (skillet) over medium heat. Add molasses and bring to a boil. Put in 3 or 4 slices of bread and let them "sizzle" for about 2 minutes. Remove slices 1 at a time with a spatula and place on a sheet of waxed paper. Put more bread slices in spider and while they are "sizzling," the first pieces will be cool enough to handle and form into rolls. Place the rolls on a lightly buttered serving plate. Cool in icebox. Makes 12 rolls.

Serve with a pitcher of heavy cream. As they are very rich, usually 1 roll per person will suffice. But 2 (or more) per serving have been enjoyed by young people with healthy appetites.

The Fine Arts Cookbook I

A windjammer is a large, fast, merchant sailing vessel. Some are pure sailing vessels with no inboard engines; wind and tide set the schedule for their cruises. In New England, the word windjammer is virtually synonymous with the fleet that carries passengers on sailing vacations.

Index

The old whaling seaport museum on the Mystic River offers a nostalgic visit back into the 19th century. Mystic, Connecticut.

INDEX

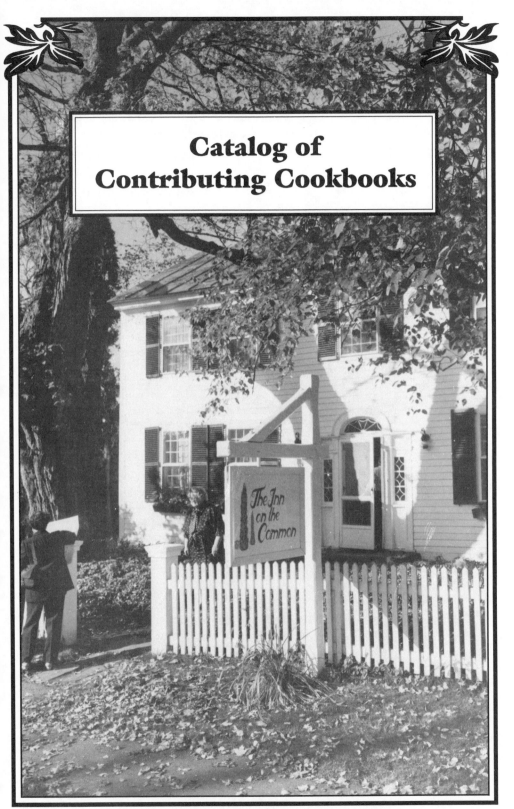

Catalog of
Contributing Cookbooks

One of the many charming country inns of New England.
Craftsbury Common, Vermont.

CATALOG OF CONTRIBUTING COOKBOOKS

All recipes in this book have been submitted from the New England cookbooks shown on the following pages. Individuals who wish to obtain a copy of any particular book may do so by sending a check or money order to the address listed. Prices are subject to change. Please note the postage and handling charges that are required. State residents add tax only when requested. Retailers are invited to call or write to same address for discount information.

ALL-MAINE COOKING
Edited by Ruth Wiggin and Loana Shibles
Down East Books
P.O. Box 679
Camden, ME 04843   207-594-9544

Contributed by people throughout the state, from celebrities to "just plain folks," these recipes are classic New England cooking. Paperback, 192 pages, index.

$ 7.95 Retail price
$ .44 Tax for Maine residents
$ 4.50 Postage and handling
Make check payable to Down East Books
ISBN 0-89272-095-6

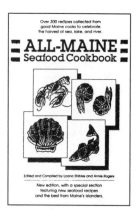

ALL-MAINE SEAFOOD COOKBOOK
Edited by Loana Shibles and Annie Rogers
Down East Books
P.O. Box 679
Camden, ME 04843   207-594-9544

Our most popular cookbook features more than 300 recipes collected from all across the state, including the Maine islands. Maine is justly famous for its seafood, so it is no wonder that for over a decade *All Maine Seafood* has been a classic. Now in its 15th printing. Paperback, 200 pages, black and white photographs, index.

$ 7.95 Retail price
$ .44 Tax for Maine residents
$ 4.50 Postage and handling
Make check payable to Down East Books
ISBN 0-89272-229-0

ALL SEASONS COOKBOOK

by Connie Colom
Mystic Seaport Stores
47 Greenmanville Ave.
Mystic, CT 06355   800-331-2665

Compiled from recipes in the private files of Mystic Seaport Museum members, this exciting cookbook offers the traditional as well as the new and unusual ideas for entertaining throughout the year. Illustrated by Sally Caldwell Fisher, the cookbook is filled with tips, culinary lore, and a treasure of recipes pertaining to each season. Spiral bound, 9¼x9.

$ 14.95 Retail price
$ .90 Tax for Connecticut residents
$ 4.95 Postage and handling
Make check payable to Mystic Seaport Stores
ISBN 0-939510-06-5

ANOTHER BLUE STRAWBERY

by James Haller
The Harvard Common Press
535 Albany Street
Boston, MA 02118   617-423-5803

The great spoon wizard James Haller is back again, stirring up the New American Cuisine with the inimitable exuberance that has become the hallmark of the famous Blue Strawbery restaurant. Haller's latest culinary brainstorms are taking the country by storm, and the cooks who use it should beware—their kitchen styles may never again be the same. Paper. 176 pages.

$ 14.95 Retail price (Hardcover only)
$ .75 Tax for Massachusetts residents
$ 4.00 Postage and handling
Make check payable to The Harvard Common Press
ISBN 0-916782-46-8

APPLE ORCHARD COOKBOOK

by Janet M. Christensen and Betty Bergman Levin
8 Pine Street/P.O. Box 297
Stockbridge, MA 01262

Easy-to-follow, healthful recipes for the everyday or the out-of-the-ordinary occasion. Features dishes for every course of the meal, all using apples!

$ 8.95 Retail price
$ .45 Tax for Massachusetts residents
$ 4.00 Postage and handling
Make check payable to Berkshire House Publishers
ISBN 0-936399-32-5

THE ART OF ASIAN COOKING
Museum of Fine Arts, Boston
465 Huntington Avenue
Boston, MA 02115

The Art of Asian Cooking was published to commemorate the hundred year anniversary of the Department of Asiatic Art. Recipes represent each country whose art is exhibited in the MFA. The book is beautifully illustrated with examples of Asiatic art. There are 228 recipes, 127 pages, plus a glossary. Book is currently out of print.

AS YOU LIKE IT
Recipes and Photographs from the Williamstown Theatre Festival Family
Williamstown Theatre Festival Guild
P.O. Box 219
Williamstown, MA 01267

Cook with the stars! 180 recipes and 50 celebrity photographs from New England's premier summer theatre festival, celebrating its 40th anniversary in 1994. Recipes from Alec Baldwin, Kate Burton, Marge Champion, Blythe Danner, Richard Dreyfuss, Paul Newman, Christopher Reeve, George Wendt, Joanne Woodward and many more. 228 pages. Book is currently out of print.

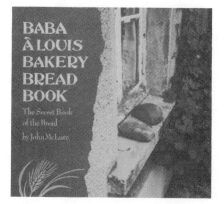

BABA-À-LOUIS BAKERY BREAD BOOK
by John McLure
P. O. Box 41   802-875-2216
Chester, VT 05143-0041   802-875-4666

This paperback 9x8 book with 132 pages shares the techniques of Baba-À-Louis Bakery. This book welcomes the reader to the culture of baking. It brings to life the day-to-day routines with 50 photos, illustrations, anecdotes, observations, historical notes, and quotations.

$ 13.95 Retail price
$ .70 Tax for Vermont residents
$ 3.50 Postage and handling
Make check payable to Baba-À-Louis Bakery
ISBN 0-9636892-0-7

THE BED & BREAKFAST COOKBOOK

by Martha W. Murphy
43 South Pier Road
Narragansett, RI 02882   401-789-1824

Without leaving home, you can sample the delectable breakfast fare that has made Bed & Breakfasts the choice of thousands of sophisticated travelers in recent years. More than 300 wonderful recipes and 200 splendid illustrations showing exteriors, interiors, gardens, and enticingly set tables laden with typical fare of B&Bs in every state in the Union, including Alaska and Hawaii. 288 pages.

$35.00 Retail price HC / $19.95 SC
$ 7%   Tax for Rhode Island residents
$ 3.50 Postage and handling
Make check payable to Martha W. Murphy
ISBN 0-88045-046-0

BERKSHIRE SEASONINGS

Junior League of Berkshire County
42 Wendell Avenue
Pittsfield, MA 01201   413-443-5151

Berkshire Seasonings is a cookbook of favorite recipes of Junior League members. It has 164 pages divided into nine different catagories with 309 recipes. These include sweets, meat and poultry, vegetables, and others. There are a number of helpful hints at the end of the book.

$10.95 Retail price
$ .55 Tax for Massachusetts residents
$ 1.50 Postage and handling
Make check payable to Junior League of Berkshire County

THE BEST FROM LIBBY HILLMAN'S KITCHEN

by Libby Hillman
Countryman Press
P. O. Box 175–QRP
Woodstock, VT 05091

The Best from Libby Hillman's Kitchen builds from the basics, teaching understanding, control, and enjoyment of the tools and ingredients in the kitchen. Raised in a tradition of recipe-less cooking, she shows how to adapt fearlessly to available ingredients, from quick-and-easy to strut-your-stuff recipes. Hardcover, 352 pages; 332 recipes with index; original illustrations; menu suggestions. Book is currently out of print.

BEST RECIPES
OF THE BERKSHIRE CHEFS

Berkshire House Publishers
480 Pleasant Street Suite 5
Lee, MA 01258   413-243-0303

Best Recipes of the Berkshire Chefs is a compilation of the finest and most unique recipes from Berkshire County in western Massachusetts. Contributors include: Roy Blount, Jr., Arlo Guthrie, and Alice Brock. Menu suggestions, preparation tips, and delightful descriptions of famed inns and restaurants are given.

$ 12.95 Retail price
$ .65 Tax for Massachusetts residents
$ 4.00 Postage and handling
Make check payable to Berkshire House Publishers
ISBN 0-936399-35-X

THE BLUE STRAWBERY COOKBOOK

by James Haller
The Harvard Common Press
535 Albany Street
Boston, MA 02118   617-423-5803

Subtitled, *"Cooking (Brilliantly) Without Recipes,"* James Haller, chef of the Blue Strawbery restaurant in Portsmouth, NH, stresses imaginative cooking. "The basic tools in my kitchen are the blender and the skillet...no need for expensive equipment...put your money into the food." A delightful book. Paper. 160 pages.

$ 8.95 Retail price
$ .45 Tax for Massachusetts residents
$ 4.00 Postage and handling
Make check payable to The Harvard Common Press
ISBN 0-916782-05-0

THE BOOK OF CHOWDER

by Richard J. Hooker
The Harvard Common Press
535 Albany Street
Boston, MA 02118   617-423-5803

Carried to America by seafaring men in colonial days, chowder was made on board from any fish combined with salt pork, hardtack, and water. This book follows its course along coastal North America, then across the continent with the pioneers, presenting authentic and delicious chowder recipes that emerged along the way. 144 pages. ISBN 0-916782-10-7

$ 10.95 Retail price
$ .55 Tax for Massachusetts residents
$ 4.00 Postage and handling
Make check payable to The Harvard Common Press

BOSTON TEA PARTIES

Museum of Fine Arts, Boston
465 Huntington Avenue
Boston, MA 02115

Tea is served in the Museum by members of the Ladies Committee. Many recipes included in this book
are great tea-time favorites! Each chapter begins with
a description and preparation techniques for that type
of baked products. This book contains 426 recipes,
154 pages beautifully illustrated with photographs of
art objects pertaining to tea. Book is currently out of
print.

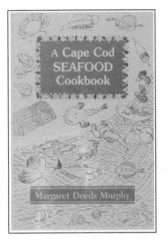

A CAPE COD SEAFOOD COOKBOOK

by Margaret Deeds Murphy
Parnassus Imprints
45 Plant Road
Hyannis, MA 02601

With its delicate and zesty appetizers, luscious soups
and chowders, ambrosial salads and cold plates, and
succulent and flavorful entrées, *A Cape Cod Seafood
Cookbook* transforms the bounty of the sea to the pleasures of the table. 176 pages, illustrated, hard cover.
Book is currently out of print.

CAPE COD'S NIGHT AT THE CHEF'S
TABLE COOKBOOK

The Provincetown AIDs Support Group
P. O. Box 1522
Provincetown, MA 02657-5522   508-487-9169

May 6, 1992 was the date of the first annual Night at
the Chef's Table benefit for the Cape Cod AIDS
Council and the Provincetown AIDS Support Group.
Presented in this book are over 100 recipes from the
40 restaurants who prepared sumptuous banquets for
this event. Plus chefs bios, photos, menus. 160 pages.

$ 5.95 Retail price
$ 2.50 Postage and handling
Make check payable to Provincetown AIDS Support Group
ISBN 0-9609814-8-9

CAPE COLLECTION–SIMPLY SOUP

Association for the Preservation of Cape Cod
P. O. Box 636
Orleans, MA 02653-0636   508-255-4142

Prepared in 1991 by a staff member and a committee of volunteers who solicited recipes from our 2500 members, some of whom live on Cape Cod year round and others who summer here and live in most of the 48 states. As our name implies, Cape Cod supplies a great amount of fresh fish and shellfish, and many of our recipes make use of them. 133 pages, 114 recipes, illustrated.

$ 8.00 Retail price
$ .40 Tax for Massachusetts residents
$ 3.50 Postage and handling
Make check payable to APCC

CELEBRITIES SERVE

International Tennis Hall of Fame
194 Bellevue Avenue
Newport, RI 02840   401-849-3990

Celebrities Serve cookbook utilizes colorful photos and drawings to showcase a cornucopia of fun recipes from tennis legends and well-known personalities who enjoy the game. The 190-page book includes 135 recipes as well as menu suggestions for tennis parties. Proceeds benefit the International Tennis Hall of Fame, a non-profit organization dedicated to preserving the history and heritage of tennis and its champions.

$15.95 Retail price
$ 1.12 Tax for Rhode Island residents
$ 4.00 Postage and handling
Make check payable to International Tennis Hall of Fame
ISBN 0-9629683-0-7

THE CHEF'S PALATE COOKBOOK

by Jayne Pettit
P.O. Box 1003
Quechee, VT 05059   802-295-1786

The Chef's Palate Cookbook focuses on the fun of cooking with lowfat, low-calorie foods for hungry people. The emphasis is on pastas with light sauces, stir-fry dishes using grains and veggies, tantalizingly easy appetizers, and hearty soups. Also has food articles and quotations on the art of fine dining along with tips on good nutrition and calorie-cutting without fasting!

$ 9.95 Retail price
$ .50 Tax for Vermont residents
$ 2.00 Postage and handling
Make check payable to Jayne Pettit-*The Chef's Palate*

CHICKEN EXPRESSIONS

by Normand Leclair
P. O. Box 356
N. Kingston, RI 02852   401-295-8804

The recipes in this book allow the hosts(esses) to enjoy their guests by making the preparations of meals easier by pre-assembling. These dishes are festive, delicious, and easy to prepare. All dishes are baked in the oven. A unique book from the owner/operator of the Red Rooster Tavern. Covered wire-o binding.

$ 9.95 Retail price
$ .70 Tax for Rhode Island residents
$ 1.05 Postage and handling
Make check payable to *Chicken Expressions*
ISBN 0-9620441-0-3

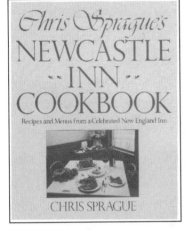

CHRIS SPRAGUE'S NEWCASTLE INN COOKBOOK

by Chris Sprague
The Harvard Common Press
535 Albany Street
Boston, MA 02118   617-423-5803

Guests come to the Newcastle Inn from all over the country for its cozy accommodations and its setting in one of Maine's prettiest coastal towns. What brings them back again and again, is the food. The culinary craft of chef Chris Sprague has earned her a loyal following among the inn's guests and a tide of accolades from the country's leading food journalists.

$10.95 Retail price (paperback) $18.95 (hardcover)
$ 5% Tax for Massachusetts residents
$ 4.00 Postage and handling
Make check payable to The Harvard Common Press
ISBN 1-55832-049-0

CHRISTMAS MEMORIES COOKBOOK

by Lois Klee and Connie Colom
Mystic Seaport Stores
47 Greenmanville Avenue
Mystic, CT 06355   800-331-2665

Block Island Turkey and Capt. Cooke's Plum Pudding are only a sampling of the recipes in this collection. Re-create imaginative variations on classic New England cooking. Great for year round entertaining and original gift ideas. Ample pages for favorite holiday menus and recipes. Spiral bound, 9¼x8. 70,000 copies in print!

$15.95 Retail price
$ .96 Tax for Connecticut residents
$ 4.95 Postage and handling
Make check payable to Mystic Seaport Stores
ISBN 0-939510-03-0

CLAMS, MUSSELS, OYSTERS, SCALLOPS & SNAILS

by Howard Mitcham
Parnassus Imprints
45 Plant Road
Hyannis, MA 02601

This book is about Clams, Mussels, Oysters, Scallops & Snails and about the preparation of all these items with usually a story to go along with the recipe. 220 pages, illustrated, paperback. Book is currently out of print.

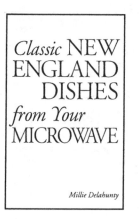

CLASSIC NEW ENGLAND DISHES FROM YOUR MICROWAVE

by Millie Delahunty
Down East Books
P.O. Box 679
Camden, ME 04843   207-594-9544

Delicious regional foods quickly prepared in today's favorite appliance, the microwave oven. The author has adapted traditional New England recipes; many dishes, such as clam chowder, meat loaf, and Boston cream pie, are even better when prepared in the microwave than by conventional methods, says the author. Comb bound, 120 pages, index.

$ 5.95 Retail price
$ .33 Tax for Maine residents
$ 4.50 Postage and handling
Make check payable to Down East Books
ISBN 0-89272-280-0

COME SAVOR SWANSEA

First Christian Congregational Church
Maple Avenue and Route #6
Swansea, MA 02777

Come Savor Swansea, a cookbook celebrating the 300th anniversary of the First Christian Congregational Church in Swansea, is a chunky, spiral-bound book (332 pages) with a brick-red cover. It is chock-full of recipes—416 in all—and spiced with snippets of Swansea history—over 150 of them—and designed to appeal to a wide audience. Book is currently out of print.

CONNECTICUT COOKS

American Cancer Society, Connecticut Division
14 Village Lane
Wallingford, CT 06492

Variety is one of Connecticut's most valuable spices. Throughout its history, the Nutmeg State has enjoyed a rich and diversified cultural heritage. Today, more than 60 separate ethnic groups provide our state with a broad and interesting personality. We are proud to present this book and are assured that all will find the recipes to be intriguing as well as delicious. Book is currently out of print.

CONNECTICUT COOKS II

American Cancer Society, Connecticut Division
14 Village Lane
Wallingford, CT 06492

The recipes in *Connecticut Cooks II*, initially printed in 1985, include many from our state's most famous restaurants. They were selected from nearly two thousand submitted by our volunteers and other friends of the American Cancer Society. We are confident that you will enjoy the wide variety of recipes. Bon appetit! Book is currently out of print.

CONNECTICUT COOKS III

American Cancer Society, Connecticut Division
14 Village Lane
Wallingford, CT 06492

Connecticut Cooks III was published in 1988. It has been very popular because in addition to traditional recipes, it includes separate sections on ethnic cuisine, recipes from inns throughout Connecticut and across the country, and simple microwave specialties to accommodate our modern lifestyles. It also contains Connecticut historical facts from *Connecticut Firsts* by Wilson H. Faude and Joan W. Friedland. Book is currently out of print.

THE COOKBOOK II

Worcester Art Museum
55 Salisbury Street
Worcester, MA 01609-3196   508-799-4406

The Cookbook II follows in the footsteps of a culinary classic, Cookbook I. Our challenge was to create a book not only with the same standard of excellence, but also with its own fresh and unique flavor. Many of these recipes cultivate the pleasures of cooking and demonstrate New England's rich blend of ethnic traditions. Having tested, tasted, and screened each of the 355 recipes, we are sure that a cooking adventure awaits you.

$14.95 Retail price
$ .75 Tax for Massachusetts residents
$ 3.00 Postage and handling
Make check payable to Worcester Art Museum Shop
ISBN 0-936042-40-0

COOKING WITH H.E.L.P.

H.E.L.P.
P. O. Box 904
York, ME 03909-0904

Our cookbook comes from historical York, Maine, and presents over 250 recipes in 75 pages. Some of the recipes are over 70 years old and come from some of the earliest families who lived in the York area. We hope you enjoy cooking with H.E.L.P. (an organization dedicated to Help Elevate Local Politics). Book is currently out of print.

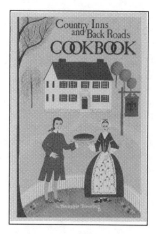

COUNTRY INNS AND BACK ROADS COOKBOOK

Berkshire House Publishers
480 Pleasant Street Suite 5
Lee, MA 01258   413-243-0303

Representing 159 inns from around the United States, reflective of local tastes, *Country Inns and Back Roads Cookbook* offers a wide selection in recipe variety. Over 150 recipes! 176 pages.

$29.95 Retail price (HC) $17.95 (paperback)
$ 5% Tax for Massachusetts residents
$ 4.00 Postage and handling
Make check payable to Berkshire House Publishers
ISBN 0-912-94456-0

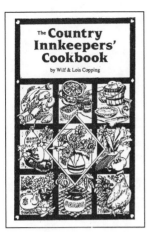

THE COUNTRY INNKEEPERS' COOKBOOK

by Wilf & Lois Copping
Country Roads Press
Main Street/P.O. Box 286
Castine, ME 04421   207-326-0897

From the Deer Hill Inn in Grafton, VT, 225 taste-tested favorites that are proven winners at the inn and at home...*your* home! These are foods with flair, from Hot Cheese Toasties to Brandy Alexander Pie. 224 pages, 6x9 paperback.

$ 12.95 Retail price
$ .78 Tax for Maine residents
$ 3.00 Postage and handling per order
Make check payable to Country Roads Press
ISBN 1-56626-015-9

CUISINE À LA MODE

Les Dames Richelieu du Rhode Island
c/o Louise R. Champigny
One Social Street, Box F
Woonsocket, RI 0289

Cuisine à la Mode contains a variety of favorite recipes submitted by members and friends of Les Dames Richelieu du R.I. Some are family keep-sakes and some are new. All reflect love of cook-ing. The unique easel-type binder is designed to stand open on the counter for ease in reading. Book is currently out of print.

A CULINARY TOUR OF THE GINGERBREAD COTTAGES OF THE MARTHA'S VINEYARD CAMP-MEETING ASSOCIATION

by Joan Davis
P. O. Box 1956
Carolina Beach, NC 28428   910-343-1180

Favorite recipes from "Campgrounders" past and present. Includes Victorian treasures, traditional Martha's Vineyard Island fare, and unique modern-day creations, many never before published. Come savor our community's special flavor of recipes, anec-dotes, and history, interspersed with reproduced pho-tographs, vintage stereoptican views, and postcards.

$ 14.95 Retail price
$ 1.50 Postage and handling
Make check payable to Joan Davis

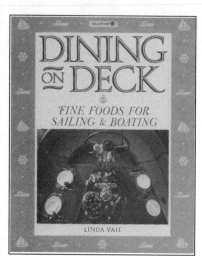

DINING ON DECK

by Linda Vail
Williamson Publishing
P. O. Box 185
Charlotte, VT 05445   800-234-8791

Casual elegance and fine foods with minimal effort!
More than 200 recipes for breakfasts, lunches, dinners, plus 90 menus for day sails, elegant weekends,
on-board brunches, and hearty suppers. Plenty of tips
on provisioning and storage. 160 pages; 8x10 with
illustrations; trade paper.

$10.95 Retail price
$ 3.00 Postage and handling
Make check payable to Williamson Publishing Co.
ISBN 0-913589-21-7

FAVORITE NEW ENGLAND RECIPES

by Sara B. B. Stamm
Country Roads Press
Main Street/P.O. Box 286
Castine, ME 04421   207-326-0897

A delicious blend of traditional and modern cooking
styles truly reflects the flavor of the region. Savory
casseroles, hearty soups, scrumptious desserts, and
more will make your mouth water! Features a chapter
on the time-honored tradition of Afternoon Tea. 322
pages, 7x10 paperback, second edition.

$15.95 Retail price
$ .96 Tax for Maine residents
$ 3.00 Postage and handling per order
Make check payable to Country Roads Press
ISBN 1-56626-036-1

THE FINE ART OF
HOLIDAY COOKING

University of Connecticut, School of Fine Arts
875 Coventry Road
Storrs, CT 06269-1128   860-486-3016

Favorite recipes by Connecticut chefs, including hu-
morist Victor Borge and Connecticut First Lady
Claudia Weicker. Designed by award-winner Peter
Good, ('93 USA Christmas and '94 Valentine's Day
stamps). A wonderfully elegant cookbook filled with
delightful recipes, a treasure for every chef! Proceeds
support artistic programming by the University of
Connecticut School of Fine Arts. 150 pages. 155
recipes.

$12.95 Retail price
$ 3.00 Postage and handling
Make check payable to University of Connecticut

THE FINE ARTS COOKBOOK I
Museum of Fine Arts, Boston
465 Huntington Avenue
Boston, MA 02115

The idea of a "cookbook as a Museum fundraiser" was from an anonymous MFA member in Newton. The 362 severely tested recipes are from the ladies committee, MFA staff, trustees, and donors. The 195-page cookbook, in five sections, reflects the life of the MFA. In seven editions, 50,000 copies, it is a 23-year-old gourmet "fundraiser." A successful "recipe." Book is currently out of print.

THE FINE ARTS COOKBOOK II
Museum of Fine Arts, Boston
465 Huntington Avenue
Boston, MA 02115

The Fine Arts Cookbook II is an extension of the fine art of dining put forth in Volume I, but with greater emphasis on dishes that can be prepared ahead, the best of recipes brought back from foreign travels, and treasured recipes passed down through Museum families. Book is currently out of print.

FRESH FROM VERMONT
Vermont Life Magazine
6 Baldwin Street
Montpelier, VT 05602

Fresh from Vermont features nearly 100 recipes developed by Chef David Miles of the renowned New England Culinary Institute. The 159-page cookbook tempts the cook with beautiful photographs and recipes organized by season. Syndicated food writer, Marialisa Calta, introduces each segment. A most useful and attractive cookbook from *Vermont Life*. Book is currently out of print.

FROM ELLIE'S KITCHEN TO YOURS

by Ellie Deaner
P.O. Box 1164
Framingham, MA 01701   508-620-1009

Easy and delicious recipes from Ellie's television shows
and cooking classes. Recipes are made from scratch;
ingredients readily available in local supermarkets. Per-
sonalized hints, how to prepare dishes in advance, how
to reduce fat and cholesterol, how to serve and garnish—makes you feel as if Ellie is in the kitchen cooking with you. 310 recipes. 216 pages.

$14.95 Retail price
$ .75 Tax for Massachusetts residents
$ 2.50 Postage and handling
Make check payable to Denell Press
ISBN 0-9631177-7-7

FROM THE INN'S KITCHEN

Deedy Marble, Chef
The Governor's Inn
86 Main Street
Ludlow, VT 05149

A warm welcoming collection of recipes, Deedy,
through her descriptions, invites the reader into her
kitchen and beautiful country inn. The book is ar-
ranged the way dinner is served—all six courses.
Charlie has his turn with his famous breakfast entrées,
and both shine as warm, generous innkeepers/chefs.
Book is currently out of print.

THE GARDNER MUSEUM CAFÉ COOKBOOK

by Lois McKitchen Conroy
The Harvard Common Press
535 Albany Street
Boston, MA 02118   617-423-5803

Fine art and flora and a scrumptious array of dishes
are available at the Gardner Museum Café. This cookbook features scrumptious recipes, reproductions from
the museum's collection, and photographs of its lush
interior garden, making it as inspiring to the eye as it
is to the palate. Enjoy a bit of Whistler with your Pear
and Celery Soup! Paper. 176 pages.

$10.95 Retail price
$ .55 Tax for Massachusetts residents
$ 4.00 Postage and handling
Make check payable to The Harvard Common Press
ISBN 0-916782-71-9

GOOD MAINE FOOD

by Marjorie Mosser
Down East Books
P. O. Box 679
Camden, ME 04843   207-594-9544

Including a foreword and notes by the late Kenneth Roberts, the famous author's niece presents his favorite dishes in a compendium of recipes well spiced with anecdotes. "Old recipes, like old friends, are usually the most dependable." Paperback, 424 pages, index.

$ 12.95 Retail price
$ .71 Tax for Maine residents
$ 4.50 Postage and handling
Make check payable to Down East Books
ISBN 0-89272-038-7

GREAT ISLAND COOKBOOK

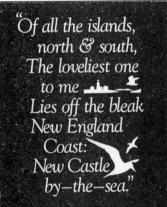

New Castle Island Church Guild
Box 39
New Castle, NH 03854-0039   603-436-3734

Great Island Cookbook is a collector's dream book, hand lettered, illustrated and in a notebook binder. A history of this unique one-square-mile island is featured. With one place of business, (a fish market), one school, one church, a town hall and small post office, no stores or malls, this is a closely knit community of 800 who wish to share their favorite recipes.

$ 12.95 Retail price
$ 3.00 Postage and handling
Make check payable to *Great Island Cookbook*

THE HAMMERSMITH FARM COOKBOOK

Hammersmith Farm
Ocean Drive
Newport, RI 02840   401-846-7346

Hammersmith Farm is on the site of the first working farm in Newport. The former home of Mrs. Hugh D. Auchincloss, it was the site of the wedding reception of daughter Jacqueline Bouvier and John F. Kennedy in 1953. The cookbook features recipes served on the farm as well as those from area caterers. 256 pages. Ringbound.

$ 12.95 Retail price
$ 3.50 Postage and handling
Make check payable to *Hammersmith Farm Cookbook*

First Congregational Church of Hancock, New Hampshire

A HANCOCK COMMUNITY COLLECTION

The Guild
20 Stoddard Road
Hancock, NH 03449-5102   603-525-6668

The book was created as a fund-raiser for our guild. We opened it to the town residents because Hancock has so many great cooks. The book has 116 pages and includes 331 recipes in all categories.

$ 5.00 Retail price
Make check payable to The Guild

THE HARLOW'S BREAD & CRACKER COOKBOOK

by Joan S. Harlow
Down East Books
P. O. Box 679
Camden, ME 04843

Joan Harlow's Bread and Cracker Company of New Hampshire makes an imaginative array of baked foods. This collection of the bakery's favorites includes soups, casseroles, and appetizers as well as breads and crackers. Paperback, 176 pages, index. Book is currently out of print

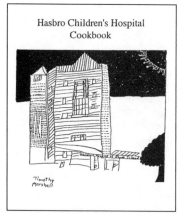

HASBRO CHILDREN'S HOSPITAL COOKBOOK

Hasbro Children's Hospital Nursing Staff
593 Eddy Street
Providence, RI 02920

Over 300 recipes on 270 pages. Compiled by the pediatric nursing staff of Hasbro Children's Hospital. A collection of recipes by busy working women. The proceeds of the sale of this cookbook are being used to purchase the stained glass windows in the chapel of our new hospital. Book is currently out of print.

HERITAGE COOKING FROM THE KITCHEN OF MARY PAUPLIS

by Mary Pauplis
147 Chapin Road
Hudson, MA 01749   508-568-0652

It is with great pride and pleasure that I share with you, family recipes from three generations of excellent cooks. Original family favorites from the Mediterranean and Baltic regions, as well as fabulous original recipes, have been documented in this book for the enjoyment of all for years to come.

$ 10.00 Retail price
$ .50 Tax for Massachusetts residents
$ 1.75 Postage and handling
Make check payable to Mary Pauplis
ISBN 0-9635383-1-4

HERITAGE FAN-FARE

Heritage Plantation of Sandwich
Museum Store
67 Grove Street
Sandwich, MA 02563-0566   508-888-3300

Heritage Fan-Fare is a collection of 284 recipes from members and friends of Heritage Plantation of Sandwich, a 76-acre indoor and outdoor museum in Sandwich, MA on Cape Cod. The ringbound book includes many family favorites. It is illustrated with sketches derived from the gardens, buildings, and exhibitions of the museum.

$ 8.95 Retail price
$ .45 Tax for Massachusetts residents
$ 3.80 Postage and handling
Make check payable to Heritage Plantation of Sandwich, Inc.

HOME COOKIN' IS A FAMILY AFFAIR

Windsor Junior Women's Club
P. O. Box 1068
Windsor, CT 06095   860-285-8137

A book of favorite recipes compiled by friends, families, members, and past members of the Windsor Junior Women's Club. Home cookin' favorites!

$ 6.00 Retail price
Make check payable to WJWC

HOMESPUN COOKERY

by Marie Carter Durant
164 North Main Street
Boscawen, NH 03303-1121   603-753-6548

Homespun Cookery, now in its third printing, has 173 pages and contains 250 recipes. These recipes are a collection gathered from many sources, plus some of Marie's originals. They are in eleven categories and are an excellent representation of good New England cooking.

$11.95 Retail price
$ 2.00 Postage and handling
Make check payable to Marie C. Durant

HOSPITALITY

North Shore Medical Center/Volunteer Office
81 Highland Avenue
Salem, MA 01970   978-741-1215 Ext. 6286

A cookbook celebrating Boston's North Shore is an impressive treasury of more than 350 recipes assembled from private and celebrity collections. Hospitality emphasizes innovative combinations of fresh ingredients. There are nine color illustrations of historic Essex County. The diversity of tastes and dishes distinguishes New England hospitality!

$ 19.95 Retail price
$ 1.00 Tax for Massachusetts residents
$ 2.50 Postage and handling
Make check payable to North Shore Medical Center
ISBN 0-9628689-0-6

THE ISLAND COOKBOOK

Stetson Laboratories, Inc.
P. O. Box 28
North Scituate, RI 02857   401-647-3616

The Island Cookbook is not just a cookbook. It is a collection of the best that the Islands of southern New England have to offer, along with anecdotes of people, places, and more than 100 years of just plain cooking.

$ 14.95 Retail price
$ 1.05 Tax for Rhode Island residents
$ 3.50 Postage and handling
Make check payable to Stetson Laboratories, Inc.

J. BILDNER & SONS COOKBOOK

by Jim Bildner
The Harvard Common Press
535 Albany Street
Boston, MA 02118   617-423-5803

Famous for his neighborhood-style groceries with their unparalleled takeout selections, Jim Bildner knows that easy-to-prepare food doesn't have to be ordinary and unimaginative. His cookbook reflects the creative exuberance of his stores. Casual feasts, terrific fast food, delicious picnic food, perfect make-ahead dinners. Paper. 256 pages.

$12.95 Retail price
$ .91 Tax for Massachusetts residents
$ 4.00 Postage and handling
Make check payable to The Harvard Common Press
ISBN 1-55832-064-4

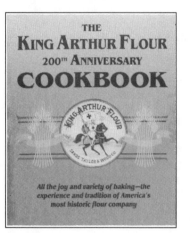

THE KING ARTHUR FLOUR 200TH ANNIVERSARY COOKBOOK

The Baker's Catalogue
P. O. Box 876
Norwich, VT 05055

A must for the beginner to the advanced baker. Over 600 pages of recipes, photographs, and illustrations. Recipes include originals by the author, friends, and family, some from before the turn of the century. Brinna Sands includes numerous "primer" sections of technical information in areas such as ingredients, utensils, and nutrition. The bread baker's bible!

$21.00 Retail price
$ 1.05 Tax for Vermont residents
Postage and handling varies, ask for information
Make check payable to King Arthur Flour Baker's Catalogue
ISBN 0-88150-247-2

THE LEGAL SEA FOODS COOKBOOK

Legal Sea Foods
33 Everett Street
Allston, MA 02134   617-254-7000

This cookbook contains many of Legal Sea Foods signature items. It is paperback, 182 pages, illustrated.

$15.00 Retail price
$ .75 Tax for Massachusetts residents
$ 3.95 Postage and handling
Make check payable to Legal Sea Foods, Inc.
ISBN 0-385-23183-0

THE LOAF AND LADLE COOK BOOK

by Joan S. Harlow
Down East Books
P.O. Box 679
Camden, ME 04843   207-594-9544

Joan Harlow has collected more than 250 of her famous New Hampshire restaurant's most popular recipes. Favorite hors d'oeuvres, salads, breads, and desserts are among the offerings, but the main feature is soup. Paperback, 228 pages, index.

$ 13.95 Retail price
$ .77 Tax for Maine residents
$ 4.50 Postage and handling
Make check payable to Down East Books
ISBN 0-89272-181-2

THE LYMES' HERITAGE COOKBOOK

Lyme Historical Society/Florence Griswold Museum
96 Lyme Street
Old Lyme, CT 06371   860-434-5542

This is not just another run-of-the-mill cookbook. It is a carefully chosen collection of favorite recipes that will appeal to both expert and novice cooks. Over 500 recipes with emphasis on New England dishes—some very old that are adapted to modern tastes, cooking methods, and ingredients.

$ 14.95 Retail price
$ .89 Tax for Connecticut residents
$ 2.00 Postage and handling
Make check payable to Florence Griswold Museum

THE MAINE COLLECTION

Portland Museum of Art Guild
7 Congress Square
Port, ME 04105   413-243-0303

The Maine Collection is a 6x9, comb-bound, hard cover book and contains 256 pages of tasty recipes contributed by Maine artists, innkeepers, and individuals from all over the state. Proceeds from the sale of this book will go toward the restoration of the McLellan-Sweat House, the original museum, and considered one of the finest works in the museum's collection.

$ 12.95 Retail price
$ .78 Tax for Maine residents
$ 2.50 Postage and handling
Make check payable to The Maine Collection
ISBN 0-9635386-0-8

MAINE'S JUBILEE COOKBOOK

Edited by Loana Shibles and Annie Rogers
Down East Books
P. O. Box 679
Camden, ME 04843

Recipes contributed by cooks from all over Maine for the celebration of the state's sesquicentennial (1970). Now in its twelfth printing and still going strong. Paperback, 256 pages, index. Book is currently out of print.

The Marlborough Meetinghouse Cookbook

THE MARLBOROUGH MEETINGHOUSE COOKBOOK

Congregational Church of Marlborough
35 South Main Street/P. O. Box 57
Marlborough, CT 06447

The Marlborough Meetinghouse Cookbook contains more than 225 favorite recipes from church members and friends, sprinkled with historical quips and sayings. The book, now in its fourth printing, was created to raise funds for the restoration of the church's 150-year-old sanctuary, recently accepted to the National Register of Historic Places. Book is currently out of print.

THE MBL CENTENNIAL COOKBOOK

MBL Associates
Marine Biological Laboratory
Woods Hole, MA 02543

One of the joys of being in Woods Hole and at the MBL is sharing good food with friends. Scientists and their families come here from all over the world and often bring with them recipes for favorite dishes. In celebration of our 100th birthday, we share in this cookbook our traditional offerings from the community, as well as cosmopolitan recipes from around the world. Book is currently out of print.

MEMORIES FROM BROWNIE'S KITCHEN

by Mildred "Brownie" Schrumpf
Magazines Inc.
1135 Hammond Street
Bangor, ME 04401

This 230-page book contains traditional Maine recipes compiled by Mildred "Brownie" Schrumpf, who, in her 90th year, still writes her weekly food column in the *Bangor Daily News*. Her collection of recipes, all made from basic ingredients, reflects more than 40 years of contributions from Maine's best cooks. Book is currently out of print.

MERRYMEETING MERRY EATING

Mid Coast Hospital, Brunswick Auxiliary
58 Baribeau Drive
Brunswick, ME 04011   207-729-0181

Enjoy the bounty of our good earth with this wonderful collection of home-tested recipes gathered in Maine. *Merrymeeting Merry Eating* is a community cookbook for everyone, making great use of the abundant harvest of our world in general and Maine in particular. 320 pages, over 400 recipes.

$15.95 Retail price
$ .96 Tax for Maine residents
$ 3.00 Postage and handling
Make check payable to *Merrymeeting Merry Eating*
ISBN 0-9620094-0-7

MORE THAN SANDWICHES

Sandwich Junior Women's Club
P. O. Box 757
Sandwich, MA 02563

Recipes for appetizers, soups and sauces, main dishes, vegetables, bread, and desserts with a Cape Cod flair. Book is currently out of print.

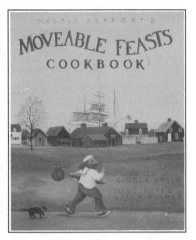

MOVEABLE FEASTS COOKBOOK

by Ginger Smyle
Mystic Seaport Stores
47 Greenmanville Ave.
Mystic, CT 06355   800-331-2665

The book for everyone who has ever planned for a concert in the park, a trek through the woods, a day on a boat, or any meal on the go. Hundreds of tantalizing recipes for all kinds of excursions, from "Pepper Soup" to "Pecan Tarts." These creative recipes and menus will make all "Moveable Feasts" an occasion to remember. Delightfully illustrated by Sally Caldwell Fisher. Spiral bound, 9¼x8.

$ 14.95 Retail price
$ .90 Tax for Connecticut residents
$ 4.95 Postage and handling
Make check payable to Mystic Seaport Stores
ISBN 0-939510-14-6

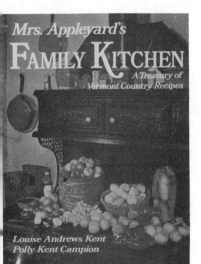

MRS. APPLEYARD'S FAMILY KITCHEN

Vermont Life Magazine
6 Baldwin Street
Montpelier, VT 05602

The ultimate "Mrs. Appleyard" cookbook, infused with time-tested insight and laced with contemporary innovation. Over 700 recipes (373 pages), along with countless tips for food preparation, unexpected guests, and elaborate parties. More than a cookbook, this home companion brings together the warmth and wisdom that grew from more than three generations of a Vermont family's country kitchen. Book is currently out of print.

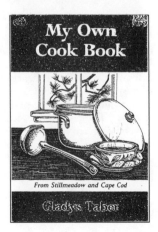

MY OWN COOK BOOK

by Gladys Taber
Parnassus Imprints
45 Plant Road
Hyannis, MA 02601   508-790-1175

The smell of a country kitchen is in these pages. Over 250 recipes with particular emphasis on the bounty of the sea. 312 pages, paperback.

$ 9.95 Retail price
$ .50 Tax for Massachusetts residents
$ 3.00 Postage and handling
Make check payable to Parnassus Imprints
ISBN 0-940160-15-3

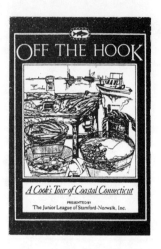

OFF THE HOOK

Junior League of Stamford-Norwalk
748 Post Road
Darien, CT 06820   203-655-8375

The Junior League of Stamford-Norwalk, Connecticut, brings the spirit of New England cooking to you with over 165 savory seafood recipes collected from local celebrities, coastal restaurants, culinary experts, and League members. Each double-tested recipe is easy to follow and will appeal to cooks of all experience levels. Ring bound. Book is currently out of print.

THE PARKVIEW WAY
TO VEGETARIAN COOKING

Parkview Memorial Hospital Auxiliary
329 Maine Street
Brunswick, ME 04011   207-729-1641 Ext. 244

The Parkview Way to Vegetarian Cooking, a 206-page looseleaf cookbook, is a collection of 660 recipes by members and friends of the Parkview Memorial Hospital Auxiliary. Recipes reflecting today's emphasis on healthful eating and the unique artwork contained within the book combine to make this a welcome addition to any cookbook library.

$ 5.00 Retail price
$ .28 Tax for Maine residents
$ 3.00 Postage and handling
Make check payable to Parkview Memorial Hospital

PERENNIALS

Falmouth Garden Club
P.O. Box 487
Falmouth, MA 02541

The Falmouth Garden Club has compiled a cookbook for the cooks of today—time-saving, vegetarian, low-fat, and low-calorie, but still gourmet and delicious. We know that in these busy days we are all happy to find new recipes that taste as though we have spent all day laboring in our kitchens. These delicious recipes for the modern cook only take a fraction of your time.

$ 7.00 Retail price
$ 1.75 Postage and handling
Make check payable to Falmouth Garden Club

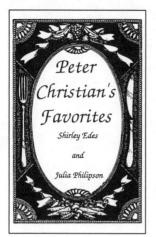

PETER CHRISTIAN'S FAVORITES

by Shirley Edes and Julia Philipson
Down East Books
P. O. Box 679
Camden, ME 04843

The three Peter Christian's restaurants of New Hampshire enjoy a widespread reputation for fine food and friendly atmosphere. In this popular cookbook you'll find exemplary fare of soups, salads, sandwiches, and desserts, plus recipes for house specialties such as Mustard Chicken Cordon Bleu, Chinese Turkey Salad, and Ham Florentine Pinwheels. Comb bound, 192 pages, index. Book is currently out of print.

PETER CHRISTIAN'S RECIPES

by Shirley Edes and Julia Philipson
Down East Books
P. O. Box 679
Camden, ME 04843

More of the famous restaurants' outstanding gustatory artistry. These recipes have been collected at the request of loyal patrons of the Peter Christian's restaurants of New Hampshire. Comb bound, 184 pages, index. Book is currently out of print.

PLUM CRAZY

by Elizabeth Post Mirel
Parnassus Imprints
45 Plant Road
Hyannis, MA 02601   508-790-1175

Here is a book about beach plums containing 70 recipes from appetizers to desserts and beverages. Jellies, jams, muffins, pies, and legumes—they are all here. 160 pages, illustrated, paperback.

$ 6.95 Retail price
$ .35 Tax for Massachusetts residents
$ 3.00 Postage and handling
Make check payable to Parnassus Imprints
ISBN 0-940160-34-X

PROVINCETOWN SEAFOOD COOKBOOK

by Howard Mitcham
Parnassus Imprints
45 Plant Road
Hyannis, MA 02601   508-790-1175

A classic in seafood preparation from the tip-end of Cape Cod written by Provincetown's best known and most admired chef. 280 pages, profusely illustrated, paperback.

$12.50 Retail price
$ .62 Tax for Massachusetts residents
$ 3.00 Postage and handling
Make check payable to Parnassus Imprints
ISBN 0-940160-33-1

RECIPES FROM A CAPE COD KITCHEN

The New England Book Co.
P.O. Box 740
Epping, NH 03042   800-386-0015

From earliest times, New England cooking has been associated with Cape Cod kitchens. Through 300 years of blending Old World recipes with New World ingredients, these kitchens have helped shape our American culinary heritage. This hard covered and illustrated book re-creates an important part of the heritage with 138 recipes from inns and homes of yesteryear.

$14.95 Retail price
$ 1.05 Postage and handling
Make check payable to The New England Book Co.
ISBN 0-9629571-0-0

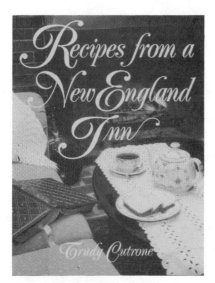

RECIPES FROM A NEW ENGLAND INN

by Trudy Cutrone
Country Roads Press
Main Street/P.O. Box 286
Castine, ME 04421   207-326-4014

An appetizing collection of over 100 of the most requested recipes from the Snowvillage Inn in Snowville, NH—some with a Central European origin (the author/chef is from Austria). Refreshing no-nonsense instructions make every recipe easy to do. 128 pages, 8½x11 paperback.

$12.95 Retail price
$ .78 Tax for Maine residents
$ 3.00 Postage and handling per order
Make check payable to Country Roads Press
ISBN 1-56626-012-4

Recipes From

Smith-Appleby House

The Historical Society
of
Smithfield, Rhode Island

RECIPES FROM
SMITH-APPLEBY HOUSE

Historical Society of Smithfield, RI
220 Stillwater Road
Esmond, RI 02917   401-231-7363

Over 400 recipes on 134 pages compiled from family
favorites of members and friends of the society, with
particular emphasis on apples, as this town is the center of "apple country."

$ 7.00 Retail price
$ 3.00 Postage and handling
Make check payable to Historical Society of Smithfield

THE RED LION INN COOKBOOK

Time-honored recipes and new favorites
from a famous New England inn.

SINCE 1773

SUZI FORBES CHASE

THE RED LION INN COOKBOOK

by Suzi Forbes Chase
Berkshire House Publishers
480 Pleasant Street Suite 5
Lee, MA 01258   413-243-0303

Time-honored favorites and new lighter recipes
from the famous Red Lion Inn in Stockbridge,
Massachusetts. From the times of stage coach
travel to today, the Red Lion Inn has been serving only the finest to its guests. Over 180 recipes. 210 pages.

$16.95 Retail price $29.95 (hardcover)
$ 5% Tax for Massachusetts residents
$ 4.00 Postage and handling
Make check payable to Berkshire House Publishers
ISBN 0-936399-28-7

RHODE
ISLAND
COOKS

RHODE ISLAND COOKS

American Cancer Society
New England Division
400 Main Street
Pawtucket, RI 02860   401-722-8480

Rhode Island Cooks is a 192-page cookbook featuring
approximately 150 regional recipes of great cooks
from local area restaurants, caterers, and the school
of culinary arts at Johnson and Wales University. It
was produced by the Rhode Island Division of the
American Cancer Society, and was the 1992 regional
winner of the Tabasco Community Cookbook award.

$ 10.00 Retail price
$ 3.00 Postage and handling
Make check payable to American Cancer Society
ISBN 0-87197-338-3

RSVP

The Junior League of Portland, Maine, Inc.
107 Elm Street Suite 100R
Portland, ME 04101

Discover the wide range of tempting treats that Maine is famous for, from hearty favorites like Fishmonger's Kettle and Brunswick Stew to such elegant specialties as Lobster Newberg and Crocked and Sherried Crab. Choose from 31 artfully planned and easily prepared menus. From Camden to Kennebunkport, Mainers have opened their hearts and their kitchens to share their most prized recipes with you. Enjoy!

$15.95 Retail price
$ .96 Tax for Maine residents
$ 4.50 Postage and handling
Make check payable to RSVP
ISBN 0-939-11455-0

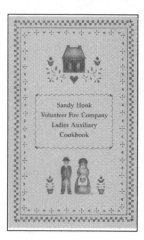

SANDY HOOK VOLUNTEER FIRE COMPANY LADIES AUXILIARY COOKBOOK

Sandy Hook Volunteer Fire & Rescue Ladies Auxiliary
P. O. Box 783
Sandy Hook, CT 06482   203-426-3744 or 426-5261

The Sandy Hook Volunteer Fire & Rescue Ladies Auxiliary has compiled over 300 favorite recipes from the firefighters of the department, their families, and their friends in a spiral bound, soft-cover cookbook.

$ 6.00 Retail price
$ 1.50 Postage and handling
Make check payable to Sandy Hook Ladies Auxiliary

SAVORY CAPE COD RECIPES & SKETCHES

by Gail Cavaliere
Gift Barn
P. O. Box 1885
N. Eastham, MA 02651-5044   508-255-7000

A guide to the many flavors of Cape Cod: seafood, berries, and more; family activities; short-cut treats; helpful information; and easy-to-read recipes. This book is for those who love Cape Cod or who plan to visit. 27 illustrations of Cape Cod scenes, 63 recipes, 64 pages.

$ 3.95 Retail price
$ 1.50 Postage and handling
Make check payable to Gift Barn

Seafood Expressions
by Normand J. Leclair

SEAFOOD EXPRESSIONS

by Normand Leclair
P.O. Box 356
N. Kingston, RI 02852   401-295-8804

Normand Leclair, owner and chef of the Red Rooster Tavern in North Kingston, presents seafood recipes reflecting his knowledge, skill, and creative ability. Guaranteed user-friendly, he invites you to write to him personally if you encounter any difficulty in preparing any of his recipes. 312 pages. Covered wire-o binding.

$12.95 Retail price
$ .55 Postage and handling
Make check payable to Seafood Expressions
ISBN 0-9620331-2-X

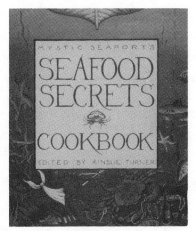

SEAFOOD SECRETS COOKBOOK

by Ainslie Turner
Mystic Seaport Stores
47 Greenmanville Avenue
Mystic, CT 06355   800-331-2665

"Martini Bait," "Luxurious Lobster," "On Board," "Main Catch," and "Top It Off" are only a beginning to the tempting chapters. From simple to elegant, these imaginative seafood recipes (over 400) can enhance cooking and dining experiences at cocktail parties, luncheons, picnics, or buffets—both ashore and afloat! Amusingly illustrated by Sally Caldwell Fisher. 9¼x8.

$15.95 Retail price
$ .96 Tax for Connecticut residents
$ 4.95 Postage and handling
Make check payable to Mystic Seaport Stores
ISBN 0-939510-08-1

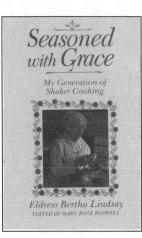

SEASONED WITH GRACE:
My Generation of Shaker Cooking

by Eldress Bertha Lindsay
The Countryman Press
P. O. Box 175–QRP
Woodstock, VT 05091   800-245-4151

Seasoned with Grace offers an authentic, firsthand profile of a way of life and worship that continues to fascinate the hundreds of thousands who visit Shaker museums and communities each year. Eldress Lindsay's cookbook mixes recipes and anecdotes in an illustrated guide to this graceful past. Chronological and biographical information. Paperback, 161 pages; 103 recipes with index.

$14.00 Retail price
$ 3.50 Postage and handling
Make check payable to The Countryman Press
ISBN 0-88150-099-2

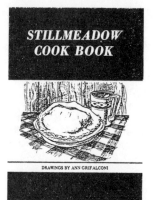

DRAWINGS BY ANN GRIFALCONI

STILLMEADOW COOK BOOK

by Gladys Taber
Parnassus Imprints
45 Plant Road
Hyannis, MA 02601   508-790-1175

A New England cookbook by Gladys Taber. Her own recipes from her homes in Connecticut and Cape Cod. The more than 300 recipes range from appetizers to desserts. 336 pages, paperback.

$ 9.95 Retail price
$ .50 Tax for Massachusetts residents
$ 3.00 Postage and handling
Make check payable to Parnassus Imprints
ISBN 0-940160-18-8

A TASTE OF BOSTON

Shank Painter Publishing Co.
650 Commercial Street
Provincetown, MA 02657   508-487-9169

A guide to Boston's finest restaurants plus more than 100 of their most popular recipes. Includes Biba, Durgin-Park, Locke-Ober, Olives, Upstairs at the Pudding, Michaela's. 96 pages.

$ 7.50 Retail price
$ 2.00 Postage and handling
Make check payable to Shank Painter Publishing Co.

A TASTE OF CAPE COD

Shank Painter Publishing Co.
650 Commercial Street
Provincetown, MA 02657   508-487-9169

A guide to Cape Cod's finest restaurants plus more than 100 of their most popular recipes. Includes the Bramble Inn, Regatta, Cafe Elizabeth, Captian Linnell House, Aesop's Tables. 96 pages.

$ 8.50 Retail price
$ 2.00 Postage and handling
Make check payable to Shank Painter Publishing Co.
ISBN 0-9609814-6-2

A TASTE OF HALLOWELL

by Alice Arlen
25 Warren Street
Hallowell, ME 04347   207-622-9745

The recipes punctuate a narrative and follow the schedule of events for "Old Hallowell Day," the town's annual summer celebration. With history, photographs, illustrations, and personal comments woven around the wonderful recipes, this book is a delightful and delicious cornucopia of Hallowell, Maine. Paper; 8x8; 256 pages.

$14.00 Retail price
$ .84 Tax for Maine residents
$ 1.00 Postage and handling
Make check payable to Alice Arlen

A TASTE OF NEW ENGLAND

Junior League of Worcester, Inc.
71 Pleasant Street
Worcester, MA 01609   508-756-4739

Within these 230 pages you'll find traditional New England favorites, as well as recipes to start new traditions. Watercolors by Robert Kennedy of Kennedy Studios highlight each chapter. There are also sample menus to fit every occasion. Proceeds provide funding for projects and programs supported by JLW.

$16.95 Retail price
$4.00 Postage and handling first book, $2.00 each additional
Make check payable to Junior League of Worcester, Inc.
ISBN 0-9637509-0-9

A TASTE OF NEWPORT

Shank Painter Publishing Co.
650 Commercial Street
Provincetown, MA 02657   508-487-9169

A guide to 15 of Newport's finest restaurants, plus more than 100 of their most popular recipes. Includes Clarke Cooke House, Le Bistro, La Petite Auberge, and White Horse Tavern. 96 pages.

$ 7.50 Retail price
$ 2.00 Postage and handling
Make check payable to Shank Painter Publishing Co.
ISBN 0-9609814-1-1

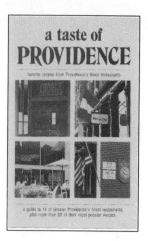

A TASTE OF PROVIDENCE

Shank Painter Publishing Co.
650 Commercial Street
Provincetown, MA 02657

A guide to 14 of Providence's finest restaurants, plus more than 80 of their most popular recipes. Includes Pot au Feu, Nathaniel Porter Inn, Angels, Hemenway's. 88 pages. Book is currently out of print.

A TASTE OF PROVINCETOWN

Shank Painter Publishing Co.
650 Commercial Street
Provincetown, MA 02657   508-487-9169

Provincetown has earned a reputation as Cape Cod's gourmet center. This book describes 15 of Provincetown's finest restaurants, with more than 100 of their most popular recipes. Includes Pepe's, Ciro & Sal's, Front Street, the Moors, The Mews. 96 pages.

$ 8.50 Retail price
$ 2.00 Postage and handling
Make check payable to Shank Painter Publishing Co.

A TASTE OF SALT AIR
& ISLAND KITCHENS

Ladies Auxiliary of the Block Island Volunteer Fire Department - c/o B. Bebby
Beach Avenue
Block Island, RI 02807

Our cookbook, *A Taste of Salt Air & Island Kitchens*, contains 381 recipes in 123 pages. It offers a sampling of clever and easy ways to prepare all foods—especially seafoods and desserts. Everyday ingredients are used in many recipes, and this book will soon become one of your favorites.

$ 6.00 Retail price
$1.05 Postage and handling
Make check payable to Ladies Auxiliary of the B.I.V.F.D.

TASTY TEMPTATIONS
FROM THE VILLAGE BY THE SEA

Holy Redeemer Guild
P.O. Box 1224
W. Chatham, MA 02669   508-945-1847

A collector's cookbook from the popular little Cape Cod village of Chatham, Massachusetts. Illustrated by local artist and guild member, Diana Fitchett, with delightful drawings of Chatham landmarks depicting scenes familiar to vacationers from around the country—lighthouse, fish pier, Friday night band concert, beaches and boating pleasures. 500 recipes; 228 pages; spiral bound.

$12.00 Retail price
$ 2.50 Postage and handling
Make check payable to Holy Redeemer Guild

TONY CLARK'S NEW
BLUEBERRY HILL COOKBOOK

Edited by Arlyn Hertz
Down East Books
P.O. Box 679
Camden, ME 04843

Vermont's Blueberry Hill Inn's reputation for fine food stretches back for decades, to Elsie Masterton, who established the inn. Under Tony Clark's management, the inn today still enjoys a reputation for outstanding food. Comb bound, 176 pages, index. Book is currently out of print.

TRADITIONAL PORTUGUESE
RECIPES FROM PROVINCETOWN

Shank Painter Publishing Co.
650 Commercial Street
Provincetown, MA 02657   508-487-9169

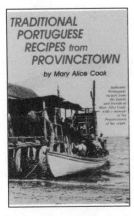

Mary Alice Cook, born in Olhoa, Portugal, presents over 70 of her family's recipes and records a memoir of Provincetown in the early years of this century. Many historic photos of Provincetown circa 1910. 88 pages.

$ 9.50 Retail price
$ 2.00 Postage and handling
Make check payable to Shank Painter Publishing

UNCLE BILLY'S
DOWNEAST BARBEQUE BOOK

by Jonathan St. Laurent and Charles Neave
Dancing Bear Books
P. O. Box 4
W. Rockport, ME 04865

Barbeque is more than a cuisine, it's an experience. In Uncle Billy's, author, chef and storyteller, Jonathan St. Laurent, tells stories, tall tales, and a few outright lies while dishing out superb barbeque recipes. Said one reviewer, "Even if I were a vegetarian allergic to wood smoke, I'd recommend this book." Paperback, 208 pages.

$12.95 Retail price
$ .78 Tax for Maine residents
$ 3.00 Postage and handling
Make check payable to Dancing Bear Books
ISBN 0-9622518-0-1

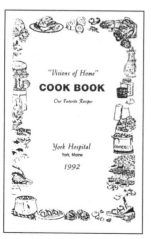

VERMONT KITCHENS REVISITED

Vermont Kitchen Publications
2 Cherry Street
Burlington, VT 05401   802-864-0471

Vermont Kitchens Revisited is a collection of 290 recipes indicative of the way Vermonters cook today. Its 282 pages reflect the modern approach to a healthy, interesting diet, but do not overlook the good old-fashioned favorites. It is beautifully illustrated throughout with original artwork by Margaret Parlour.

$14.95 Retail price
$ .75 Tax for Vermont residents
$ 2.00 Postage and handling
Make check payable to Vermont Kitchen Publications
ISBN 0-9627253-0-7

VISIONS OF HOME COOK BOOK

York Hospital
15 Hospital Drive
York, ME 03909

Our *Visions of Home* cookbook was initiated and accomplished by the entire York Hospital family. The project is dedicated to our new Vision of Service to our patient: "Through the Patient's Eyes, Caring, Listening, Satisfying...One by One," and presents 97 pages with 250 recipes. Book is currently out of print.

WASHINGTON STREET EATERY COOK BOOK

LuAnn Neff
521 Portsmouth Avenue
Greenland, NH 03840   603-427-2595

Our book was created due to many requests from customers to print recipes used in our restaurant located in historic Strawbery Banke Museum, 61 Washington Street in Portsmouth, New Hampshire. The menu changes daily, offering a wide variety of choices. Since the first printing in 1989 of the 90 recipes, we've often had requests for a second edition of recipes.

$ 12.95 Retail price
$ 2.00 Postage and handling
Make check payable to LuAnn Paquette

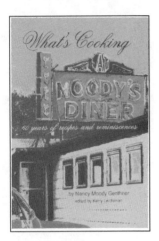

WHAT'S COOKING AT MOODY'S DINER

by Nancy Moody Genthner
Moody's Diner, U.S. Route 1
Waldoboro, ME 04572   207-832-7785

When *What's Cooking at Moody's Diner* was first published, the *Bangor Daily News* declared the long wait for the diner's cookbook finally over. Nancy Genthner, daughter of founder Percy Moody, spent three years compiling the book's recipes and memorabilia. Now in its 8th printing! Paperback, 112 pages. Published by Dancing Bear Books.

$ 8.95 Retail price
$ .54 Tax for Maine residents
$ 2.50 Postage and handling
Make check payable to Moody's Diner
ISBN 0-88448-075-5

WINDJAMMER COOKING

by Dee Carstarphen
Pen & Ink Press
P.O. Box 235
Wicomico Church, VA 22579   804-580-8723

Windjammer Cooking is not only a cookbook. It's also a history and a guide. Included—a day-by-day description of life aboard a windjammer, and brief sketches of the fleet of Maine Windjammers. A major portion of the book is given over to recipes used on the schooner *Adventure* when the author was cook. 158 pages.

$11.95 Retail price
$ 2.00 Postage and handling
Make check payable to Pen & Ink Press
ISBN 0-9607544-3-1

The Old North Church (1723), where the two lanterns were hung—"One if by land, two if by sea"— before Paul Revere embarked on his midnight ride. Boston, Massachusetts.

Preserving America's Food Heritage

BEST OF THE BEST COOKBOOK SERIES

Best of the Best from
ALABAMA
288 pages, $16.95

Best of the Best from
INDIANA
288 pages, $16.95

Best of the Best from
MISSISSIPPI
288 pages, $16.95

Best of the Best from
PENNSYLVANIA
320 pages, $16.95

Best of the Best from
ARKANSAS
288 pages, $16.95

Best of the Best from
IOWA
288 pages, $16.95

Best of the Best from
MISSOURI
304 pages, $16.95

Best of the Best from
SOUTH CAROLINA
288 pages, $16.95

Best of the Best from
COLORADO
288 pages, $16.95

Best of the Best from
KENTUCKY
288 pages, $16.95

Best of the Best from
NEW ENGLAND
368 pages, $16.95

Best of the Best from
TENNESSEE
288 pages, $16.95

Best of the Best from
FLORIDA
288 pages, $16.95

Best of the Best from
LOUISIANA
288 pages, $16.95

Best of the Best from
NEW MEXICO
288 pages, $16.95

Best of the Best from
TEXAS
352 pages, $16.95

Best of the Best from
GEORGIA
336 pages, $16.95

Best of the Best from
LOUISIANA II
288 pages, $16.95

Best of the Best from
NORTH CAROLINA
288 pages, $16.95

Best of the Best from
TEXAS II
352 pages, $16.95

Best of the Best from the
GREAT PLAINS
288 pages, $16.95

Best of the Best from
MICHIGAN
288 pages, $16.95

Best of the Best from
OHIO
352 pages, $16.95

Best of the Best from
VIRGINIA
320 pages, $16.95

Best of the Best from
ILLINOIS
288 pages, $16.95

Best of the Best from
MINNESOTA
288 pages, $16.95

Best of the Best from
OKLAHOMA
288 pages, $16.95

Best of the Best from
WISCONSIN
288 pages, $16.95

Cookbooks listed above have been completed as of January 1, 2000.

Special discount offers available!
(See previous page for details.)

To order by credit card, call toll-free **1-800-343-1583** or send check or money order to:
QUAIL RIDGE PRESS   P. O. Box 123   Brandon, MS 39043
Visit our website at **www.quailridge.com** to order online!

- -

Order form

Send completed form and payment to:
QUAIL RIDGE PRESS P. O. Box 123 Brandon, MS 39043

❏ Check enclosed

Charge to: ❏ Visa ❏ MasterCard
❏ Discover   ❏ American Express

Card #_____

Expiration Date _____

Signature _____

Name _____

Address _____

City/State/Zip_____

Phone # _____

Qty.	Title of Book (State)	Total

Subtotal	_____
7% Tax for MS residents	_____
Postage ($3.00 any number of books)	+ 3.00
Total	_____